Mapping Kurdistan

Since the early twentieth century, Kurds have challenged the borders and national identities of the states they inhabit. Nowhere is this more evident than in their promotion of the 'Map of Greater Kurdistan', an ideal of a unified Kurdish homeland in an ethnically and geographically complex region. This powerful image is embedded in the consciousness of the Kurdish people, both within the region and, perhaps even more strongly, in the diaspora.

Addressing the lack of rigorous research and analysis of Kurdish politics from an international perspective, Zeynep N. Kaya focuses on self-determination, territorial identity and international norms to suggest how these imaginations of homelands have been socially, politically and historically constructed (much like the state territories the Kurds inhabit), as opposed to their perception of being natural, perennial or intrinsic. Adopting a non-political approach to notions of nationhood and territoriality, *Mapping Kurdistan* is a systematic examination of the international processes that have enabled a wide range of actors to imagine and create the cartographic image of greater Kurdistan that is in use today.

ZEYNEP N. KAYA is Senior Teaching Fellow in the Department of Development Studies at the School of Oriental and African Studies; Visiting Fellow at the Middle East Centre, London School of Economics and Political Science; and Academic Associate at Pembroke College, University of Cambridge. Her research focuses on the Kurds and identity politics in the Middle East from an international relations perspective and gendered drivers of conflict in Iraq.

Mapping Kurdistan

Territory, Self-Determination and
Nationalism

ZEYNEP N. KAYA
London School of Economics and Political Science

CAMBRIDGE
UNIVERSITY PRESS

CAMBRIDGE
UNIVERSITY PRESS

University Printing House, Cambridge CB2 8BS, United Kingdom

One Liberty Plaza, 20th Floor, New York, NY 10006, USA

477 Williamstown Road, Port Melbourne, VIC 3207, Australia

314–321, 3rd Floor, Plot 3, Splendor Forum, Jasola District Centre, New Delhi – 110025, India

79 Anson Road, #06–04/06, Singapore 079906

Cambridge University Press is part of the University of Cambridge.

It furthers the University's mission by disseminating knowledge in the pursuit of education, learning, and research at the highest international levels of excellence.

www.cambridge.org
Information on this title: www.cambridge.org/9781108474696
DOI: 10.1017/9781108629805

© Zeynep N. Kaya 2020

First published 2020

A catalogue record for this publication is available from the British Library.

ISBN 978-1-108-47469-6 Hardback

To Elif

Contents

Maps

Acknowledgements

Several wonderful people inspired and supported this book with whom I have discussed many of its aspects and who have given me immensely useful advice: my doctoral supervisors Fred Halliday and John Sidel and doctoral adviser John Breuilly, my doctoral examiners Charles Tripp and James Mayall and the two anonymous reviewers whose comments transformed the way I present the ideas in this book. Working with Fred Halliday was one of the biggest privileges of my life – he was a great source of intellectual wisdom and inspiration, a huge support and a wonderful friend. I am also indebted to the editorial team at Cambridge University Press for taking me through the process with such expertise and ease, especially Maria Marsh, Daniel Brown and Atifa Jiwa. I would like to thank David McDowall, Mehrdad Izady, Laris Karaklis, The Kurdish Project for generously allowing me to use their maps in the book.

Big thanks go to my friends and colleagues at the London School of Economics: Robert Lowe for always being there for me throughout my career and the writing of this book; Ribale Sleiman-Haidar, Sandra Sfeir, Chelsea Milsom and Courtney Freer for being the best colleagues and friends; Toby Dodge for the wonderful guidance. It is impossible to mention all those who been part of my journey in writing this book, intellectually and emotionally. I am worried about omitting names but here it goes: to Jennifer Jackson-Preece, Margot Light, Denise Natali, Güneş Murat Tezcür, Lily Ling, Djene Bajalan, Brendan O'Leary, Joost Jongerden, David McDowall, Katerina Dalacoura and Yaniv Voller for discussing ideas that formed this book; to Jasmine Gani, Naz Masraff, Natali Pagliari, Claire Beaugrand, Outi Keranen, Chris Phillips, Kevork Oskanian, Ramon Pacheco-Pardo, Jeffrey Reeves for being wonderful PhD friends; and to Kimberly Hutchings, John Hutchinson and Christine Chinkin for supporting me throughout my career.

Special thanks also go to my family of friends who have surrounded me with love, laughter and wisdom. I am especially grateful to Charlie

Miller, Rubina Fur, Sarah Latimer-Sayer, Bene Lassartesse-Jones and Marie Morice for being there for me in the final, most painful years of writing.

There are many other friends and colleagues whose names haven't been mentioned here, and many scholars, researchers and practitioners I have met and with whom I have discussed the book and exchanged ideas. Their ideas and insights have inspired this book so much.

This book would not have been possible if it wasn't for my family, who deserve the biggest thanks – special thanks to my parents and brother in Turkey for the limitless love and support, and putting up with the stressed version of me and my distractedness during holidays, as well as to my Irish family who have always been equally loving. Also thanks to my husband Matthew for reading (several!) earlier versions of the book, talking about it for numerous hours and for always encouraging and supporting me. I dedicate this book to my daughter Elif who has always cheered me up and was always ready to provide gems of 'wisdom' in the hardest hours.

No work is ever entirely owned by one person, and I am indebted to all those fantastic people. Of course, any errors that remain are my own.

Note on Text

Transliteration was a challenging task for this book because it covered a long historical period (from mid-nineteenth century to present), a large geography and a wide range of different transliterations of Kurdish words in multiple languages – Kurdish, Persian, Arabic, Turkish and Ottoman Turkish. This book is meant for both specialists and general readers; therefore, I adopted a basic transliteration method. I have preserved Ottoman Turkish, Arabic, Kurdish and Persian terms where possible for words commonly used in English as well as for place names, personal names, treaties, historical textbooks, names of associations, rebellions and movements. I have not used diacritics. I have followed the transliteration guidelines of the *International Journal of Middle East Studies*. My choice of transliteration is not intended to impose identity or nationality on the individuals, names and locations.

Abbreviations

AKP	Justice and Development Party (Adalet ve Kalkınma Partisi)
BCE	Before Common Era
CUP	Committee for Unity and Progress (İttihat ve Terakki Cemiyeti)
DFNS	Democratic Federation of Northern Syria
ECHR	European Court of Human Rights
HDP	Peoples' Democratic Party (Halkların Demokratik Partisi)
HEP	People's Labour Party (Halkın Emek Partisi)
HPG	People's Defence Forces (Hêzên Parastina Gel)
IR	International Relations
ISIS	Islamic State of Iraq and Syria
KCK	Association of Communities in Kurdistan (Koma Civakên Kurdistan)
KDP	Kurdistan Democratic Party
KDPS	Kurdistan Democratic Party of Syria
KDPT	Kurdistan Democratic Party of Turkey
KHRP	Kurdish Human Rights Project
KJ	Kurdistan Resurrection Organisation (Komalay Jiyanaway Kurd)
KNCL	Kurdistan National Congress
KNK	Kurdistan National Congress (Kongra Netewiya Kurdistan)
KRG	Kurdistan Regional Government
KRI	Kurdistan Region of Iraq
KSSP	Kurdish Society for Solidarity and Progress (Kürt Teavün ve Terakki Cemiyeti)
LGBTQI	Lesbian, Gay, Bisexual, Transgender, Queer and Intersex
MPs	Members of Parliament
PDKI	Democratic Party of Iranian Kurdistan (Partiya Dêmukratî Kurdistanî Iran)
PKK	Kurdistan Workers' Party (Partiya Karkerên Kurdistan)

PUK	Patriotic Union of Kurdistan
PYD	Democratic Union Party (Partiya Yekîtiya Demokrat)
SAK	Society for the Advancement of the Kurds (Kürt Teali Cemiyeti)
SDF	Syrian Democratic Forces
SFR	Socialist Federal Republic of Yugoslavia
TİP	Turkey Labour Party (Tűrkiye İşçi Partisi)
UN	United Nations
UNHCR	United Nations High Commissioner for Refugees
YPG	People's Protection Units (Yekîneyên Parastina Gel)
YPJ	Women's Defence Units (Yekîneyên Parastina Jin)

Introduction

Since the early twentieth century, Kurds have challenged the borders and national identities of the states they inhabit. Nowhere is this more evident than in their promotion of the map of greater Kurdistan, a unified ideal homeland which encompasses large swathes of Turkey, Iraq, Syria and Iran, and a small part of Armenia, in a region with a complex history of ethnic, cultural and political background. The main Kurdish political actors in each of these states claim some ownership or control over a part of a state's territory and they are usually careful to restrict their claims to within the state they reside. All these Kurdistans have been geographically, economically and culturally marginalised in each state and have historically been buffer zones between regional and colonial powers. The idea of greater Kurdistan combines these areas and puts Kurdistan at the centre rather than in the margins.

The map of greater Kurdistan is embedded in the consciousness of the majority of Kurdish people, both within the region and, perhaps even more strongly, in the diaspora. The territory it depicts, Kurdistan, has never been a recognised state and does not have a unified political leadership. Yet the concept of Kurdistan, as a cultural and political abstract, survives the reality and exists in the minds of Kurdish nationalists, their supporters as well as those who deny it. The territory depicted on the map is a heterogeneous geography inhabited by different ethnic and religious groups such as Arabs, Turks, Persians, Assyrians, Armenians, Yazidis, Christians and others. The map projects a historical continuity of Kurdistan, overlooking historical conflicting claims, for instance between Armenians, Assyrians and Kurds. The Kurds do not constitute one group with a similar culture, language, religion and political goals. Tribal divisions are important, sometimes more so than Kurdishness. Kurdish political parties and Kurdish societies in each state face different problems that emerged as a result of distinct political, social, historical and economic circumstances of the state they are in.

1

The map of greater Kurdistan is frequently used in Kurdish political programmes, on political party flags, on the walls of homes and offices, and its silhouette is even used on accessories such as key rings, brooches or necklaces. What is particularly noteworthy is that it is not only Kurdish nationalists who use this map, but also outsiders use it to show the location of the Kurdish homeland or to show the Kurdish demographic presence in the area. What is interesting is the almost identical cartographic depiction of maps showing Kurdish demography and maps showing the political aspiration of Kurdistan. Indeed, non-political maps that show the demographic distribution of the Kurds have similar contours in which the silhouette that emerges from coloured parts indicating Kurdish habitation looks very similar to the political map of Kurdistan. Although maps showing Kurdish habitation through the image of Kurdistan do not seek to make a political point on the existence of a Kurdish territory, the similarity of the contours of the demographic and political maps of Kurdistan is usually overlooked by outsiders using these maps.

This raises two fundamental questions about the Kurdish political project, both of which have important implications for thinking about national self-determination and how this is pursued by non-state nationalists. Why and how has the map of greater Kurdistan become a widespread image; and what is the perceived underlying relationship between territory and people that bolsters the greater Kurdistan map? Widespread use of this map does not mean that all Kurds aim for a unified Kurdish statehood in the Middle East or those outsiders who use it to support the idea of a unified Kurdistan. Many would claim the relationship is straightforward in that such a map merely depicts a people's natural and actual homeland. For most Kurds, this is certainly the case. For its supporters, the map of greater Kurdistan makes the case that Kurds are a nation without a state whose homeland is divided by four states.

Yet it is worth pushing beyond the question of the actuality or viability of a greater Kurdistan. The focus of this book is not to establish whether such a territory actually exists or not. Clearly, imaginations of homelands are socially and politically constructed, rather than being natural and perennial, and the same can be said for state territories. The fact that states have internationally recognised boundaries does not make their territories less constructed or more natural. The aim of this book instead is to examine the imagination and presentation of the Kurdish homeland through its cartographic depictions within the contexts of internal Kurdish dynamics and the international normative framework since the nineteenth century. Through this, it seeks to examine the resultant political, cultural and social effects of this construction and historically trace how the Kurdistan map(s) are constituted by Kurdish nationalist politics as well as international norms.

Political maps have the power to influence our imaginations about where territories and states lie in the world because maps are seen as objective and scientific, and they are powerful in making constructed ideas look natural (Agnew, Livingstone and Rogers 1996: 422). They are cultural and political discursive formations and represent percep-tions, political discourses, ideologies and aspirations (Crampton 2001; Harley 1989, 2002). The narratives maps present create the lenses through which we see, understand and interpret territoriality, under-stood as the relationship between people and territory in this study. The power of maps derives from their embeddedness in the narratives of nation and identity. Conceptions of nation, identity and territoriality and how they define political realities and the rules of state legitimacy change over time. Their different meanings in different periods have implications for how we perceive political maps, both existing and aspirational. Kurds and outsiders imagine the Kurdish homeland through contemporary norms related to nation and territoriality, spe-cifically self-determination. Fuzzy and changeable, this norm has influ-enced national politics, as well as the conception of Kurdistan and its map, in different ways over time.

The map of greater Kurdistan and the Kurds are an apt case to explore wider questions around maps, self-determination and territory. This map is a useful tool to navigate through a complex temporal and conceptual field in which ideas of self-determination and territoriality have changed and evolved, both in the case of Kurdish nationalism and internationally. Through this analysis, the book links politics around Kurdish nationalism to international-level politics and normative fra-meworks. The interaction of Kurdish nationalist groups, both in the region and in the diaspora, with international actors does not take place simply through the regional states they are located in. Their interactions with the international society of states, multilateral and international organisations and sub-state actors occur in a normative and political context that influences both states and non-state actors.

This book contributes to the scholarly work on self-determination, nationalism and territoriality by integrating the Kurdish case into the debates on these phenomena. The Kurdish case is underrepresented in the discipline of International Relations (IR) and in the study of Nationalism despite its potential for generating new insights and lessons. The book approaches the study of Kurds in a way that has been neglected to date by offering a new perspective to the study of territoriality and presenting an in-depth historical case study from an IR perspective. It connects the evolution of Kurdish territoriality and Kurdish politics to the international level.

The analysis developed in this book also contributes to the scholarly work on Kurdish politics. The existing work in this literature with an international angle examines the Kurds in each state and looks at how Kurdish politics influences the domestic, regional and international relations of these states (Voller 2014; Gunter 2011a; Natali 2010, 2005; Barkey and Fuller 1998; Kirişçi and Winrow 1997). The literature also offers valuable analyses with different disciplinary perspectives, such as history, politics, sociology and anthropology.[1] However, an IR analysis of Kurdish politics is missing in the literature. This book meets this gap and it looks at Kurdish politics in totality, rather than country-by-country and situates this case in an international context.

Additionally, the book's focus on Kurdish territoriality fills another gap in Kurdish studies. Even though territoriality is a significant feature of Kurdish nationalism and its politics, there is limited literature on territoriality, except social and political geographers O'Shea's (2004) and Culcasi's (2010, 2006) works that study Kurdistan from a political geography perspective. This book builds on O'Shea and Culcasi's useful insights but situates the case in an international framework. O'Shea argued that the map of greater Kurdistan does not reflect the realities of Kurdish society or the region as a whole. She defined this map as a 'propaganda map' and saw it as a symbol of the effort to construct a Kurdish nationalist myth based on historical and territorial

---

[1] Literature on the Kurds with historical, political, sociological and anthropological perspectives has been growing since the 2000s. Some examples are Stansfield and Shareef 2017; Eppel 2016; Galip 2015; Tezcür 2016; Allsopp 2014; Bajalan 2013; Bengio 2014; King 2013; Entessar 2009; Lowe and Stansfield 2010; Olson 2009; Tejel 2008; Heper 2007; Tahiri 2007; Jabar and Dawod 2006; Jwaideh 2006; Romano 2006; O'Leary et al. 2005; Özoğlu 2004; Vali 2003.

perceptions or imaginations (O'Shea 2004: 4). In her book, O'Shea examined the maps of Kurdistan and historical narratives about the origins of the Kurds as constructions created in order to produce a sense of unity in the minds of the people and to enable them to connect their identity to the territory they inhabit. Culcasi looked at the role of orientalist discourses in the American journalistic geography of Kurdistan in presenting the Kurds in a way that supported and verified the United States' geopolitical and ideological position. Yet what is neglected is the international dimension and the international normative context in the construction of this map and how it is perceived.

The Kurds and Their Territory

One of the most common phrases that define the Kurds is 'the largest nation without a state'[2] spread in a huge geography encompassing large swathes of Turkey, Iraq, Iran and Syria and a small part of Armenia.[3] Even if practical support and demand among the Kurds for a unified pan-Kurdistan is low, the idea that four states (five if Armenia is included) currently exist across what is 'naturally' Kurdish territory has resonance in the minds of both Kurds and some outsiders as the continued and widespread use of the map of greater Kurdistan shows. The idea of territorial homeland played an important role in the emergence and development of Kurdish nationalism and it is central to understanding Kurdish nationalist groups' activities today. Despite this, the territorial aspect of Kurdish nationalism remains understudied and unproblematised in the academic literature. Existing studies depict the history of the region as the history of Kurdistan but fail to interrogate the basis and suppositions underpinning the assumption that a minority nationalism simply has a right to a territorial expression. In other words, most of these studies see the history of Kurdistan as identical to the history Kurdish nationalism (Hassanpour 2003),

---

[2] Despite the existence of possibly larger peoples without states such as the Tamils, an estimated population of 70 million spread across Sri Lanka, Mauritius, India, Malaysia and Singapore.

[3] There is also a large Kurdish diaspora in Europe and the United States, and substantial and long-standing Kurdish communities in Central Anatolia in Turkey, Khorasan in Iran, in Central Asia, Azerbaijan, Lebanon, Georgia and Armenia as a result of imperial deployments and forced deportations, and migration to escape persecution or conflict. In Turkey, a large proportion of Kurds live in big cities such as Istanbul and Izmir.

essentialising this territorial identity and underestimating the prevalence of political claims behind it.

The concept of Kurdistan refers to a space, an area or a region, but in this book, this concept is used for ease of description. Space is '*structural*' not territorial (Agnew 1994: 55, emphasis in the original). The territorial conception of space takes its representation for granted and this conception is quite dominant in the study of societies and politics. The structural conception of space, on the other hand, acknowledges its fluid and changing nature and its relationship with other social, economic and political factors (Agnew 1994: 55). The use of the concept of Kurdistan, therefore, does not imply that the region was historically defined as Kurdistan, or its inhabitants were all Kurdish, or the area had clearly demarcated borders/or its extent was clear. The concept of Kurdistan does not refer to ahistorical and ontologically permanent locations or territories but to the geographical context upon which social, economic and political interactions take place and in return, to a territory or geography shaped by these interactions (Agnew 1994: 56).

Territory is usually understood to be obvious or self-evident (Elden 2010). Mainstream perspectives in IR usually do not define territory – instead they see it as state territory defined in terms of jurisdictional control over a physical area and the people living on it (Kadercan 2015: 128). In this book, a political geography definition of territory is adopted, which connects territory directly to human agency and relations of power. In that sense, territoriality, the link between territory and society, is the primary concern here. The way Kurdistan and its map have been framed, used and interpreted throughout history have depended on how the relationship between nation and territory was understood in each period. The meaning and function of self-determination, a key international norm related to the legitimacy of political authority in international relations, had constitutive roles in shaping the relationship between the people and territory. In other words, the changes in the meaning and function of this international norm have, in turn, changed the way the relationship between a national people and 'their' territory – territoriality – is perceived.

Kurdish nationalism asserts self-determination claims to territorial autonomy or independence based on a distinct cultural and ethnic identity. Kurdish activists, especially since the second part of the twentieth century, have disseminated the idea of Kurdistan to the international community through framing this promotion in the language of human rights, democracy and self-determination. This was done to enhance the legitimacy of their claims to democratic countries whose endorsement and support they seek. Kurds have been more successful than other smaller groups in the Middle East, such as the Assyrian Christians in Turkey, Syria and Iraq or the Turkmens and Yazidis in Iraq, in drawing attention to themselves and generating support and sympathy for the issues they have in each state and their desire to be recognised as a distinct people.

Today, Kurds in Iraq enjoy official or de jure autonomy as a region in a federal Iraq. They have their own government, parliament, administration and military forces. Meanwhile, although heavily suppressed in the past, since the onset of the war, Kurds in Syria have carved a de facto autonomy in the north of the country, labelled as Rojava by the Kurds. In Turkey, the military conflict between the Kurdistan Workers' Party (PKK, *Partiya Karkerên Kurdistan*) and the state army has been ongoing since 1984, interrupted by a short period of talks between 2012 and 2015. The PKK gave up on its goal for independence since early 2000s and now seeks decentralisation within a system it calls 'democratic confederalism'. In Iran Kurdish political activists are facing a struggle to survive under an oppressive regime, but Kurds have historically benefited from some degree of cultural and linguistic rights in this country. Each of these groups faces different challenges, have different leaderships and pursue different goals. What is more, these goals and leaderships have often come into conflict with one another in the past and the war in Syria has exacerbated these divisions further in many key respects (Kaya and Whiting 2017).

Given this picture, it is a fair statement to say that each Kurdish nationalist organisation typically defines its goals and problems in a way that is limited to the country they reside in, with regional activities pursued especially by the PKK, but also by the Kurdistan Democratic Party (KDP) and the Patriotic Union of Kurdistan (PUK) in Iraq at a more limited level. No contemporary Kurdish nationalist party in the Middle East so far has made an explicit demand to establish a greater Kurdistan that would unite all the Kurds living in different states within a new single political entity and each Kurdish political movement has its own understanding of the boundaries of the territory they wish to have full or administrative control over. Despite this, the map of greater Kurdistan has gained resonance in both Kurdish and international discourses and is a highly influential tool in advancing Kurdish separatist and autonomist demands.

The Map of Greater Kurdistan

Kurds have been using the map of greater Kurdistan since the early twentieth century to depict the Kurdish homeland, much to the annoyance of the states in which they are located. Kurdish nationalists see the map of greater Kurdistan as the cartographical reflection of the Kurdish territory. Kurdistan as a homeland and its maps are commonly used in the rhetoric of almost all Kurdish nationalist organisations and activist groups, both in the region and in the diaspora. Kurdish nationalist historiography claims ownership of this territory since 4,000 BCE. Like other nationalisms it has a subjective view of national existence that goes back to 'time immemorial' and deploys past geographic and administrative terms to promote the idea that a Kurdish nation existed centuries ago (Nezan 1996; Izady 1992). In so doing, Kurdish nationalist historiography associates pre-modern meanings of 'Kurdistan' or 'Kurdishness' to the contemporary uses of national, territorial and political identity (O'Shea 2004: 2–3; McDowall 1996b: 3).

Kurdish activists have produced many historical, sociological and political texts to legitimise and prove the Kurdish right to statehood and have created and distributed multiple maps of Kurdistan. Maps are useful tools for presenting nationalist views. The cartographic image of a territory with clear boundaries and a name that makes reference to a people gives the message that the territory and the people inhabiting it are related. In fact, this usage has moved beyond the discourse of Kurdish nationalists. For example, Bob Filner, Democrat Congressman for California's 51st District pleaded for the recognition of Kurdish self-determination at the United States Congress on 1 May 1997. The justification he put forth was that Kurds have been ruling the area they inhabit since 2,000 BCE and the Kurds (then Gutis) ruled today's Persia and Mesopotamia 4,000 years ago. He declared that despite this historical legacy, Kurds have been denied the right to nationhood and self-determination. Frank Pallone, Congressman for the 6th district of New Jersey, in a speech also on 1 May 1997, appealed for Kurdish self-determination and requested the United States government stop giving Turkey military support and making arms deals with it. Pallone gave another statement to the Congress on 6 April 2000, referring to his 1997 address and referring to the 'lands of Kurdistan' and calling for support for action to stop the persecution of Kurds and violation of their rights in the hands of states.

The map of greater Kurdistan has become one of the prominent features and symbols of Kurds. It has become synonymous with the idea of 'Kurdistan' in the minds of the Kurds and become a significant feature of Kurdish nationalist discourse. Kurdish parties do not promote this map or include it as a territorial goal in their party programmes, but they use it to justify the ethnic presence of Kurds on the territory the map depicts. There is a striking similarity between Kurdish nationalists' and outsiders' descriptions of Kurdistan. The idea that there is a direct link between the area represented on these maps and the people living in that area has become embedded in both Kurdish and international political discourses. As it has come to be seen as a natural territory, it has come to 'inscribe boundaries and construct objects that in turn become our realities' (Pickles 2004: 145).

The Power of Political Maps and Territoriality

The power of political maps partly comes from their perceived objectivity and naturalness. We see the world through maps. The world, from a traditional IR perspective, is composed of state territories that frame the nation and the space it controls. The world political map reifies the idea of a world divided into sovereign domestic spaces of control and political authority (Black 2000: 12). Political maps are widely used in state offices, schools, newspapers and other forms of media, internet, flags and political pamphlets, which in turn further perpetuate our image of the world (Vujakovic 2002: 377–9). In this process, particular understandings of politics, society or the world a map depicts become common sense, as if the map reflects reality in a neutral and transparent way (Weldes 1996: 303). Because of the perception that maps are scientific, the sense of territorial control and the boundaries of states appear both objective and natural.

Critical geographers challenged the idea that maps reflect objective cartographic information (Pickles 2004; Crampton 2001; Black 2000). They argued that the mapping process produces the territory and the identity of the people that live in that territory. Maps, including state maps, are social and political constructs shaped and understood through temporal, social and political contexts and discourses

(Crampton and Krygier 2006: 15–17). Social constructions are things
we consider as common sense because they appear to reflect reality, like
gender roles or identity. Societies usually take social constructions for
granted, as something natural, and hardly question their origins
(Weldes 1996: 279–80). In the case of maps, those who are inside the
boundaries of a map are considered to share an identity, different from
those who are outside those borders (Anderson 1991), overlooking the
fact that historically boundaries change, and do so more often than
assumed.

The power of political maps also derives from the discourse through
which we see cartographic images. There is interplay between the map
and our knowledge of shared ideas and dominant discourse (Weldes
1996: 286). The overlap between dominant narratives of national
identity and territoriality, in other words the idea that the world is
composed of nations and their territories, is at the source of the power
of political maps. Conceptions of nation and homeland constitute the
context through which we understand maps. These conceptions are
underpinned by notions of nationhood and territoriality, which change
over time and in turn shape the way we perceive cartographic
information.

Our conceptions of national identity and territoriality not only shape
how we see the maps of states but also maps of aspirational territories,
claimed homelands of aspirant nations. The contemporary international system builds on territorially defined national units and nation-
states represented on the world map, which are perceived to have
internationally   recognised   sovereignty   (Krasner   1999:   9–25).
Separatist nationalists use the same logic; they use maps of their imagined homeland to show their location in the world and imply that they
deserve sovereignty over their territory in the same way that other
recognised sovereign entities have. In that sense, cartographic images
can become political tools not only for recognised states but also for
those who seek recognition, such as separatist and autonomist nationalists. Maps become tools for showing competing understandings of
territorial reality on the same land (Culcasi 2006: 681), making maps
divisive.

Separatist and autonomist nationalists aim to achieve autonomy or
devolved authority within the state or to form their own state on behalf
of their nation on the territory over which they claim ownership (Breuilly
2001: 32). In that sense, when demanding self-determination, they claim

their own territoriality and sovereignty and challenge the sovereignty of the ruling state (Mayall 1990: 51, 69). Here the tension is between a people's right to self-determination and another people's right to existing sovereignty (Bishai 2004: 7), in other words, between two different claims on territoriality.

By definition, the democratic enterprise is based on a defined group of people, and for the last couple of centuries this group is understood to be the nation. Popular sovereignty, a product of the French and American democratic revolutions, moulded into the nineteenth-century concept of nationalism in the transition from the sovereignty of monarchs to that of the peoples. Throughout the transformation of the doctrine of sovereignty in the nineteenth century, different types of sovereignties co-existed (Benton 2010: 1–2). But by the early twentieth century, people and popular sovereignty became the legitimate source of a state's sovereignty and absolute control within its territory in most parts of the world (Krasner 2001; Philpott 2001: 16; James 1999: 458–9).

With the devolution of states and empires into nation-states, the idea of popular sovereignty became associated with nationality, consent of the governed, and later, self-determination. People, or the nation, emerged as the source of state power, and state territoriality became defined as linked to the nation. The 1789 Declaration of the Rights of Man and of the Citizen by the National Assembly of France defines nation as 'essentially the source of all sovereignty; nor can any individual, or any body of men, be entitled to any authority which is not expressly derived from it'. The association of sovereignty with a specific group of people, the nation, brought with it challenges to existing sovereignties, in the form of self-determination demands.

The principle of self-determination is a critically important principle. It is part of the rules and principles that bind or guide state relations. It has a geographical aspect because it involves people and territoriality. It pertains to processes both within the states and at international level (Knight 1985: 251). On one hand it stresses continuity of the territorial integrity of each state or, for instance, territorial administrations, but it also challenges the status quo, because according to United Nations (UN) documents, it is the right of all peoples. Self-determination, the right of peoples to 'freely determine their political status and freely pursue their economic, social and cultural development', as defined in Article 1 of the UN International Covenant on Civil and Political Rights, has had a determining role in the proliferation of nation-states in the twentieth century.

Demand for secessionist self-determination, or the 'desire of minority nations to demand sovereignty' in the form of administrative regions or independence, increased dramatically in the post-1918, post-1945 and post-1991 periods (Griffiths 2014: 580). The number of states in the world in 1912 was 51; as of May 2018, this number was 195, according to the United States Department of State.[4] Woodrow Wilson's, then President of the United States, ideal of self-determination, which he introduced as a pathway to statehood for small nations in the aftermath of the First World War, turned into an international framework for forming new states out of existing ones (Moore 2014, 2015; Miller 2014; Moynihan 2002). Enshrined as an international legal norm in the UN Charter of 1945, the principle was implemented in ex-colonial territories in the 1950–70s, and subsequently in ex-communist territories after 1991. Today some consider self-determination as applicable to certain territories that are neither ex-colonial nor ex-communist (Fabry 2010: 180). With the 1990s, the pressure to prioritise people over territory increased again with the return to Wilsonian self-determination. Although this last trend has not gained much legitimacy and traction globally, instances of people demanding self-determination, unilaterally declaring it (Kosovo in 2008) or gaining autonomous self-rule (Kurdistan Region of Iraq) have certainly increased. Within this context, the territory-nation link turned into something perennial for nationalists and their supporters, even if it challenges existing state territories.

Claims for self-determination actually are made to advance the sovereignty and territoriality of a new people in the form of independence or autonomy. Such claims assume the existence of a clearly definable territory that belongs to a people, or the possibility of drawing clear boundaries for such a territory, despite the fact that it is hard to define 'people', let alone where their territory lies. However, for a new people to attain legitimate sovereignty, recognition by other states, or in Krasner's words 'international legal sovereignty', is necessary. International legal sovereignty is recognition of a state's rule over a specific territory and people by other states (Krasner 1999: 14–20).[5]

---

[4] www.state.gov/s/inr/rls/4250.htm
[5] Krasner defines different types of sovereignty – a complex concept with multiple and changing meanings throughout history – 'domestic sovereignty', 'Westphalian sovereignty' 'interdependence sovereignty' and 'international legal sovereignty' (Krasner 1999: 9–25).

Then the issue is with deciding which people a state is entitled to wield legitimate authority over.

Self-determination reifies territoriality – the assumed link between the territory and the people. After all, the 'purpose and value of the division of the world into territorial jurisdictions is self-determination' (Banai et al. 2014: 103). Self-determination provides the pretext for assumptions on the nation-territory link, whether this link is understood in the context of a traditional state model or in relation to more plural forms of governance or separatists' demands. In all these cases, a link is assumed to exist between territory and people. This is despite the fact that assuming any such link can be problematic due to the obvious question of defining who the people are, the existence of multiple cultural groups on a piece of land, and the normative and subjective questions around who has territorial rights.

The Link between Nation and Territory

Interrogating the link between the nation and territory is necessary for generating a nuanced understanding of self-determination in separatist cases. Assumptions on an intrinsic link between the nation and territory actually hinder theoretical discussions on self-determination and on the implications of separatism or autonomism. Therefore, an empirically grounded theoretical interrogation of the link between nation and territory can shed a new light on debates around self-determination and claims to sovereignty.

Separatist or autonomist nationalists perceive their national boundaries as different from the existing boundaries of the country they inhabit. Their claims emphasise that the people who are attached to a territory should have the right to exercise sovereignty over it. Most separatists bolster this claim with an assertion that they have distinct cultural, territorial and linguistic identities, arguing that the only way to protect their identity is through the democratic right to sovereignty over a specific territory. The right emerges from the process in which people's usage and habitation of a specific territory generates, or is believed to generate, a territorially defined identity. Territory, from this perspective, is seen as a material necessity to enforce laws and policies through which the national or cultural identity of people can be protected (White 2000: 22; Kacowicz 1994: 7), basically echoing the idea that 'the political and the national should be congruent' (Gellner 2006: 6).

How can we explain this assumption that group identity and territory are linked? Why are ethno-national separatist movements associated with territory, or why is the right to self-determination usually framed around territorial identity? The existing literature in IR on self-determination provides useful explanatory and normative insights to some other relevant questions but has not necessarily interrogated how the link between territory and group identity came to be taken for granted. These scholars emphasise the resonance of self-determination, the rightfulness of such claims and the conditions under which such claims are given international recognition (Buchanan 2003; Griffiths 2003; Castellino 2000; Heraclides 1997; Shaw 1997). Others focus on the liberal and democratic underpinnings of self-determination demands, and solutions for territorial disputes (Tamir 2003; Moore 1997; Horowitz 1994), or the relationship between sovereignty, territoriality and self-determination (Griffiths 2014; Fabry 2010; James 1999; Mayall 1990).

There is also a more recent body of work that tries to develop a theory of territory and to understand what constitutes attachment between people and territory and what justifies the territorial rights of states and non-state groups (Banai 2014; Miller 2014, 2012; Moore 2014; Elden 2013). This body of work builds on previous attempts by political geographers to theorise territory (Agnew 1994; Anderson 1988; Knight 1985), and this is a useful starting point to interrogate the assumption between territory and nation. Moore (2014) offers a theoretical perspective to territory and explains the different perspectives of the 'nationalist theory' and 'legitimate state theory' on territory. Nationalist theory of territory argues, according to Moore, that nations are perennial entities that have existed throughout history and therefore should be the foundational units in the organisation of the world. As such, the nation-state system is defensible. Although this theory does not claim to offer answers to all territorial disputes or to provide justification for all territorial claims, it asserts that a state can claim territorial rights only if it represents a people, a nation, understood as culturally integrated and continuous over time. According to this approach, basically, nations' ownership of territory comes from the material and symbolic value they add to the land (Miller 2012: 107); nation and territory are attached because they shape each other and people mix their culture with territory by creating cultural and political rules and institutional structures on that territory (Moore 2014: 124).

The assumptions about the link between nation and territory in the nationalist theory, as described by Moore, have resonance in the ethno-symbolist and primordial accounts of the concept of nation in the study of Nationalism. These accounts argue that the core of nations existed in the past before the division of the world into nation-states. Smith, whose definitions and theories have had a huge influence on contemporary work on nationalism, called this an *ethnie*, the pre-modern basis of nations, and emphasised territorial attachment as one of the significant characteristics of *ethnie*s (Smith 1986). Although Smith distanced himself from less-respected primordialist accounts of nationalism, his concept of *ethnie* as the precursor of nationalism gave resonance to nationalist ideals about national awakening. Both separatist and state nationalists make reference to the historical existence of their distinct ethnic identity and territorial ownership, and both invoke democratic rights for their people. For these accounts, Smith's approach has a huge appeal, including Kurdish nationalists and parts of the Kurdish nationalist scholarship. As Alexander and Smith put it, 'Smith's approach to nationalism satisfies the emotional gap that primordialism's collapse left behind' (Maxwell and Smith 2015: 784). Though they also emphasise that Kurdish experts have overlooked the finer details of Smith's thinking about how complex phenomena *ethnie* and nation are, instead focused on the 'idea of the transition *ethnie* → nation'. (Alexander and Smith 2015: 774).

Scholars who adopt the ethno-symbolist perspective see territorial control and jurisdiction as a material necessity for the protection of the national and cultural identities of peoples (White 2000: 22). It is essential, for them, that new governing institutions represent the ethnic and cultural identity of the people (Kacowicz 1994: 7). Smith argued that 'ethnospaces', defined as sacred sites, mountains, battlefields, tombs and monuments, are significant in the construction of national identities or in the 'territorialisation of memory' (1996: 454). He accepted that territorial identity is socially constructed and that it is humans who give meaning to that territory. But he also argued that territorial associations asserted by nationalists should have implications on the political life of their people on whose behalf they talk. According to Smith, this is not particularly destabilising. On the contrary, what provokes instability is the failure to implement the national ideal (Smith 1981: 199). Ethno-symbolist (and primordialist) arguments draw on the idea that a homeland is one of the key traits of ethnic or national groups. Most separatist nationalists aspiring to have their own sovereignty, use the idea of an ethnically defined territory as the content and justification for their aspirations. Territory and its history are central for ethno-nationalist groups and they believe that their objectively perceived territorial identity gives them the right to exercise sovereignty and jurisdiction over that territory (Buchanan 2003).

The other theory Moore describes, the legitimate state theory, adopts a different view on the territory and nation link, or territoriality. Legitimate state theory argues that people or non-state communities alone cannot be rights holders over territory. The state and people living on its territory are the legitimate rights holders of land (Stilz 2011), and the state and its institutions generate a collective body of people, the nation. So here, the link between territory and people is established via a legitimate state, and is not assumed to exist already and naturally. Only nations with a legitimate state can claim ownership over a territory. National culture is also important for legitimate state theory in that nation and territory ultimately become connected, but the crucial distinction from nationalist theories is that the key justification for people's ownership of the territory is the legitimate jurisdiction of the state. This view echoes the modernist accounts of nations, which emphasise the constructed nature of nations and national identities – constructed through historical processes of state formation, capitalism, print-capitalism and the transition from monarchical systems to republican and democratic states (Gellner 2006; Breuilly 1993; Anderson 1991; Hobsbawm and Ranger 1983). However, the legitimate state theory remains limited in accounting for non-state nationalist claims and offers a statist perspective in which states could also be the representative of a majority identity at the expense of others.

The division between nationalist and legitimate state theories builds on the widely used civic–ethnic typology in the study of Nationalism. The civic type has more in common with the legitimate state theory while the ethnic type corresponds more to nationalist theory. The civic understanding of nations (also known as solidarist or political) emphasises citizenship, while the ethnic understanding (also known as cultural) emphasises the common 'objective' traits of a group of people (Calhoun 2007; Kohn 1929). Although this ideal typology does not always apply to real cases and many cases incorporate elements from both types (Zimmer 2003: 177–81), it provides a conceptual frame for understanding claims made on behalf of a nation. The civic type is generally associated with the individual choice to be part of a nation and the significance of state institutions and political culture in constructing collective identity. The ethnic type on the other hand is associated with a belief in the perennial existence of a distinct group. It assumes the objective national or ethnic features of a group to be given and continuous throughout history.

Crucially, despite different emphasises between the nationalist and legitimate state theories, what they both have in common is that neither actually questions the assumption that nation and territory are linked. They disagree on the processes that create the connection between nation and territory, but both consider the nation–territory attachment, or territoriality, as an existing core feature of a people. Similarly, although the two approaches differ in how they justify the territorial rights of people, again they both fail to interrogate this link. Instead they assume a territory-people link exists in theory and in practice. When assessing whether this attachment can be turned into a right to ownership for non-state peoples, they try to verify the existence of that attachment in empirical terms. As such, neither approach asks the bigger question of whether such attachments, in the case of states or non-states, should be accepted in either theoretical, conceptual or practical terms in the first place.

Again, the point here is not to discuss whether a link between territory and people actually exists or not. The question is why such a link is perceived to exist and how the perceived nature of this link changes over time and influences territorial politics of non-state nationalist actors. Assumptions embedded in the discourse and narrative on nations and territoriality shape how we see the world map or the cartographic depictions of aspirational homelands. These assumptions are two-fold as explained so far. One is the belief in the objectivity and accuracy of maps, which lends political power to these tools of communication. Second, and most important, the international normative and political context that shapes these perceptions have changed historically. International narratives of self-determination and territoriality, and their new meanings in different periods affected the way both Kurds and outsiders perceived the Kurdistan maps and Kurdish territoriality. The rest of this book explores the changing dynamics between international justifications for people's claims to territorial self-determination and perceptions of Kurdistan and its maps.

Conclusion

The map of greater Kurdistan conveys the message that the territory it demarcates belongs to the Kurds. Its influence comes from the assumed natural link between 'nation' and 'territory'. Though, it is more likely to be politically constructed because we see the world map through our assumptions about nation, territory and territoriality. Political maps have the power to shape people's images of the world in a manner that text alone fails to. They are visual expressions of apparently homogeneous national territories. In reality, political maps are not simply reflections of how the world territory is partitioned; they are the outcomes of political projects and imaginations, and in return, they shape our perceptions of the world territory.

The argument the map of greater Kurdistan makes – that the boundaries depicted on the map reflect a Kurdish territory – is a political and subjective argument. Nonetheless, the widespread use and reproduction of the map bolsters the Kurdish struggle to generate support for their cause and raise awareness about their issues. This raises key questions relating to: How has the map of Kurdistan become a widespread symbol of Kurdish territorial identity? Where does the idea of the map of Kurdistan come from? What messages does this map give? How is it perceived, and why? And has its purpose, use and reception changed over time?

The map of greater Kurdistan has been developed and communicated through the use of dominant international norms that give legitimacy to nationalist demands. The key international norm that shapes the rules of legitimacy on territorial and national rights is self-determination. This principle and related concepts such as sovereignty and territoriality influence the meaning of 'nation' and 'territory', and the relationship between them. Shifts in their meaning and in their relationship shape how maps are perceived.

The rest of the book historically traces the changes in the meaning of self-determination and in its relationship with territoriality and explains how these changes affected the use and reception of the map of Kurdistan by the Kurds and outsiders in different historical periods. Over time, self-determination expanded from being applicable to nations (initially understood as peoples of states) to include peoples with distinct ethnic, linguistic and territorial characteristics. This transformation increased the traction the map of greater Kurdistan has had in international society. The book tells the parallel and interlinked stories of the map of greater Kurdistan and self-determination since the late nineteenth century until today. It argues that in its transformation, the idea of Kurdistan and its map have been a constant term of reference for Kurdish nationalism. But, the framing, use and interpretation of both self-determination and the idea of Kurdistan have depended on how the relationship between nation and territory was understood in each period.

What follows now, in the second chapter 'Kurdish territoriality under Ottoman rule', is the analysis of the conceptual and historical underpinnings of the idea of Kurdistan and its later cartographic manifestations. This chapter explains the attribution of modern meanings of territory and nation to the past references of Kurdistan in the Kurdish nationalist historiography and examines the territoriality of the tribal leaders who revolted against the Ottomans in the nineteenth century. The third chapter, 'Orientalist views of national identity and colonial maps of Kurdistan' focuses on the maps of Kurdistan produced in the nineteenth and early twentieth centuries by Western travellers and colonial officers. Colonialist understanding of what constitutes national identity shaped the territorial identity of the peoples of this region. This perception shaped the construction of a retrospective view on Kurdish national identity later in the twentieth century. The maps European travellers produced were later adopted and used by Kurdish nationalists and became the key sources of mapping the Kurdish nation.

The fourth chapter, 'Wilsonian self-determination: The rise and fall of hopes for Kurdistan', is about how Kurdish nationalism adapted to the international framing for legitimate statehood in the first half of the twentieth century. This period was the height of Kurdish hopes for statehood, which did not come to fruition. The Kurdish political elite presented their Kurdistan maps to international authorities to receive support for their project, similar to many other groups across the world in this period. The fifth chapter, 'Kurdish nationalism during decolonisation and the Cold War', is about another significant period of state formation worldwide, when Kurdish nationalism transformed from being an elite project to a grassroots movement and different movements emerged in the four countries in which Kurds reside.

The sixth chapter, 'Kurds and the international society after the Cold War', looks at the evolution of self-determination and new state formation process in the post-Cold War period and the international norms of democracy and human rights that framed and shaped the goals of each Kurdish nationalist group. The seventh chapter, 'Kurdish diaspora: Kurdistan map goes global' looks at the role of Kurdish activists in the diaspora in making the map of greater Kurdistan a widely used symbol of Kurdish territoriality. The Kurdish diaspora combined the prevalent normative and political discourse of human rights, justice and democracy with their identity-based territoriality and promoted pan-Kurdish ideas more strongly than the Kurds in the region. The concluding chapter offers a re-cap of the historical case study of the map of Kurdistan and its alignment with the evolution of the international normative framework, specifically self-determination, and looks at the situation of Kurdish politics today and the divisive impact of the war in Syria on the Kurds.

1 | *Kurdish Territoriality under Ottoman Rule*

Introduction

Kurdish territoriality under the Ottoman rule was tribally defined, localised and based on tribal authority. Kurdish nationalist historiography and some of the Kurdish scholars, however, usually apply a retrospective reading to Kurdish territoriality, attributing modern meanings of territory and nation to the past uses of the concepts of Kurdistan and Kurds. They consider references to the concept of Kurdistan in historical texts, privileges Kurdish tribal leaders had under Ottoman rule and the nineteenth-century Kurdish rebellions as the verification of the existence of a Kurdish national consciousness and national territoriality in the past. Kurdish nationalists use similar interpretations as historical justifications for asserting the existence of a historical Kurdish homeland. These scholars and the nationalist historiography also define the Kurdish revolts in the late Ottoman period as nationalist and claim that the leaders of these revolts aimed at Kurdish statehood. However, while arguing about this, they emphasise the nationalistic characteristics of these movements, partly overlooking the complexity of tribal and political affiliations. Such retrospective interpretations can lead to assumptions, usually in the non-academic field, that the population living in Kurdistan is more or less homogeneously Kurdish, that the boundaries of Kurdistan can be demarcated based on Kurdish demographic distribution and that a Kurdish ethnic or national territorial homeland existed at least since the twelfth century.

Language, religion and culture are also important sources of Kurdish identity, but territorial attachment has always been a prominent aspect of it. The variety of languages, religions and political goals and affiliations across different Kurdish groups renders them relatively weaker sources of identity when it comes to making an argument for one

21

Kurdish nation. Substantial differences exist within Kurdish society, most notably the existence of different Kurdish dialects, which include Kurmanji, Sorani, Gorani and others (Van Bruinessen 2006: 24–5), as well as religious differences between the Sunni Islam, Shi'a Islam, Alevism, Ahl-i Haqq and the Yazidi religion (Tahiri 2007: 5; Van Bruinessen 2006: 25–6). The fluidness of boundaries of Kurdish identity can also be evidenced from the fact that identities such as Dimili, Zaza, Bakhtiyari, Luri, Alevi, Yazidis and Kaka'i are now considered distinct even though they used to be considered as Kurdish (Hassanpour 2003: 117; Limbert 1968: 47).[1]

The importance of the territorial element, Kurdistan, partly derives from a strong attachment to the place of habitation and to the physical environment. Geographic features are deeply integrated into the social life of Kurdish culture (Jwaideh 2006: 291). Environmental, geographical and rural features serve as strong expressions of identity, not only for Kurds in the region but also for Kurds in the cities and diaspora. Children are often named after rivers, mountains and rural symbols. Many Kurdish proverbs dwell on the character of the Kurdish territory, with typical declarations such as 'the Kurds have no friends but the mountains' and 'level the mountains and in a day the Kurds will be no more' (O'Shea 2004: 5).

Kurdish national identity, like other nationalities, is in many ways a modern phenomenon constructed with the political purpose of nation-building and achieving sovereignty. It is the result of the emergence of Kurdish nationalism in the early twentieth century. While most nationalisms in the Ottoman territories emerged in the nineteenth century, the dominant opinion in the scholarly literature is that Kurdish nationalism started to take its nationalist form in the early twentieth century or after the First World War. What is more, with the emergence of Kurdish nationalism Kurdish territoriality began to transform from solely tribal and local into national and imagined. Tribal territoriality can be observed in the relationship of the Kurdish tribal leaders with the Ottoman Porte in the nineteenth century. This interaction gives significant insights into how Kurdish tribal leaders defined their

---

[1] Linguistic and religious variety among Kurdish society is generally attributed to the very mountainous geography of the region, which made contact and communication very difficult in the past. Also, the absence of a Kurdish political entity in history hindered the creation of a common literature and a historical construction of identity.

territoriality, which implied attachment to tribal territorial dominion and authority, rather than simply nationalism.

This chapter explains the conception of Kurdish territoriality in the Ottoman era and how Kurdish nationalist historiography interprets these conceptions today. Through an analysis of existing accounts of the history of the Kurds, it derives insights on the meaning of territoriality and Kurdistan under Ottoman rule. This background complements the way Western officers who produced the first maps of Kurdistan in the nineteenth century perceived Kurdish identity and territoriality through the lenses of Western conceptions of national identity and territoriality.

Past Uses of the Concept of Kurdistan

Kurdish nationalist historiography assumes that a nationalist state of mind already existed, independent of the development of Kurdish nationalist politics. It perceives Kurdish identity as a constant and distinct identity synonymous with a historic Kurdish territory that has been unjustly partitioned (Edmonds 1971: 88). There is thus a clear attempt to link Kurdish identity etymologically to the historical inhabitants of the region. This leads to a fusion of the history of Kurdistan and the history of the Kurdish people in dominant historiographical accounts. Nationalist historiography claims that the historical continuity of Kurdish people goes back to the time of the Guti (beginning of second millennium BCE) and the Medes (circa 678–549 BCE), the indigenous peoples of this geographic area (Izady 1992: 32). Such primordialist understandings of identity involve claims to a direct ethnic link to ancient peoples of the region and see the Kurds as the indigenous people of this geographic area (Houston 2008: 16). Therefore, in the Kurdish case, as in almost all other nationalist ideologies, a historical link between an ideal territory and a people is constructed.

Kurdish historiography developed by 'nationalist scholarship' (Vali 2003: 59–60) interprets historical events related to Kurds and references to the 'Kurds' or 'Kurdistan' in historical texts as indicators of the existence of a Kurdish ethnic self-consciousness in the past. These scholars (Hassanpour 2003; Nezan 1996; Izady 1992) draw a direct connection between these past references and contemporary Kurdish identity and nationalism. In other words, they frame particular past uses within contemporary conceptions of nationhood and territorial identity. For them, tracing the origin of the Kurds is crucial because the historical origin of a nation is what determines it, echoing perennialist and ethno-symbolist approaches to nationalism in the literature.

Kurdish nationalist historiography refers to the creation of a Kurdistan province by the Seljuks in the twelfth century and the privileges Kurdish tribes enjoyed under the Ottoman rule from the sixteenth to nineteenth centuries to illustrate the existence of a Kurdish consciousness and some form of territorial ownership or control in the past. This historiography also refers to historical texts written in the sixteenth to nineteenth centuries, such as *Sharafname* (1596), *Seyahatname* (1656), *Mem u Zin* (1695), Koyi's work (1817–97) and *Kamus-ul Alem* (1889), to prove the existence of a nationalist state of mind and awareness of a distinct Kurdish identity in the past. Most importantly, they argue, these documents show that Kurdish national awareness was territorially confined. References to the territory of Kurdistan and the descriptions of its boundaries are seen as indicators of this.

Eppel traces earliest mentions of the Kurds to Arab chronicles and books by historians such as Al-Baladhuri (d. 892) and Al-Tabari (838–932). These historians wrote about pastoral tribal populations inhabiting the mountainous areas to the north and northeast of the Tigris and Euphrates in the context of Muslim conquest of the region. These peoples, referred to as *al-akrad*, the Kurds, were described as peoples with no central government, dialects close to Persian, a nomadic lifestyle and multiple religious practices (Eppel 2016: 15–16). Another argument about the origin of the Kurds and Kurdistan refers to the first official use of the term 'Kurdistan' in the twelfth century when Sultan Sanjar of Turkic Seljuk State, the dominant power in the area then which controlled big chunks of today's eastern Anatolia, Syria, the Arabian peninsula, Iran, Pakistan and Afghanistan,[2] created a province called 'Kurdistan' in 1157 (Houston 2008: 19–20).[3] Seljuks' Kurdistan province was located in the eastern

---

[2] Seljuk dominance in Anatolia began after their victory over Armenia and Byzantium in the 1071 Battle of Malazgirt (also Battle of Manzikert), which led to the Turkish domination of Anatolia.

[3] Kurdish nationalist historiography makes references to an even earlier use of Kurdish land, the use of the notion of 'the land of the Kurds' and its cartographic definition by a Central Asian geographer, Ali Kashari, in 1076 (O'Shea 2004: 165).

parts of the Zagros Mountains and covered parts of the territories of modern Iraq and Iran, a much smaller area compared to the desired borders of Kurdistan today. Its capital was Bahar, and it encompassed the Sinjar, Shahrazur, Dinawer and Kermanshah *vilayet*s (a large administrative division) (McDowall 1996a: 23; Nezan 1996: 10). Sultan's nephew, Süleyman Shah, governed the province as the Seljuks administered their provinces through Turkmen officers (Nezan 1996: 23).

The Seljuk province of Kurdistan raises the question of whether this name was given to the province because of the identity of the people living there. Nezan argues that this province was created because Sultan Sanjar was already aware of the distinctive personality of the Kurdish people (Nezan 1996: 10). Some of the scholarly work on Kurdish history overrules ethnic considerations and Kurdish ethnic consciousness in the creation and naming of the Kurdistan province (Özoğlu 2004: 26–7; Tezcan 2000). These arguments build on the accounts of Hamd-Allah Mustawfi of Qazvin, who indicated that the province did not include major Kurdish-populated towns and that it simply was an administrative arrangement (Özoğlu 2004). According to Özoğlu, the Arab chronicles (which, according to Eppel, show Arab historians' awareness of the Kurds) did not use the term 'Kurdistan' and referred to the region as 'Jibal (Mountain), Zozan (Summer Pastures), Azerbaijan, and Armenia' (Özoğlu 2004: 26). He wrote that these chronicles gave the names to the peoples inhabiting the area based on 'tribal or clan name of the particular region or valley they were living, or from the mountain chain along which they were nomadizing' (Arfa 1966: 7). In any case, it would be fair to say that, even if the Seljuks named the province 'Kurdistan' and Arab historians described the people in the area as *al-akrad*, it is hard to ascertain whether Kurds had a collective ethnic consciousness then.

An important development in the thirteenth and fourteenth centuries that deeply affected the region was the Mongol invasions. Nomadic life and disparate and scattered small tribal communities became the rule for many communities for centuries as a result of constant upheaval and instability, agricultural decline and economic deterioration due to changing trade routes (McDowall 1996a: 24–5; Chaliand 1994: 23). Kurdish and non-Kurdish tribes moved away from urban areas and spread out to the north and west, reaching both Greater and Lesser Armenia, and the Anatolian plateau (McDowall 1996b: 8). This nomadic lifestyle and organisation of society around small tribal communities hindered the emergence of institutions and relations that would have helped to transcend linguistic, cultural and religious fragmentation within Kurdish communities.

An important process that reinforced this fragmented and tribal structure among Kurdish communities was the Ottoman–Safavid rivalry from the mid-fifteenth to mid-sixteenth centuries. After the Mongol invasions, the Ottoman Empire (1299–1922) in Anatolia and the Safavid Empire (1501–1722) in Persia tried to increase their influence in eastern Anatolia. This resulted in conflict and rivalry between the two states over the control of the region. The Kurdish tribes benefited from this rivalry by changing alliances between the two empires when it suited their interests. This hindered their integration into one of the empires, which perpetuated their fragmented status.

Increased Ottoman control in eastern Anatolia after the Ottomans defeated the Safavids at the 1514 Battle of Chaldiran did not alter the tribal and fragmented nature of Kurdish societies. This is because the Ottomans preferred an indirect rule in these peripheral areas and offered tribal leaders fiefdoms, principalities and greater local power. The Safavids wanted to govern this area through Turkmen and Persian administrators, while the Ottomans relied on local chiefs (McDowall 1996b: 26–7). Other factors that led to Kurdish tribal leaders siding with the Ottomans are the Ottoman military strength and the mutual religious suspicion between Sunni Kurdish tribes and the Shi'a Safavid rulers. As a result, many Kurdish tribal leaders saw Ottoman control as preferable to Safavid control (Ateş 2013).

The Ottoman Sultan Selim entrusted the integration of Kurdish tribes into the imperial system to Kurdish Ottoman diplomat İdris Bitlisi. Following İdris Bitlisi's approaches before the conquest, some Kurdish leaders had already declared their allegiance to the Ottomans in advance of the Chaldiran victory (Bajalan 2012: 803). İdris formed alliances between the Ottomans and several Kurdish tribes against the Safavids. Kurdish nationalist historiography considers the efforts by İdris as an indicator of Kurdish national consciousness, arguing that he was flagging Kurdish national interests (Jwaideh 2006: 291). However, such views overlook the fact that İdris Bitlisi was an Ottoman diplomat rather than a nationalist and many Kurdish nationalists today label him as a 'traitor' because they believe he failed to serve, or even betrayed, the Kurdish cause and hence cannot be considered Kurdish (Hassanpour 2003: 147).

Sharafname, written in 1596 about a century after the Ottomans began to dominate eastern Anatolia, is an important historical source that contemporary Kurdish nationalist historiography refers to in constructing Kurdish national identity. Written by Sherefhan Bitlisi, the ruler of the Ottoman Emirate of Bitlis, *Sharafname* is a significant historical source on the Kurdish chiefdoms and emirates. From the perspective of Kurdish nationalist historiographers, *Sharafname* is a nationalist text written in reaction to the control of Kurdistan by non-Kurdish (Ottoman) powers (Hassanpour 2003: 114–15). Bitlisi defines what he labels as *Kurdistan Eyaleti* (Kurdistan province) as follows:

The boundaries of the Kurdistan province begin at Hürmüz and ends at the borders of Malatya and Maraş. To its north lies the Arran province [Persia, today's Azerbaijan] and to its south lies Mosul and Iraq. (Şerafeddin Han [Sherefhan Bitlisi] 2006: 74)

Kurdish scholars see *Sharafname* as a proof of the existence of Kurdish ethnicity and Kurdish ethnic territory. They argue that Sherefhan had a Kurdish 'geo-ethnic entity' in mind when defining the areas where Kurdish families lived (Jwaideh 2006; Hassanpour 2003). Bajalan argues that in writing *Sharafname*, Sherefhan aimed to defend the autonomy of Kurdish principalities and believed the argument that he wanted 'to assert a form of *Kurdish statehood* is farfetched' (Bajalan 2012: 808). Interestingly, Sherefhan writes that many Kurdish families originally belonged to the Arabic dynasties of the Umayyad and Abbasid. Therefore, his use of the 'Kurd' could be indicating a collective identity linked to a geographical region, Kurdistan, rather than to an ethnic group (Özoğlu 2004: 27–8).

The Ottoman–Safavid rivalry offered several opportunities to tribes located in the mountainous areas where neither empire was able to fully penetrate. These tribes were able to shape things on the ground by pragmatically allying themselves with one or the other empire, whoever offered a better deal. Moreover, the 1639 Zohab Treaty, which is argued to have ended the conflict between the Ottomans and Safavids (Ateş 2013: 96–100), generated a status that resembled autonomy for several tribes around the Zagros Mountains. The Treaty created a broad border from the Zagros in the east to the Tigris in the west (about 100 miles), and this zone provided a peripheral location for

Kurdish tribes (Chaliand 1994: 24) for about two centuries. The Kurdish historiography records this period as a golden time for Kurds.

Seyahatname is another historical source that mentions the term 'Kurdistan' and therefore is deployed by Kurdish nationalist historiography to indicate the existence of a Kurdish territorial consciousness. *Seyahatname* is a compilation of famous Ottoman traveller Evliya Çelebi's (1611–85) travel notes. Its first proper publication goes back to 1896, and the full publication of all his notes was completed in 2007.[4] *Seyahatname* includes observations about the eastern territories of the empire. Çelebi undertook extensive travels in this area after the Ottoman–Safavid conflict ended. He defined Kurdistan, which he referred to as 'vilayet-i Kurdistan', as follows:

> It is a vast country. Its one end starts in Erzurum and it spreads on the area including Van, Hakkari, Cizre, Imadiye, Mosul, Şehrizor, Harir, Erdalan, Baghdad, Derne and Derteng reaching to Basra covering a seventy-camp distance. It would have been easy for the Acems [Safavids] to invade Anatolia if it was not for the rocky land between the Ottomans and Arabs in Iraq inhabited by six thousand Kurdish tribes and clans. (Özoğlu 2004: 34)

Yet rather than portraying the region as homogeneously Kurdish and the territory of a clear ethnic people, Çelebi defined the inhabitants of the region as a culturally and religiously mixed population (Van Bruinessen 2000). For example, he discusses the large number of Armenian Christian quarters in the city of Bitlis (Houston, 2008: 59; Köhler 1989: 43).

Another historical text used by Kurdish nationalist historiography to prove Kurdish ethnic consciousness is *Mem u Zin* written in 1695. This is a love story written by Kurdish intellectual Ahmed-i Hani that made references to the Kurds, the Kurdish land and the political status of the Kurdish people (Hani 2016). Although Hani did not define the borders of Kurdistan, he assumed that Kurdistan was a coherent territorial region, albeit not a politically united one, lying in the middle of Persian (*Ajam*), Ottoman (*Rum*), Arab and Georgian land (Van Bruinessen 2003a: 44). Eppel describes Hani's writing as an early expression of modern nationalist characteristic of desire for statehood and argues that Hani used the term 'Kurds' 'in the ethno-nationalist sense' (Eppel

---

[4] History of the publication of *Seyahatname* is available on the website of the Turk Tarih Kurumu (Turkish Historical Association).

2016: 42). Nationalists today define Hani as an early advocate of national self-determination as he demonstrated the existence of group consciousness. This is because, they argue, Hani distinguished Kurds from Arabs, Turks and Persians and criticised the divisions and rivalries among Kurdish tribal leaders calling for solidarity. However, declaring Hani a Kurdish nationalist could be considered a stretch as it is hard to speak of a Kurdish nation, or any nation, in Hani's time (Van Bruinessen 2003a: 54–6), especially in the areas under Ottoman control in the east.

Finally, two other historical works cited by Kurdish nationalist historiography are the writings of Haji Qadir Koyi (1817–97) and Şemseddin Sami (1850–1904). Koyi, an Ottoman intellectual, is considered the earliest proponent of Kurdish nationalist ideas (Edmonds 1971: 89) and came up with a detailed description of the boundaries of Kurdistan which encompassed a very large area:

Iskenderun and the Taurus mountains to the west, Black Sea, Ardahan and the River Aras to the north, Alvand peaks and the River Aras, Euphrates to the east and Hamrin Mountains, Sanjar and the Nassibin road to the south. (O'Shea 2004: 170–1)

In the same period, Şemseddin Sami, a famous Ottoman intellectual, described Kurdistan in his *Kamus-ul Alem (Özel Adlar Ansiklopedisi, Encyclopaedia of Custom Names)* (Sami 1996). During his time, the Ottomans created the Province of Kurdistan. It was established after the Ottomans defeated the Bedirhan Pasha Revolt in 1847. The province was short-lived, however, and was dissolved in 1867. Sami defines Kurdistan as follows:

Kurdistan is a large area that is generally known in relation to the name of the Kurdish people living on it. It is located in western Asia and part of it is ruled by Iran. This name covers the area that we [Ottoman Empire] used to call Kurdistan Province and the current Kurdistan Province in Iran. However, since Kurds are dispersed and mixed with other peoples in the area, it is difficult to fully ascertain the boundaries of Kurdistan. (#Tarih Dergi, 2014)

References to Kurds and the Kurdish land in *Şerefname, Mem u Zin,* Koyi's writings and *Kamus-ul Alem,* together with the Seljuk Kurdistan province, and references to Kurds in Arab chronicles, the short-lived Ottoman province of Kurdistan and the privileges Kurdish tribes had under the Ottoman rule are some of the key examples used in the Kurdish historiography to construct a Kurdish past. Kurdish historians

and nationalist scholars consider these usages as indicators of an existing Kurdish ethnic consciousness and a sense of territorial ownership.
In doing this, they adopt an ethno-nationalist and perennial view of
nations. They see the features of nations, such as their territoriality or
culture, as continuous throughout the history. However, when doing
this, they interpret these accounts and descriptions via conceptions
loaded with modern meanings of nations and territoriality.

It is hard to distinguish between the presumed identities of the people
defining where Kurdistan lies or the perceived boundaries of Kurdistan.
Today, Kurdishness has mainly linguistic and territorial meanings and
is attributed to the speakers of Kurdish and people who live in the
'Kurdish region'. But where is the Kurdish region, and who are its
inhabitants? The question is whether co-ethnics living side by side in
a territory can be retrospectively declared to have a nationalist consciousness when there was no overarching sense of shared cultural,
political or territorial affiliation within this diverse group of people at
the time. However, concepts such as 'Kurdish region', 'Kurdistan' and
'areas inhabited by Kurds' are abundantly used retrospectively in the
literature despite the multi-ethnic structure of the societies in the past
and today. Adding to this complexity is the tribal character of Kurdish
society under the Ottoman rule, to which the next section turns.

Kurdish Tribes in the Ottoman Local Administration System

Despite the wide linguistic and cultural variations throughout history
(and at present), the argument that Kurds had a sense of common
identity among the tribes long before the age of nationalism is not
convincing. Such a statement overlooks the multiple forms of divisions
among the societies in this region throughout the Ottoman era and
today. Tribal structure has been an important source of division in this
region, dividing populations along tribal and non-tribal lines, as well as
along separate tribal associations, which reinforced territorial attachment and control of areas at localised levels.

Traditionally, Kurds have been defined as the 'tribesmen of eastern
Asia Minor and the Zagros, settled as well as nomadic, who were not
Turkish, Arabic or Persian-speaking' (Van Bruinessen 2006: 25). The
Kurdish tribal structure has been mostly based on culturally distinctive
large families centred on kinship and common descent (King 2013:
80–92). A significant aspect of this structure is the hierarchical order of

society. Tribes, or *ashirets*, are typically composed of 'a leading lineage, a number of commoner clans/lineages, client lineages and subject non-tribal peasantry' (Van Bruinessen 2002). The leaders of these tribes were *beys* (owners of the land), who used their revenues to recruit and maintain military units for the Ottoman Porte, the central government of the Ottoman Empire.

Tribes in the eastern territories of the Ottoman Empire were considered as different from the non-tribal peasantry defined as *köylü* (peasant) or *reaya* (Ottoman term for commoners) (Van Bruinessen 1992). The *reaya* could not carry arms and worked as labourers in the land of their *beys*. The *reaya* population was of a very heterogeneous background, including Kurdish, Turkish, Arabic, Armenian-speaking and religiously diverse groups (Van Bruinessen 1992: 107–9). It has been suggested that peasants often consisted of the old populations of these territories who were now subject to new lords (O'Shea 2004: 36–7). For instance, Claudius James Rich wrote in 1836:

I had to-day confirmed by several of the best authorities, what I had long suspected, that the peasantry in Koordistan are a totally distinct race from the tribes, who seldom, if ever, cultivate the soil; while, on the other hand, the peasants are never soldiers. The clannish Koords call themselves Sipah, or military Koords, in contradistinction to the peasant Koords; but the peasants have no other distinguishing name than Rayah or Keuylees, in this part of Koordistan. (Rich 1836: 88–9, quoted by Jwaideh 2006: 27)[5]

In addition to the tribal/non-tribal division of the society, there was (and still is) a considerable degree of overlap between different levels of identity. For instance, *ashiret* leaders (*bey* or *agha*)[6] could be Kurdish, Turkish, Ottoman, Sunni or Arab simultaneously. At a wider level, some tribes over time have become Kurdish or have changed their religion, and therefore their identity. Therefore, the tribal structures and identity affiliations are and were fluid. Another type of division in the region that somehow overlapped with the tribal/non-tribal distinction was the one between the townspeople and the rural populations. Like non-tribal peasantry, the identity of the townspeople was also ambiguous (Van Bruinessen 2006: 31–2).

---

[5] Rich, Claudius James. (1836). *Narrative of a Residence in Koordistan*, 2 vols. London: James Duncan, Volume 1: 88–9.
[6] *Bey* and *agha* are traditional titles for tribal or non-tribal leaders in the Ottoman Empire with varying degrees of authority.

Today, Kurdish nationalists tend to consider urban and rural Kurdish communities as a unit. This is especially the case with the intensification of mass nationalist and political mobilisation since the 1960s. Government centralisation policies and land reforms, urbanisation and immigration also rendered urban–rural divisions since the late Ottoman Empire and the establishment of the Turkish state less important over time. Still, the division between 'dominant tribal group' and 'subject peasant group' has prevailed in different forms throughout most parts of the region. Even today, many Kurds dwelling in rural areas do not consider those living in the cities as 'proper Kurds'.[7]

Another feature of Kurdish society is the prevalence of tribal structures throughout history. Tribalism and different tribal traditions, cultures and dialects played constitutive roles in the development of Kurdish identity. Although it is impossible to define Kurdish identity with a number of common cultural features, it is remarkable that separate Kurdish identities – in linguistic, religious, ethnic and tribal terms – managed to prevail throughout the centuries. This was enabled through the ability of tribes to preserve their way of life, thanks to their peripheral location and the geographical inaccessibility of the territories where the two empires met. Most of these tribes were not fully integrated in the social and political systems of the two empires and often changed alliances between the two. This geographical inaccessibility also limited interactions and led to extensive variation in Kurdish culture, language and identity. Moreover, rivalry over territorial control among tribes contributed to this dividedness and variety. These factors perpetuated the continuation of the tribal divisions and inhibited the formation of a uniform Kurdish identity and nationalism in the long term.

The tribal structure of Kurdish society and the difficulty in controlling peripheral areas led Ottoman rulers to create a somewhat different administrative arrangement in this region compared to other parts of the empire. The creation of Kurdish principalities was a result of the Ottoman administrative system, which was flexible enough to

---

[7] This is actually a typical topic of conversation among the inhabitants of the area that I came across on my visits to the region. For instance, once I met two Kurdish men, one living in a large town, in the province of Van, and the other living in the rural area close to that town. They argued and joked about who was a real Kurd. The one from rural areas adamantly claimed that due to his rural and tribal associations he was not Turkified, whereas his friend was.

accommodate local circumstances and existing practices. The remoteness of this area, its harsh topography and the deeply embedded tribal structure required intermediary figures in its governance. Therefore, even though the general administrative principle was direct rule by Ottoman officials who held non-hereditary positions, the Ottoman state created nine autonomous Kurdish principalities or fiefdoms as part of *Eyalet-i* Diyarbakır (Province) in the nineteenth century (Houston 2008: 40). These fiefdoms were administered and ruled by their holders. The main Kurdish principalities in the seventeenth and eighteenth centuries were Botan, Hakkari, Badinan, Soran and Baban (Entessar 1992: 3). The *emir*s (heads of emirates or principalities) and the *aghas* and *beys*, who controlled the more remote areas, had some degree of autonomy from the Ottoman Porte within the territory under their authority. They were exempt from taxes and were able to maintain hereditary succession (Tahiri 2007: 35).

The usual administrative practice in other parts of the Ottoman Empire was different. For territories outside the capital the general rule was to divide the territory into administrative provinces, provinces into *sancak*s (districts) and *sancak*s into fiefs or principalities.[8] Head of provinces (*beylerbeyi*) and *sancak*s (*sancakbeyi*) were directly appointed by the Sultan. These positions were not hereditary, and the main duty of *beylerbeyi* and *sancakbeyi* was to raise and command troops and maintain order (Houston 2008: 38). In 1847, the Ottomans created the 'Eyalet-i Kurdistan' (Kurdistan Province). The Diyarbakır province was united with Van, Muş, Hakkari *sancak*s and Cizre, Botan and Mardin districts to create this Province. It was established right after a major Kurdish rebellion, the Bedirhan Pasha Revolt. The province was abolished in 1968 and the Diyarbakır Province was reinstituted (Dinç 2009: 158–60).

Under Ottoman rule, there was no continuous administrative province or district named 'Kurdistan'. The Ottoman policy of sustaining principalities headed by local leaders in certain parts of this region remained more or less unchanged in this period, except the Kurdistan Province, which lasted twenty years in the mid-nineteenth century. Historical accounts indicate that the Ottomans united tribes in order

[8] In 1527 the Ottoman provinces were: Rumelia (capital Edirne), Anadolu (Anatolia, capital Kütahya), Rum (capital Amasya) and Karaman (capital Konya), Egypt, Syria and Diyarbakır (İnalcık 2007).

to create confederations that did not exist before and appointed tribal leaders to these new establishments (Houston 2008: 45). They were directly bound by the Ottoman authority in terms of military responsibilities, but still, this period led to the reinforcement of the authority of Kurdish tribes and their leaders thanks to their relative autonomy in their positions as tribal leaders and their peripheral location away from the direct control of the centre (McDowall 1996b: 14). Kurdish nationalist historiography considers this period as Kurdish semi-independence and autonomy and sees the creation of provinces headed by local Kurdish tribal leaders as an indicator of the distinct Kurdish identity of the territory in question.

Kurdish Tribal Revolts

Some of the Kurdish scholarly work traces political mobilisation around Kurdish national consciousness back to the Kurdish revolts in the nineteenth century led by tribal leaders, who were Ottoman subjects and officials (Jwaideh 2006; Hassanpour 1992). They argue that these were nationalist rebellions reacting to the destruction of emirates and principalities by the Ottomans. Other scholars argue that tribal groups and their leaders with their strong desire to maintain their territorial control and self-interested ambitions used nationalism as a 'cover' and were not necessarily motivated by ethnic fraternity, even in the case of most famous of these rebellions, the revolt of Sheikh Ubeydullah (Ateş 2014; Edmonds 1971: 88). The period of the tribal revolts and the decades that followed these rebellions were accompanied by increasing political activism of Kurdish intellectuals in Istanbul and Europe, who were members of leading Kurdish tribes. Some scholars, such as Bajalan, trace the emergence of Kurdish nationalism to this period and perceive a Kurdish consciousness of a kind among educated Kurds and consider this as a form of nationalism (Bajalan 2013: 20). He frames this nationalism within the complex identity politics of the Ottoman Empire rather than through the widely accepted correlation between Ottoman collapse and the rise of minority nationalisms (Bajalan 2013: 4).

The timing of the emergence of Kurdish nationalism is a contested topic in the literature on the Kurds and there is no consensus about which theoretical model of nationalism Kurdish history fits (Maxwell and Smith 2015: 771). Different views on the emergence of Kurdish nationalism derive from various definitions of the nation and models of nationalism. If nationalism is seen as ethnic self-identification or consciousness, the emergence of Kurdish nationalism can be traced back to the sixteenth century (Hassanpour 2003: 148). On the other hand, if it is defined as directly associated with the notion of popular sovereignty and the idea of attaining a nation-state, Kurdish nationalism cannot be said to have emerged until the early twentieth century.

Nonetheless, the Kurdish nationalist historiography considers the Kurdish revolts in the nineteenth century, namely the Mir Muhammad[9] (1833–7), Bedirhan Pasha Revolt (1847) and Sheikh Ubeydullah (1880–2) revolts, as nationalist. These revolts were a response to the Ottoman centralisation policies, which were initiated in the mid-nineteenth century. The imposition of these centralisation policies led to many rebellious movements in different parts of the Empire, not only among the Kurdish emirates. Centralisation aimed to revive the power and strength of the Empire in the face of its decline in terms of foreign influence and domestic control and of the increasing power of the *ayan*s (local lords) as well as the Kurdish *emir*s, who did not welcome increased state control and loss of power. The most important of these policies were a series of administrative, taxation and military reforms, called *Tanzimat*, initiated by Sultan Mahmud II (reigned 1808–39) in 1839 and continued by Abdulmecid (reigned 1839–61).

The Kurdish nationalist discourse claims that Mir Muhammad, Bedirhan and Ubeydullah were conscious of their people's Kurdish identity and that their overarching aim was to establish a Kurdish state. According to this view, Kurdish tribal groups had a relatively autonomous status in the form of privileges granted to Kurdish *bey*s and *agha*s by the Ottomans before the beginning of the centralisation policies. It also asserts that Kurdish communities had common territorial, linguistic and cultural bonds that were akin to an *ethnie* (Houston 2008: 32; Smith 1986: 191). Indeed, Smith's concept of *ethnie* appealed to many scholars writing on the Kurds, who generally interpret the Kurdish *ethnie* as the source of Kurdish nationalism today. The rebellion of Sheikh Ubeydullah in 1881 is seen as a particularly important event showing Kurdish awakening (Jwaideh 2006). Their autonomous status combined with an ethno-national consciousness led tribal leaders to react to the centralisation policies. So,

---

[9] Also known as Kör (Blind) Muhammad Pasha.

according to this view, the revolts did not just aim to protect and continue existing positions: they were nationalist reactions and the Kurdish leaders had the vision of a different future for their people.

However, these rebellions can be partly understood as the result of Kurdish tribal leaders' attempts to protect their power or to force the Ottoman Sultan to keep their status in the new administrative arrangements. The policy of centralisation was partly an attempt to fix the weakening Ottoman system and rule, and partly a reaction to the efforts of the *emirs* and tribal leaders to further their control by, for example, appropriating local revenues instead of handing them over to the central authority (Van Bruinessen 1992). New policies, especially giving the authority of the *emirs* to centrally appointed *valis* (governors), threatened the former (Jwaideh 2006: 54–5). In this way, Kurdish leaders resorted to revolts to regain authority or come up with a new arrangement with the state. Leaders of the revolts, after their defeat, would be deported to other parts of the Empire or to Istanbul (Hakan 2007: 237–9). Mardin's notion of 'tacit contract', which explains the traditional centre-periphery relations where the Ottoman state and the rebels perceived resistance as a means of bargaining and negotiation (Mardin 2008: 108), fits well with this interpretation. Based on this, Kurdish leaders aimed to force the state for a new deal in order to regain the status and authority they lost due to centralisation policies. Bozarslan, supporting this point, argues that the Kurdish revolts were means to renew the type of relations between the state and the tribal leaders (2003: 186). However, although these revolts were typically tribal in many respects in seeking to maintain autonomy from an increasingly centralising government, their leaders and participants in the revolts also had reasonably good understanding of identity politics around nationalism (Bajalan 2013).

Another factor that led to Kurdish revolts was the increased recognition of non-Muslim communities by the western powers and the Ottoman Porte. Mahmut II's *Tanzimat* reforms in administration, taxation and within the legal system, promoted the idea of Ottomanism, a formula created in elite and intellectual circles in Istanbul to stop the Ottoman Empire from weakening and potentially dissolving and to alleviate the negative impact of nationalist movements in the Balkans and dissident revolts in other parts of the empire (Ortaylı 2007: 15–17). An important provision of these reforms was equality among Ottoman *millets*, which improved the status of non-

Muslim populations but disturbed Kurdish tribal leaders. Moreover, the 1878 Berlin Treaty that ended the Russian–Ottoman War promised Armenians certain 'improvements and reforms' and guaranteed their 'security against Circassians and Kurds' (Jwaideh 2006: 80–3). Kurdish leaders felt threatened by the changing status of the Christians (Nestorians and Armenians) and increased Christian missionary activities, thinking these might lead to a Christian state (Strohmeier 2003: 11). Both Bedirhan and Ubeydullah's violent actions towards the Christian populations during their revolts illustrate such concerns (Houston 2008: 56).

The earliest large Kurdish revolt in the nineteenth century against the Ottoman state after the centralisation policies were initiated was the Mir Muhammad Pasha Revolt (1833–7). Mir Muhammad Pasha was from Soran principality in today's northern Iraq near the Iranian border and succeeded his father in 1814 as an Ottoman *emir*. The Pasha expanded his control very quickly within two decades taking over the Amadiyah Emirate, Erbil, Zakho and Duhok (Ateş 2013: 67). He established armies and tried to develop alliances with other tribes to increase his dominance. According to some historians, the Pasha's aim was to create unity (Nezan 1996: 45). His increasing power concerned the Ottomans because of the state's weakening power combined with the offers of support Mir Muhammad Pasha received from the Qajars and Russians for his goals. Nationalist scholars argue that underlying the Pasha's rebellion was the idea of Kurdish nationality, and he revolted with the aim to acquire all the Kurdish provinces of the Ottoman Empire (Jwaideh 2006: 55, 291–2).

In response to Mir Muhammad Pasha's revolt, the Ottoman forces appeared in the region in large numbers, but the revolt was suppressed through diplomacy. This is partly because the Ottomans realised they would not be able to defeat the Pasha because of the international support he received (Galip 2015: 47) Interestingly, after his defeat Mir Muhammad Pasha was brought to Istanbul and was appointed governor-general of a wide area in east Anatolia and was 'acknowledged to be ... one of the pillars that sustained the throne of the Sultan' (Jwaideh 2006: 61). His brother took over the Soran principality, but the principality was abolished a few years later (Galip 2015: 48). The way the revolt led by Mir Muhammad Pasha emerged and finalised appears to fit in with Mardin's theory of 'tacit contract', meaning the Pasha might have revolted partly to increase his bargaining ability against the state and was eventually given concessions that brought the rebellion to an end.

Soon after the Mir Muhammad Pasha's rebellion ended, another Kurdish *emir*, Bedirhan Pasha, revolted in 1843–7. The Bedirhan Pasha Revolt also followed a similar pattern to Muhammad Pasha's in terms of fitting in the 'tacit contract' framework. Bedirhan Pasha was the Ottoman *emir* of the Botan Principality and controlled this strong emirate throughout the first half of the century. Bedirhan's family had been dominant in the area for several centuries. Bedirhan was a loyal *emir*, for example he was given an official rank in the Ottoman army for a campaign in Egypt, but he opposed the centralisation policies of the Ottoman state (Galip 2015: 48; Özoğlu 2001: 397). After his revolt was suppressed, Bedirhan Pasha was appointed to another Ottoman post and sent to Crete to suppress the Greek uprising in 1856. After that, he was allowed to return to Istanbul (Jwaideh 2006: 74). It is widely accepted that Bedirhan Pasha revolted against the Ottoman's new administrative arrangements in the region within the context of centralisation policies, as the new arrangements divided the land under Bedirhan Pasha's authority and reduced his power (Özoğlu 2004: 71). Although Bedirhan Pasha claimed that his aim was to liberate Kurdistan, it has been argued that his intention was to regain the status he lost as a result of the centralisation policies (Tahiri 2007: 35–6).

After the suppression of Bedirhan Pasha's revolt, no Kurdish leader gained much power in the region until Sheikh Ubeydullah. Bedirhan Pasha's suppression marked the end of the power of *emir*s. The gap created by the disappearance of the emirates was filled by leaders with religious authority, the *sheikh*s, who from then on, were to be found at the head of all the important Kurdish rebellions (Jwaideh 2006: 145, 212; Chaliand 1994: 24). They were closely associated with the Sufi orders, the tribal lineage and landed property (Van Bruinessen, 1992: 203). Due to their religious nature, the *sheikh*s were able to exert authority because their followers saw them as saviours (*mehdi*), who would end the chaos and bring justice during difficult periods (Olson 1991: 393). Sheikh Ubeydullah was one of the first of such leaders in this region. A Naqshbandi Sufi from the Şemdinan family, he had an extended control over a large area including parts of previous principalities of Botan, Badinan and Hakkari in the Ottoman territories and Ardalan in Persia (Jwaideh 2006: 80–3).

Most importantly, the historical context in the region generated suitable circumstances for *sheikh*s to emerge as leaders. First, the Ottomans, in their attempts to centralise power, failed to replace Kurdish principalities with effective political and administrative structures and reforms. The *vali*s appointed by the Ottomans did not have the traditional legitimacy *emirs* and tribal leaders had. These factors resulted in internal chaos among Kurdish tribal communities, leading to the division of the emirates into separate confederacies and smaller tribal units and intensified rivalry (Van Bruinessen 2003b: 167). Second, the huge social, political and economic chaos in the 1877–8 Russian–Ottoman War increased people's tendency to cluster around and support religious leaders who offered them protection and salvation. Third, the 1878 Berlin Treaty provisioned improvements and reforms for the protection of Armenians against the Circassians and Kurds, and this increased the Kurds' fear of increased Armenian/Christian power in the region (Van Bruinessen 1992: 250).

Ubeydullah is defined as a nationalist who aimed to unite the Kurds and set up an independent Kurdish state (Jwaideh 2006: 80), and his revolt against the Ottomans and the Qajar Iran is considered to have 'nationalist undertones' (Edmonds 1971: 96) or to represent the first stage of the development of Kurdish nationalism (Olson 1991). Indeed, some of its features indicate that the Sheikh Ubeydullah Revolt might have been a nationalist resistance. It was different from previous Kurdish revolts because, while Bedirhan aimed at greater autonomy under Ottoman administration, Ubeydullah expressed his desire to create an independent Kurdish state (Olson 1991: 392). In a letter to Dr Cochran, an American missionary in the Hakkari region, the Sheikh wrote: 'The Kurdish nation, consisting of more than 500,000 families, is a people apart ... Their religion is different, and their laws and customs are distinct.' The British vice-consul Clayton wrote: '[the Sheikh] has a comprehensive plan for uniting all the Kurds in an independent state under himself' (Jwaideh 2006: 80–1). Therefore, despite not having a specifically nationalist ideology or goal, the Sheikh nonetheless used the language of nationalism to draw support and present his movement to outsiders (Bajalan 2013: 6). Wider contextual factors that enabled the revolt are identified as reaction to centralisation policies, Sunni-Shi'a rivalry and a 'gradual articulation of a Kurdish nationalist sentiment' (Ateş 2006: 319–20).

However, in some other ways, the Sheikh Ubeydullah Revolt is similar to previous Kurdish revolts in the sense that it aimed to increase or secure the power and control of the Kurdish elite and it was partly a reaction to an increase in the prominence of Christianity in the area. When the Sheikh wrote 'the Kurdish nation', the concept probably did not have similar connotations attributed to the same concept today. In fact, it is highly likely that the Sheikh did not even use the word 'nation' as it did not have an equivalent in the language in that part of the Empire then, especially among the Muslim Ottoman subjects. If the Sheikh used *umma* (literally 'community', which was used to denote all Muslims, or Arabs) or *millet* (meaning different religious components of the Ottoman *reaya*), it is hard to ascertain on what conception the translator, probably Dr Cochran, used the concept of the 'nation' (Özoğlu 2004: 75). Even if we assume that the Sheikh used the term 'nation', Dr Cochran and Sheikh Ubeydullah probably attributed different meanings to this term, or alternatively, maybe the Sheikh used the term strategically, having some understanding of how using the word 'nation' might evoke a positive response from a British diplomat (Özoğlu 2004: 75–6).

Moreover, similar to the way the Mir Muhammad Pasha and Bedirhan Pasha revolts ended, after the suppression of the rebellion, Sheikh Ubeydullah was brought to Istanbul, was granted honours by the Sultan and awarded a new position within the Ottoman state. What followed the Sheikh's capture also seems to support Mardin's 'tacit contract' theory. Therefore, it could be argued that although Ubeydullah might have aimed for an independent principality, he was ready to accept a deal that recognised his authority in the region while remaining under Ottoman rule (Natali 2005: 11). This shows the priority given by tribal leaders to their own personal and tribal gains. There is contradicting archival information about the Sheikh's intentions, but, even if he thought about an independent state, 'he was ready to settle for the recognition of his authority in Kurdistan within the Ottoman state. He wanted to be the ruler of a principality similar to those of the earlier Kurdish emirates but greater in its territory to match his influence in the region' (Özoğlu 2001: 391).

The territorial goals of the Kurdish leaders in the nineteenth century look like pre-national/tribal/territorial goals that emerged during centralisation in the Ottoman Empire and the local tribal elite's efforts to bargain a better position. Although the idea of 'Kurdistan' as a regional but ambiguous entity existed in the minds of these tribal leaders, their emphasis on territoriality appears to have had a different meaning to national territoriality. Moreover, their focus on tribal forms of control and authority hindered the unification of different Kurdish groups and the development of a more encompassing political goal defined in nationalist terms. Therefore, although territoriality is the most crucial aspect of Kurdish nationalism both in terms of self-identification and of projection of this identity to the outside world, its very nature was tribal and divided in the nineteenth century.

Conclusion

Kurdish nationalism is a modern phenomenon and is the result of the political purposes of nation-building and achieving sovereignty. Like other nationalisms, it builds on features emphasising a historic continuity. Particularly important in the Kurdish case is the idea of Kurdistan in the construction of a historic community. Kurdish nationalism perceives Kurdish habitation in the area since ancient times as clear proof that the history of the territory of Kurdistan reflects the history of the Kurdish people (Vali 2003: 67). This identification overlooks the presence of Persian, Arab, Turkish, Assyrian and Armenian claims over the same region. It labels this territory 'Kurdistan' with today's notions of ethnicity and nation.

Many Kurdish and non-Kurdish scholars working on Kurds conceptualise and perceive the terms Kurd and Kurdistan in perennial and ethnic terms. This is despite the fact that there are disagreements, even among the Kurds, about who constitutes the Kurdish community and where Kurdistan lies (O'Shea 2004: 45). The idea of a continuous historical Kurdish identity is tacitly based on essentialist theories that place emphasis on revealing the origin of the Kurdish identity, which is believed to lie in their language, culture and territory. Such views propagate the idea of an ethnic origin, defined in territorial and cultural terms. They then directly associate this idea with nationalism. According to this view, for example, the use of the notion of Kurdistan in the past implies the existence of an identity-based territory. The historical texts about Kurds and Kurdistan, and the rebellions led by Kurdish tribal leaders are interpreted as expressions of nationalist claims and the existence of a Kurdish identity waiting for realisation (Vali 2003: 61–2). This interpretation of the past provides the foundation for contemporary Kurdish nationalist views.

It is problematic to presume a linear history for nations – meaning an ethnic group develops its self-consciousness, becomes a nation and, then, matures enough to deserve its own nation-state (Halliday 2006; Vali 2003). Nations and their features, such as territorial attachment, language, culture and ethnicity are contingent, and develop and change as a result of historical factors and circumstances (Halliday 2000: 39). Therefore, whether nations have common distinct features or not is unimportant in understanding and explaining nationalisms (Gellner 2000: 367–8). Here, Kurdish national identity is seen as a constructed phenomenon, like all other national identities, rather than something perennial and primordial.

Indeed, it is hard to assume that the concepts of 'Kurd' or 'Kurdistan' used in the past had nationalist connotations in the way we understand nations and nationalism today. Tracing the linguistic, cultural or ethnic origins of a group of people does not automatically mean that all the activities carried out by that group in the past were nationalist, that they had nationalist goals and they were executed by leaders or groups who were conscious of a national identity. Structural socioeconomic factors, historical circumstances and local and international politics are significant in generating and driving the emergence and development of nations and nationalism, and Kurdish nationalism today is the result of such factors more so than claims on the authenticity of identity. Kurdish nationalist revolts in the late nineteenth century reflect the complexity of this contextual background and reveal the ways in which identity interacted with these factors and how the idea of a national identity evolved.

2 | Orientalist Views of National Identity and Colonial Maps of Kurdistan

Introduction

This chapter focuses on the maps of Kurdistan produced by Western travellers and colonial officers in the nineteenth and early twentieth centuries, the period of the end of the empires. It seeks to connect a colonialist understanding of what constituted national identity, which had strong perennialist and civilisationalist underpinnings, with constructions of Kurdish identity and projections of Kurdistan by Western travellers and states. Western map-making in this period was shaped by colonial powers' conceptions of nationhood and civilisation, as well as their political, economic and geostrategic interests in the region. Western travellers' and states' perceptions of nationality and colonisation and their view of the peoples of this part of the Ottoman Empire informed the construction of a retrospective view on Kurdish national identity today. Western maps of Kurdistan were adopted and used by Kurdish nationalists in the early twentieth century and onwards which became key sources for mapping Kurdistan in the twentieth century.

The geographical and ethnographic studies undertaken by Western travellers and how they informed European imperialist powers' policies in the period leading up to, during and after the First World War significantly influenced most of the territorial demarcations in the Middle East and the fate of Kurdistan. European imperialism laid the groundwork for the world today and in this historical process geography played a significant role as 'none of us is outside or beyond geography' (Said 1994: 6). Cartography had huge power in this process because it allowed for 'achieving ideological supremacy over space' (Wintle 1999: 137). Maps reflect the wider ideological and political discourses and they are the outcome of communication between cartographers, the goals of their study, the political offices and wider society

(Wintle 1999: 138). Therefore, a critical geopolitical perspective (Culcasi 2006) is adopted here to understand how geographical knowledge about Kurdistan and its cartographic depictions was produced in the nineteenth and early twentieth century.

Neither territory nor its cartographic depictions can be taken for granted as static and ahistorical things. Maps are components of a 'visual language' that communicates strategic interests and ideologies (Harley 1989).[1] Even when the aim for the production of a map is not propaganda (Tyner 1982), maps are produced based on unconscious biases and assumptions situated in the particular values, ideologies and political interests of the producer and the institutions and history they are situated in (Harley and Woodward 1987: 2). It is neither possible to escape geography nor the political and economic values and interests that shape its depictions and imaginations.

The relationship between mapping and the construction of a nation is a continuous process that evolves and changes throughout history. This relationship is framed by global and regional power configurations and ideas about the world, its components and the relationship between its components in different historical periods. Long-term historical processes and structures of the international order frame assumptions, ideologies, perceptions and interests that underlie maps and their interpretations. Political and ideological discourses at international, regional and local levels provide the supporting context for the production of geographical knowledge (Crampton 2001: 235). In different international orders the meaning of the territorial state differs; states have distinct economic structures and different dynamics that shape the relationship between states in each international order. Agnew (1994: 67) identifies three such international orders in recent world history: 1815–75, 1875–1945 and 1945–90. The first and part of the second period are relevant for the focus of this chapter.

In the 1815–75 international order, according to Agnew, European states had reached a period of balance of power in their relationship, the Concert of Europe (a consensus among the European monarchies to

---

[1] According to Agnew this is important for avoiding the 'territorial trap': 'Even among "globalist" perspectives (including dependency theories and world-systems theory) only "critical" international relations theory (e.g. Cox 1987; Gill 1993) avoids the "territorial trap" [which refers to the] importance of the *territorial* state and the similar ontological roles (including fixed identity) it performs' (Agnew 1994: 56).

maintain territorial and political status quo), which was underpinned by the policy of non-interference. Nationalism as an idea and ideology already had emerged as a force for the centralisation of European states. Nationalism came to be seen as the most apt ideology for states and as an indicator of more superior systems and values of the Western world vis-à-vis others. In this period, Italian, German and French travellers, missionaries and states were already active in the Middle East, including in the areas where Kurdish communities resided alongside other communities. Britain's colonial power was on the rise and, as the century progressed, the British became increasingly more involved in the Middle East. European travellers used their own discourses about national identity and the orientalist view of the world in their explorations and study of the region. They were mainly driven by the goal of learning about the areas and people they visited. They were particularly interested in the fate of Christian populations and carried out large-scale missionary activities which continued into today. Their focus on Christian communities generated or increased tension between Christians and other communities and led to conflict in the second half of the nineteenth and early twentieth centuries in the Ottoman Empire.

Agnew's second international order from 1875 to 1945 is one of intensified rivalry between imperialist powers over control of and access to areas, trade routes and resources (Agnew 1994: 67). In this period, especially until the end of the First World War, European explorations were made mainly for strategic purposes to promote and protect state interest against other states' interests in the region. Explorations and studies conducted by the Europeans in this period were mainly done to facilitate their states' activities and strategic interests or these explorations were co-opted for these goals. Also important in this period is the increasing strength of nationalism, both in the form of state nationalism as well as separatist nationalisms in the Ottoman and Habsburg territories, which resulted in the creation of several new states in the territories of these empires. European powers were heavily involved in the demarcation of the territories of the new states and in identifying the specific colonial power's position and role in the governance of the new territory.[2] In both these periods,

---

[2] The third international period Agnew refers to from 1945 to 1990 is outside the focus of this chapter. This period was one in which 'interstate competition and conflict were largely transformed by the US reconstruction of the industrial capitalist state along liberal capitalist lines'. (Agnew 1994: 67).

namely nineteenth and early twentieth century, an orientalist view of the non-Western world and ideas of civilisation and underdevelopment shaped the perspective of the European travellers and their states, and informed the mapping and study of the region.

Nationalism and Its Impact on the Orientalist Perspective

Nineteenth- and early twentieth-century Europe is characterised by increased centralisation of political and economic power and decision-making under militaristic nation-states and a form of imperialism that was driven by rivalry between these nation-states in most of the rest of the world (Laughlin 1986: 322). In this world, nationalism was one of the most significant political forces and ideologies,[3] and it has continued to shape the international system until the modern day. Nationalism has been a key cause in the transformation of monarchical and colonial empires into new states since the eighteenth century (Wimmer and Feinstein 2010: 764).[4] In the late eighteenth century, the British colonies in North America rejected the monarchical authority of the British Empire and declared an independent United States of America which took the form of a sovereign nation. Similarly, in Europe, the French Revolution was based on the ideas of nationhood, republicanism and liberty. Both revolutions saw the republican nation as the only legitimate form of political order to realise this latter goal of liberty.

In the nineteenth century several central and south American states gained independence from Portuguese and Spanish colonial empires. In 1830, Greece and Belgium were recognised as independent states, and in the second half of the nineteenth-century Italy and Germany unified, and Romania, Luxembourg, Serbia, Montenegro, Germany, Bulgaria, Norway, and Albania became states (Barkin and Cronin 1994; Knight

---

[3] Although according to Freeden (1998) nationalism is not a full ideology, the way it was used to justify state formations and policies in the nineteenth century could qualify it as an ideology. In other contexts, nationalism can also be a sentiment or a movement.

[4] In the last two hundred years more than 140 new states formed in total in the form of nation-states. In the twentieth century, the number of states tripled. In 1800 there were about 20 states, by 1900 there were about 50 states and by 1960 the total number of states in the world reached about 140. Since the collapse of the Union of Soviet Socialist Republics (the Soviet Union), new states emerged in ex-communist states in the Balkans, Caucasus, and Central Asia, and other parts of the world. Today there are about 180 states in the world.

1985: 253). After the First World War, the dissolution of the Habsburg, Russian and Ottoman Empires led to the formation of new states based on the principle of nationality.[5] Basically, most modern European nation-states emerged in the nineteenth century during significant social and economic change following the consolidation of industrial capitalism combined with nation-building (Laughlin 1986: 299).

Initial nationalisms in Europe were rooted in countries with already distinct social, political and economic systems within well-defined territorial boundaries. This model of nation-state and the types of nationalism in Europe (for instance, the well-known civic and ethnic types, exemplified by the French and German nationalism respectively) (Kohn 1929) in the nineteenth century and early twentieth century, are historical outcomes that emerged and formed within specific political, economic and ideological settings. Therefore, the perceived homogeneity of the nation and the idea that this homogeneity led to the development of nation-states is misplaced. Nations have fragmented pasts and a sense of shared identity was forged in the nineteenth century through modernising forces (Weber 1976). Such nation-building processes, whether the state was already present or not, were elite-led. This form of nationalism had a distinctive logic – to integrate the masses into the constructed identity of the elite middle class. This logic resulted in a specific political character, ideology and values among European states in the late nineteenth and early twentieth centuries, which were not politically neutral (Laughlin 1986: 302, 311).

Key characteristics of the logic of the state in nineteenth-century Europe were industrial capitalism/development and centralisation. The emergence of nationalism in place of feudal and monarchical affiliations coincided with industrial capitalism. This led to the perception that industrial development and nationalism go hand in hand, and a centralised economy, education system, military, police and bureaucracy were seen as the outcomes or products of the consolidation of national integration. The reverse is also possible; nationalism could be

---

[5] However, Irish and Polish nationalisms were not allowed to gain independence, and colonial rule in Africa, Asia, and the Pacific islands continued. In the twentieth century, nationalism became an internationally recognised principle for new states, which legitimised the formation of new states in other parts of the world in the decolonisation period and later, following the collapse of the Soviet Union.

considered as the outcome of these centralising forces (Tilly 1994; Breuilly 1993). As a result of the coincidence of industrial capitalism, development and nationalism, the ideas of development and civilisation became associated with the nation, and its distinct identity, territory, culture, language and values. In this context, racial and ethnic groups were perceived to overlap with such processes. If this perceived overlap was present, a nationalist movement was seen to be a legitimate force or an entity to be taken seriously in the nineteenth century.

This coincidence between nationalism, development and industrial capitalism generated the lenses through which European colonial forces imagined the political future of non-European territories. They assumed that the consolidation of nation-states around specific identities within well-defined territories under a clear national leadership was an appropriate model for these areas as well. Most colonial officers and travellers, including writers, anthropologists, linguists and geographers, saw the areas they explored and visited from this perspective and their writings, and their approaches to the subject, research methods and interpretations of the information they gathered were shaped by such ideological positions.

As a result, European colonial officers and travellers projected an understanding of the nation as experienced (or thought to be experienced) in Europe and they understood dissident or rebel groups and the groups with distinct cultures and customs through these lenses. National communities were thought as entities with common language or religion with a historical attachment to a defined territory and shared culture. This understanding of the nation was accompanied by the belief that nationalism and the nation-state are natural and progressive (Laughlin 1986: 300). If such a people exist and if they have a nationalist leadership espousing these ideas, then they were seen to deserve being categorised as a national liberation movement. However, such a perspective overlooked the possibility that nationalism or liberation movements are 'one strategy among several adopted in concrete historical-regional contexts' to deal with socio-economic and social changes (Laughlin 1986: 307).

Accompanying the orientalist and colonial views on national identity and territoriality was the idea that the ability to form national unity around a specific identity and on a demarcated territory required a certain level of civilisational attainment. The lack of apparent shared identity or a nationalist leadership among a community or people were considered as indicators of backwardness. This rendered, in the orientalist perspective, these people as unable to govern themselves. European state officials, travellers, traders and geographers often wrongly 'projected upon local parochial communities the belief that national concerns not local issues should be at the forefront of local consciousness' and where that appeared to be missing, they were considered as being unready for national attainment (Laughlin 1986: 308).

Ideas that Underlay the European Perspective of the Nation: Liberal Democracy and Self-Determination

Liberal ideology is a key component of the ideal of the nation-state with a demarcated territory and a society with shared identity, an ideal that came to be seen as a universal standard among the European states by the end of the late nineteenth century. Liberalism is an intellectual and political philosophy that embraces individual human liberty and equal rights as key political values. There are several strands within liberalism, but at its core is the belief in the unconstrained individual. The adjacent and peripheral aspects of the liberal ideology (Freeden 1998) is belief in institutional arrangements that ensure the freedom of the unconstrained individual, such as constitutional government, equality and the right to private property. In different historical periods liberalism and nationalism appear to have been at odds,[6] and at a conceptual level, the contradiction between the two is constant. Liberalism singles out the individual and therefore divides the community, while nationalism singles out national communities and therefore divides humanity. Liberalism aims to enhance individual liberty; nationalism aims to create a coherent national and communal identity and tends to overlook the differences within a defined national community. The idea of 'liberal

---

[6] An important historical period that put liberalism and nationalism at odds was when racist forms of nationalism and later the appropriation of the national principle by the Soviet Union for administrative purposes became central during the interwar period and after 1945 respectively (Resnick 1992: 511). The experience of fascism and Nazism led most liberals after the Second World War to denounce nationalism (Kymlicka 1989: 4). Another historical reason for liberalism's denunciation of nationalism is the association between national self-determination and the Third World in the decolonisation process. This led many liberals to portray nationalism as a 'backward ideology' given the underdeveloped and seemingly tribal nature of these new states (Nodia 1994: 14).

nationalism' seeks to combine the two ideas and presents nationalism as the best form of ensuring individual liberty by protecting the communal identity of which an individual is part of (Tamir 2003).

Still, historically, both national acts and liberation movements are seen to be undertaken in the name of protecting individual rights due to the connection between the collective right of self-determination and individual freedom (Resnick 1992: 511). Nationalism provides the collective ideology and legitimacy for the state to undertake the endeavour to accomplish individual freedom through institutional arrangements. In this sense, liberal nationalist thought today sees self-determination as a liberal principle with roots going back to Grotian solidarity, to Kant's visions for peace through republican federalism, to Wilson's definition of collective security and to the UN Charter (Mayall 1990: 30). Liberal nationalists envision the possibility of a community bound together through common memories, therefore they see nationalism as a benign force. Although this implies that a civic understanding of nationhood (where state identity supersedes diverse linguistic, religious and ethnic identities) is more compatible with liberalism, some scholars argue that, historically, the coexistence of nationalism and liberal democracy has worked best in countries where the dominant culture is more or less racially and culturally homogeneous (Fukuyama 2006: 23–39, 1994: 26–7), or that in homogeneous polities, it is easier to establish and consolidate liberal democracy (Dahl 1971: 108–13).

The ideal of a nation-state was (is) also perceived to be imbued with certain values such as liberalism, capitalism, democratic institutions and popular sovereignty. Nineteenth-century classical liberals saw popular sovereignty and the general will of the people as the best and only option against dynastic rule. In this model, the state could ensure a harmonious society and is seen as progressive if it embraces popular citizenship instead of imperial rule (Agnew 1994: 61–2). Historically, this idea emerged with the French Revolution. Indeed, in the eighteenth- and nineteenth-century thinking, the emphasis was on the group over the individual, and liberal ideals and democracy could be achieved through a focus on the 'collectivity', the nation (Williams 2002: 1–3). Collective governance, or democracy organised on national lines, defined as 'the institutional arrangement for arriving at political decisions in which individuals acquire the power to decide by means of a competitive struggle for the people's vote'

(Schumpeter 1976: 250), it was believed, could better protect liberal values and individual freedom (Nodia 1994: 3).

Democracy and nationalism complement each other because nationalist groups or movements who claim self-determination see this right as a democratic collective right (Nodia 1994: 8–9). By definition, the democratic enterprise has always been based on a defined group of people. As a result, constructing and defining a distinct nation came to be seen as a prerequisite for the formation of a democratic state. In turn, determining who belongs to 'us' and who should form the nation is seen as a prerequisite for this democratic endeavour.[7] Building a democratic state based on a claimed distinct identity is perceived as a rational route due to the belief that it brings solutions to political problems, and provides suitable political and social circumstances for the advancement of freedom of thought and civil liberties. In this context, self-determination as a political principle is understood as a democratic right of peoples with distinct ethnic, national, cultural or religious identities.

Self-Determination

Self-determination as an idea emerged building on the eighteenth- and nineteenth-century conceptions of nationalism, liberalism and democracy (Whelan 1994: 99–100). It has become one of the most crucial international norms in relation to nationalist claims to justify separation from empires in the nineteenth century, gaining independence through decolonisation in the nineteenth and twentieth centuries, and in shaping borders during the dismemberment of communist states at the end of the Cold War, as well as secessionist, irredentist or autonomist demands in other contexts.

Self-determination as a concept is widely discussed in the literature, and one thing that is agreed upon is the difficulty in defining this concept whether it is defined as a legal, political or analytical term. As a *principle* of international law, it is generally understood in a way that prioritises the stability of the international system and protects the sovereignty of states other than in exceptional circumstances. Politically, it is interpreted as

---

[7] Yet, history shows that the act to determine who belongs to the nation has resulted in non-rational actions such as dictatorial or extreme forms of nationalism that utilised suppressive and non-democratic methods on people (Nodia 1994: 8).

a *political goal* to achieve the rights of people to determine their political future, as a people of a state or in the form of autonomy or secession. Nationalist groups and their supporters (lobby groups, diasporas, states or international organisations) are proponents of this meaning of self-determination. Lastly, self-determination as an *idea*, as an analytical concept, is utilised to understand state formation, nation-building, ethnic conflict, nationalist political movements and other related issues, especially in the study of international relations, nationalism and conflict resolution.[8]

Discussions concerning nationalism and self-determination as an idea are certainly not new, and go back to thinkers like Mazzini, Mill and Lord Acton in the nineteenth century during the French and English nation-building processes, German and Italian unifications and the wave of romantic nationalism ideology that subsequently swept through central and eastern Europe and spread to the Ottoman Empire. The meaning of the concept of self-determination is related to the 'nationality principle'. Mazzini argued that the individual has an intimate connection to the people with whom he/she shares a common identity. In his view, the community or nation has a common and homogeneous nature and this collective existence needs to be recognised (Mazzini 1898: 61). Mazzini put special emphasis on the connection between the individual and national self-esteem. He saw nations as given units of humanity and assumed that individual identity can only be realised within a national community and a country.[9] From a Mazzinian perspective, the nation is a community that shares objective features based on culture and national consciousness, and members of a nation have the right to protect their distinct existence within a communal life in line with their distinct identity.

Mill, on the other hand, adopted a more civilisational interpretation of the 'nationality principle' and argued that not all peoples are ready for self-governance. Only when they reach a required level of civilisational development should the nationality principle apply to a people (Mill 1872: 284–93). Mill's view resonates with the orientalist view of Western civilisation described earlier. According to Mill's perspective

---

[8] Throughout this book, self-determination is used in relation to all these different meanings depending on the context.
[9] 'The individual is too insignificant, and Humanity too vast. . . . He [God] gave you a country . . . he divided Humanity into distinct groups or nuclei upon the face of the earth, and creating the germ of nationalities' (Mazzini 1898: 58).

the nation refers to a group of individuals living under the same system of rule, and self-determination is the right of the governed to participate in the governing process. While Mazzini attributed a natural existence to the nation, Mill had a more civic, liberal and individualistic view of the concept. However, both saw the nation as the legitimate source of political rule and both seem to assume that the division of mankind into collective units is a given (Mayall 1990: 51).

By the end of the nineteenth century, the idea of a national identity had become a common sensical idea,[10] and self-determination, defined as the 'nationality principle' or 'self-governance' at the time, became a principle used in liberation movements against the imperial powers, notably the Habsburgs and the Ottomans, as a justification for over-throwing the ruler or the ruling class and establishing a new state. It was believed that when an independence movement achieves separation, it would be deemed a nation and would be able to establish its popular sovereignty over a defined territory and thus realise the ideal of popular national sovereignty (Knight 1985: 252).

This national idea played an important role in the formation of new states in the nineteenth century in Europe and South America (Wimmer and Feinstein 2010; Meyer 1980: 109–38).[11] Although self-determination did not enjoy widespread general acceptance as a political principle at this time, it was now being followed as a goal in a growing number of cases. These state formations reinforced the idea that popular sovereignty belongs to the nation and, especially after the First World War, nationalist ideology and self-determination became directly linked to popular sovereignty and modern liberal democracy (Diamond and Plattner 1994: xii). A combination of Mazzini's and Mill's views of the nation – the nation's natural existence combined with a democratic right for political recognition – gave national self-determination its meaning in the First World War era and throughout the rest of the twentieth century.

National self-determination derives its meaning from the idea of popular sovereignty. Here it is important to define what sovereignty is because international political rules and norms are centred on a complicated

---

[10] Mill also highlighted the difficulties in applying the national idea. The main difficulty he raised was geographic since in many places members of different nations are so mixed that it is almost impossible to divide them geographically.

[11] Wimmer and Feinstein provide a detailed account of the history of the formation of states in the last two hundred years and discuss the reasons behind the proliferation of nation-states.

relationship between sovereignty and self-determination in the international system. Sovereignty, in its most basic sense, is territorial control or
supreme authority within a territory concept and a concept 'without
which modern international relations does not exist' (Philpott 2001:
16). The difficulty in defining 'the people' is the reason why self-
determination poses a challenge to sovereignty (Mayall 1990: 51). If the
national boundaries of a people appear to be compatible with the boundaries of the state, in theory, no conflict arises between self-determination
and sovereignty. The problem arises when a group claims that their
national boundaries are different from the state(s) they live in. This causes
a tension between the people's right to self-determination and the state's
right to territorial integrity, depending on how the people is defined
(Bishai 2004: 7).

Definitions of sovereignty vary widely from the absolute sovereignty
defined by Hobbes and Bodin to Rousseau's popular sovereignty and to
modern sovereignty defined in national covenants of states and international law (Philpott 2001: 16). Throughout the past century, sovereignty
has come to apply only to territories formally constituted, accepted and
internationally recognised as states (Crawford 1979: 88). Krasner's typology of sovereignty – domestic sovereignty, Westphalian sovereignty,
interdependence sovereignty and international legal sovereignty – reflects
the transformation of the meaning and function of sovereignty throughout history (Krasner 1999: 9–25). Domestic sovereignty refers to its
classical meaning – the control of domestic affairs and territory and it is
linked to the Weberian conception of sovereignty that sees the state as the
institution with the monopoly of coercive and administrative control over
a specific territory. Westphalian sovereignty, on the other hand, alludes to
the historical importance of sovereignty as a concept in international
history. It goes back to the 1648 Treaties of Westphalia and Osnabrück
where a state's domestic administrative, political and economic control
over its territory together with the idea of the sanctity of its borders and
immunity from external intervention was adopted. Therefore, the only
difference between Westphalian sovereignty and domestic sovereignty is
the emphasis on the international dimension. These two conceptions of
sovereignty together constitute the meaning of sovereignty as it was
understood in the nineteenth and early twentieth century.[12]

---

[12] These definitions continue to constitute the concept of sovereignty today, but the
concept has become more complicated and comprehensive over time. Krasner's

Popular sovereignty is about the legitimacy of a state and is a product of the French and American revolutions, moulded into the nineteenth-century concept of nationalism. It emerged as a principle in Hobbes, Locke and Rousseau's writings on the social contract and general will. Popular sovereignty's emphasis on the consent of the governed and general will was well suited to a political rule that relied on a wider social stratum, therefore, this concept has been crucial in transitions towards democratic political regimes in Europe – in other words, transitions from the sovereignty of monarchs to the sovereignty of people (Benton 2010: 1–2). The people, or the nation, came to be seen as the source of state power and established itself as a source of all sovereignty (Knight 1985: 252). This meaning and usage became internationally widespread particularly after the dissolution of empires following the First World War and during the wave of decolonisation in the 1960s and 1970s (Philpott 2001: 3, 28).

What Do These Ideas Mean for Territorial Imaginations in This Period?

The values and ideals that crystallised around nationalism, popular sovereignty, democracy and industrial capitalism in the nineteenth-century European context were framed within a concept of a clearly demarcated territory inhabited by people that share an identity, language, institutions, history and culture. These altogether came to define the idea of the nation-state. Such a state came to be considered as the natural and progressive (and therefore desirable) model that should be followed across the world. This idea led to the geographic imagination of the state territory in more concrete ways. The process of drawing clear boundaries in Europe in the nineteenth century underpinned such imagination. This view was carried to non-Western contexts as well,

other two typologies of sovereignty refer to its expanded aspects. Interdependence sovereignty refers to a state's ability to control its boundaries and particularly it describes state's decreasing ability to control movements and issues that cut across its boundaries mainly due to the increasing accountability and responsibility of states to the outside world. The emergence of this meaning of sovereignty has led to discussion on the weakening sovereignty of states in the contemporary world (Castellino 2000: 97; Held et al. 1999: 7–14; Heraclides 1997: 501). Krasner's fourth type of sovereignty, international legal sovereignty, refers to the issue of the international recognition of a state, which is particularly important for 'popular sovereignty' and its contemporary conflation with self-determination.

and European colonial states tried to imagine the future of non-Western territories also in terms of clearly demarcated boundaries.

The idea that the modern nation-state is natural and progressive has led to 'state-centred political geographies', and social science and geographers in the nineteenth and early twentieth century contributed to this perception (Laughlin 1986: 301, 307–8). Nationalism or national identity, in this period, was believed to have an essence, an origin, which the nationalist intelligentsia tried to revive – an idea contemporary perennialist and ethno-symbolist approaches in the nationalism studies have explained (Smith 2004; Hechter 1998). Envisioning a national ideal and its 'essence' as a universal phenomenon (as autonomous, ahistorical and natural) has become an integral component of explaining state-building processes or attempts to form a state in the nineteenth century. The success of the German and Italian unifications and the maturing of the British and French (and American) nationalisms confirmed and naturalised the idea that the nation-state is the progressive and universal political unit. The sociological thinking in the nineteenth century further reinforced the idea of a political territorial state (Agnew 1994: 64, 69).

In nineteenth-century Europe, three geographical assumptions were crystallised: (1) state territories became fixed units of sovereign space; (2) binary divisions set in such as national/international or domestic/foreign; (3) and the state came to be seen as a prior to and a container of society (Agnew 1994: 53–9). Enabled by these assumptions, a link between spatially demarcated territories and state sovereignty led to the 'territorial trap', and the fragmentation of the world into territorial states served as a justification for this trap (Agnew 1994: 60). The idea of the territorial state as the container of society has become 'common sensical' and has been reproduced. Popular sovereignty over an inhabited territory created a people–territory relationship in which territory began to define the people (Knight 1985: 250–1).

This ideal state unit was filled with values that represented progress, liberalism, development and civilisation. Liberal democracy, nationalism and self-determination were at the heart of this view of a new ideal of state. These values and ideals underpinned the colonial powers' perceptions of the other, their engagement with non-European contexts and the way they interpreted their findings and information they gathered through their explorations and studies. Peoples that do not appear to be progressed, liberal or civilised were deemed not ready to attain the status of nationhood and establish their state. These values also informed Western states' and their agents' visualisation of the future of the Middle East and the Kurds in line with their strategic interests and the configurations shaped by the heightened imperial rivalry both leading up to and after the First World War.

Colonial Mapping in Kurdistan

The European travellers' explorations, activities and studies in non-European territories in the nineteenth century informed the way their states exerted power to reshape the political division of the Middle East in the early twentieth century.[13] Orientalist constructions of geography were shaped and informed by political and cultural values in the European context, as explained in the previous section, the interests of the states and the different sources of information, including local informants and inter-communal perceptions on the ground. Such information and perceptions influenced the Western travellers' biases.

The orientalist geographic studies and interpretations of this period were complex and multidimensional. The European philosophical thinking and perspectives on the ideal and most progressive form of governance and the political unit were integral to colonial geographical studies and map-making. Western cartography presented Europe as civilised and powerful, at the centre of the earth, while the rest of the world was presented as uncivilised and weak. For instance, in the seventeenth- and eighteenth-century maps, Europe was put in a central and dominant position and it was even sometimes decorated into the physical shape of a queen stretching Europe's tentacles around the globe with the world submitting to it (Wintle 1999: 152). The European self-image presented in these maps, imbued with symbols, writings and drawings of peoples, depicted Europe as 'powerful, civilised, clothed, and cultured; the rest of the world [as] subdued, exotic, savage, half-naked and primitive' (Wintle 1999: 160). Although this kind of iconography became less prominent in nineteenth-century maps, the orientalist view that informed earlier maps continued to exist in the studies of colonial officers and travellers.

[13] This section uses O'Shea's excellent analysis of the European engagement with the Kurds and other peoples in the area, and her archival research on European mapping in eastern Ottoman territories in the nineteenth century.

In the colonial era, European powers and their agents were heavily interested in objectifying, classifying and charting/mapping (Sidaway 2000: 592; Said 1978). Colonial explorers, officers, engineers, geographers and anthropologists were driven to create rational and universal knowledge about the world. Therefore, map-making and geographic work even for purely exploratory and economic reasons tried to identify unifying or dominant identity markers such as language, customs and religion in their study of the peoples in the Middle East in Ottoman and Iranian imperial territories. They usually depicted the non-Western as underdeveloped, uncivilised, tribal and primitive, therefore, undeserving of national self-determination, which in their thinking justified colonisation.

European travellers and writers visited the Kurdish populated region as state agents, army officers, scientists, researchers or journalists in the eighteenth, nineteenth and early twentieth centuries, and they created numerous definitions and cartographic depictions of Kurdistan. They were interested in Kurdistan for several reasons and these reasons influenced their findings and the way they conducted research. Initially, the Western interest in the region was for economic and religious purposes. Kurdistan is located on important communication and trade routes. They produced several writings, reports and maps for economic purposes, which included references to and observations about the Kurds and Kurdistan.

Italian merchants were among the earliest travellers to Kurdistan and they were interested in the trade routes going through the area and the region's economic potential. They wrote the oldest European accounts, including the first Kurdish grammar book and dictionary in 1789 and produced several other writings on the political structures and geographical location and features (O'Shea 2004: 109–14). German travellers also had been writing about Kurdistan since the eighteenth century based on their study of the region and its features, particularly the transport routes. German engagement was further facilitated by its close relationship with the Ottoman Empire from mid-nineteenth century onward.[14] Germans invested a big share of funding for the Baghdad Railway Project envisioned to go through Kurdistan. The British were also interested in trade and economic benefits initially;

---

[14] The railway connecting Berlin and Istanbul and the role of German military in the reformation of the Ottoman army were important factors.

for instance, the East India Company was very active in the region. Similarly, the French were engaged in economic activities and they had extensive economic links with the Ottoman Empire. The French had built railway lines in Ottoman territory[15] and had a 40 per cent share in the Baghdad Railway Project. Russians produced the earliest accounts of the routes in the region (O'Shea 2004: 114).

Western states, particularly Italy, France and the United States, and later the British, have also been heavily engaged in missionary activities in the eastern territories of the Ottoman Empire. They were particularly focused on the Christian communities and other minority groups. American missionaries had been active in Kurdistan since the early nineteenth century and they published several studies and reports on the Kurds. Italian and French Catholic missionaries carried out activities in the region, especially in the Mosul Province of the Ottoman Empire, and members of these missions wrote about different aspects of the Kurdish way of life, religion and geography (Meiselas 2008: 2–50). European missionary activities were mainly directed to Christians and other minority groups and they produced a great deal of writings about these populations. Their close focus on local Christians and their shared religious affiliation with them influenced Western missionaries' and travellers' perspective of Kurds and Muslims and this played a role in the deterioration of inter-communal relations in the region. The Russian and the French devoted particular attention to the Armenians in the late nineteenth and early twentieth century, which added to the tension in communal relations between Kurds and Armenians (O'Shea 2004: 108–13).

The maps and reports the Europeans produced mainly relied on their studies and observations, but it is likely that they came across earlier descriptions of Kurdistan by imperial historians and travellers such as Sharafhan, Evliya Çelebi and Koyi. There was limited writing and cartographic work on Kurdistan produced by local researchers in the nineteenth and early twentieth century. The lack of cartographic awareness among the Kurds and the highly multicultural, multi-ethnic, multi-religious composition of the region throughout history made it difficult for the Kurds (as well as for other communities such as Assyrians, Nestorians, Arabs and Armenians) to imagine a clear and widely accepted cartographic vision about the extent of their

---

[15] 1,266 km by the end of the nineteenth century.

homeland. Therefore, it is safe to say that Europeans' cartographic study of the area and its people mainly relied on their orientalist point of view and colonial epistemologies and methodologies of geography. Such a perspective projected and interpreted information gathered through a colonial perspective, essentialising what is studied. For instance, European travellers and writers adopted the myth that Kurds were the descendants of the Medes despite lack of historical evidence indicating to that (O'Shea 2004: 65).

In the second half of the nineteenth century and early twentieth century, the European states became even more interested in these areas due to intensified imperial rivalry. Therefore, their strategic interests played a significant role in their interpretations of the local context. Each imperial state wanted to gain political and economic supremacy in the region. Particularly, the building of the Baghdad Railway increased the importance of the area and escalated imperial rivalry as each power wanted to enjoy the highest benefit from this new transport and communication route (McMurray 2001). Russians further expanded their interests in Caucasia and its south due to increasing European engagement in the area. Western powers as well as Ottoman and Iranian powers considered this a threat (O'Shea 2004: 112–13). The imperial rivalries in the region shaped the future of most of the region, which eventually overlooked the Kurdish desire to statehood.

European travellers produced several maps of the region, including maps depicting Kurdistan. One of the first maps produced by a Western traveller was that by English traveller Claudius Rich who visited the Middle Eastern territories of Ottoman and Iranian Empires in the first two decades of the nineteenth century (O'Shea 2004). The Germans in 1854 later produced an ethnographic map of Armenia, Azerbaijan and Kurdistan, which illustrated trade routes (O'Shea 2004: 108). Karstov, a Russian military officer, produced a map of Kurdish tribes in 1896 (O'Shea 2004: 112). The first map that specifically focused on Kurdistan was produced by F. R. Maunsell, a British military officer, after his travels in the region in 1892. The map provided detailed information on the geography of Kurdistan, Kurdish habitation and habitation by other communities (O'Shea 2004: 110). The British government used Maunsell's projections of the ethnographic composition of the area when plans about the region were being made in the period before the First World War. The British Foreign Office's ethnographic map of the area, produced in 1919 (but relying on data from prior to the First World War) reflected the Foreign Office's position, showing extensive Armenian habitation that was not necessarily the case by 1919. O'Shea states that this was because at the end of the War, the Allied forces wanted to weaken Ottoman territorial claims in eastern Anatolia and therefore produced a map that indicated large Christian habitation in the region (2004: 48).

The colonial and imperial powers also took a direct role to influence boundary drawing in the eastern territories of the Ottoman Empire as early as the mid-nineteenth century. The boundary between the Ottomans and Persians was set in 1639 with the Zohab Treaty and demarcated a wide border area in which several Kurdish tribes were located. This location provided the Kurds some degree of autonomy and they were able to change alliances between the two empires as it fit them. This location made the Kurds and other communities living in this zone vulnerable because they were easily manipulated by external imperial powers and their specific interests. The maps produced in this period played an important role in the drawing of boundaries before and after the First World War, including Maunsell's maps (O'Shea 2004: 125).

In the early twentieth century and after, Western states continued to engage with the Kurds, to carry out their missions and interests in the region. However, they did not give full support to Kurds to form their state like they did to Arabs in Iraq or Syria. In this context, the association of development and civilisation with nationalism and the idea of a distinct culture, language and unified leadership in the European context informed the decisions of the Western powers in the region and their treatment of the Kurds. As a result, European colonial officers and travellers projected a European understanding of the nation and they understood dissident or rebel groups and the groups with distinct cultures and customs through these lenses. In this perspective, the Kurds were not considered to have the characteristics of a nation and were not seen as a legitimate force to deserve national liberation because of the Kurdish society's 'under-developed', tribal and divided nature. The discussions about the Kurds during the First World War period are clear indicators of those perceptions.

The studies and explorations undertaken in Kurdistan and the reports and outputs produced by European travellers and their governments' officials in the nineteenth and early twentieth centuries were used to formulate European states' policy with regard to the Kurds before, during and after the First World War. Crucially, the cartographic information on the Kurds and anthropological studies on their distinct features also constituted the foundation of Kurdish nationalist cartography and historiography later in the twentieth century. Kurdish nationalists replicated these maps or improvised on them to imagine the Kurdish homeland and its extent. Maunsell's and other travellers' maps became widely accepted and used by Kurdish nationalists, who improvised on them and produced their own maps (O'Shea 2004: 107). For instance, O'Shea states that Sherif Pasha's map included in the Memorandum demanding Kurdish self-determination in 1919 at the Versailles Conference was constructed based on the maps produced by Western travellers, British and German armies and entrepreneurs in the region.

Conclusion

Maps and geographic studies typically 'reflect and recreate dominant geopolitical discourses' (Culcasi 2006: 680) and in the nineteenth century these were linked to orientalist discourses. In the orientalist discourse of the time, national identity had begun to be geographically imagined and territorialised, which was the outcome of constructions of national identity and nationalism in the nineteenth century. Spatial categories began to be used to categorise peoples and their ethnic and linguistic characteristics. Such categories started to attain significant explanatory power in studying and mapping nationalism and ethnicity not only in Europe but in other parts of the world as well. Ethnographic maps produced by European travellers and geographers are excellent examples of this kind of thinking. The idea of national territory in the state-centred political geography became an essential and taken-for-granted entity and its presence was seen as a stage (and component) in the social and national advancement and development of a people (Laughlin 1986: 321) to reach to the level of civilisation as experienced in the European context. Such perspectives were ingrained into the nineteenth-century and early twentieth-century political geography and map-making by colonial geographers and officials.

European travellers' accounts reflect the values and perceptions of the travellers who were representatives of the states that ultimately decided the political future of the region. The orientalist view of the world perceiving non-European peoples as less civilised and under-developed informed these accounts. The civilisational understanding of nationalism that considers national consciousness, the degree of shared history, language and culture as an indicator of readiness and criteria for being considered as candidates to join the family of nations constituted the lens through which the European travellers and officers saw the Kurds and other peoples of the region. These European cultural and political values were considered as universal and this perception of universality and superiority informed their views. In addition, their own bias towards Christian and other non-Muslim communities also informed their accounts and their view of the Kurds.

3 | *Wilsonian Self-Determination*
The Rise and Fall of Hopes for Kurdistan

Introduction

The first half of the twentieth century is the second period that significantly shaped the production and use of Kurdistan maps. In this period, Kurdish political groups and intellectuals replicated colonial maps of Kurdistan in support of their demands for self-determination in the form of secession or some form of self-government. It is also in this period that self-determination was internationalised as a principle for shaping the new world order after the First World War. In order to legitimise their desire for self-rule, several groups across the world demanded their right to self-determination, including the Kurds. The idea prevalent in the conception of self-determination in this period was that the nation has the right to have its own state and gain sovereignty if it so wishes and if it is capable of forming one. This idea and its internationalisation aligned with the dissolution of the Ottoman Empire and the creation of new states on its territories. As a result, Kurdish hopes for statehood rose, however, these hopes did not come to fruition when the political map of the Middle East took shape after the War.

The First World War period was additionally important for the Kurds because Kurdish nationalism as a political movement began to emerge during this time. The re-organisation of the Ottoman territories around nation-states and the involvement of Western powers in this process created a context for the emergence of Kurdish nationalism. The Kurdish elite linked nationalism to the aim of attaining state power, initially within the context of the dissolution of the Ottoman Empire and after the war in the form of separatist nationalism in the newly established states. In this period, for the first time, Kurdistan and creating a Kurdish state was discussed in international political platforms. This led the idea of Kurdistan to consolidate in the minds of Kurdish political activists as a national

64

homeland and become a significant component of the Kurdish nationalist discourse.

The international political circumstances of this period were mainly defined by major political processes such as the dissolution of the empires and formation of new states in their place, the rivalries between European states, the First World War, the post-War negotiations and settlements, and the internationalisation of the United States' President Wilson's principle of self-determination. In this large-scale international political and normative transformation, the Allied Powers in the war – Britain, France and Russia, and later the United States – were directly involved in shaping the political map of Europe and the Middle East. In doing this, they juggled between their own interests and rivalries with each other, the demands and pressures from different local political factions and powerful elites, and the international normative context that included the idea of self-governance for all nations.

However, the process of shaping the political map of Europe and the Middle East was undertaken without any clear criteria of what constitutes a 'nation'. In this period, the ethnic interpretations of the 'nation' were dominant, and self-determination was understood to be applicable to groups with distinct ethnic identities and cultures with habitation in a clearly identifiable territory. Although this remained only as an ideal and proved impossible to implement, such interpretations shaped the conception of Kurdistan and Kurdish identity, as well as other identities, in this period. Through this process, the perceptions of territoriality and identity with origins in the nineteenth- and early twentieth-century European discourses on nations and national territoriality were carried into new areas. Such conceptions determined the engagement of the European powers with the populations of the ex-Ottoman territories and their designs in redrawing boundaries in this region. This chapter explains the impact of these international normative factors and the realities of the international politics on the development of Kurdish nationalism and the political fate of the Kurds. It also looks at the events that led to the consolidation of the idea of Kurdistan and its cartographic depiction as a core symbol and ideal of Kurdish nationalism in this process.

Kurdish Politics before the First World War

Although the question of when Kurdish nationalism emerged is debated, the general consensus is that Kurdish political mobilisation can be traced back to the First World War when the Ottoman Empire collapsed. The lead up to the war was a crucial period that prepared the foreground for the emergence of Kurdish nationalism. Kurdish nationalist historiography considers the First World War period as a defining moment in Kurdish history and a missed opportunity for statehood. The general international political and ideological circumstances of this era raised the hopes of the Kurds and the principle of self-determination had a significant influence on the articulation of Kurdish demands during the war. However, by the time the First World War ended and the Paris Peace Conference began on 18 January 1919, there was still no agreement on whether to create a Kurdish political entity nor, if it was to be created, on its location or territorial extent. The proceedings of the Conference lasted more than a year but throughout this time the situation of Kurdistan and the Kurdish people was dealt with only in general terms and mostly within the framework of its relation to the destiny of the Ottoman-controlled areas (Ahmad 1994: 196–7). At this stage, Kurdish activities started to take a more nationalistic character, but it is hard to ascertain the existence of a sense of national identity among the Kurdish masses during this time.

In the two decades before the First World War, internal turmoil and external pressures generated new political agendas that aimed to redefine the Ottoman identity, such as pan-Turkism, pan-Islamism and Ottomanism.[1] These agendas sought to find solutions to the Ottoman Empire's ills and create or renew a sense of state loyalty. Kurdish elite and intelligentsia took part in these different ideological positions and their organisations. Several members of the Kurdish tribal elite who were politically active were also part of the Ottoman administration as members of parliament, governors and military officials. For instance, Committee for Unity and Progress (CUP), *İttihat ve Terakki Cemiyeti*), a political organisation established by the *Young Turks* (*Jön Türkler*), had two Kurdish founders and many other Kurds joined the CUP later (Tahiri 2007: 43). The *Young Turks* was a coalition of various reform groups critical of Abdulhamid II's (reigned 1876–1909) suppressive rule and led the 1908 revolution, which reinstituted constitutional monarchy and reopened the Ottoman parliament.[2] The CUP became the ruling power after the 1908 revolution.

---

[1] Ottomanism was a formula created by the Ottoman Porte, elite and intellectual circles in Istanbul in order to stop the dissolution of the Ottoman Empire.

[2] Abdulhamid II had promulgated the Ottoman Parliament in 1878.

Some of the Kurdish elite had been undertaking Kurdish-related activities in exile since the early twentieth century and more Kurdish activities flourished in the era of cultural, intellectual and political freedom after the 1908 revolution. The Kurdish elite in Istanbul in this period belonged to families of tribal leaders who revolted against the Ottoman Porte in the late nineteenth century (discussed in the previous chapter). They were educated and had careers in Europe and Istanbul, through which they became aware of the intellectual and political views of their time. They published journals and established societies. Among these, Abdurrahman Bedirhan and his family's activities are notable. Bedirhan and his family's critical position towards the Porte was fuelled by the bitterness they held due to loss of territory and influence in eastern Anatolia after the Tanzimat Reforms and the suppression of the Bedirhan Pasha Revolt in 1847 (Strohmeier 2003: 22).

Abdurrahman Bedirhan carried out several activities that sought to raise awareness of the importance of education, literacy and Kurdishness. He and his brothers published a journal called *Kürdistan* between 1898 and 1902 in Switzerland, then in Cairo and some other European capitals. The journal included writings on Kurdish suffering under Abdulhamid II's reign. Although *Kürdistan* could be considered as a nationalist journal due to its emphasis on the distinctiveness of Kurdish identity and its effort to create Kurdish consciousness, it saw Kurdishness as part of Ottoman society (Van Bruinessen 1992: 7–8; Edmonds 1971: 89). Rather than being a political journal, it mainly aimed to educate and enlighten the uneducated and mostly illiterate Kurds and to explore and promote the Kurdish language, literature, history, and culture (Bozarslan 2003: 167). In the first issue of the journal, Midhat Bedirhan wrote:

Today whatever happens in the world is reported in newspapers from which we learn a great deal. Unfortunately, the Kurds, brave and intelligent though they are, live without knowing what is going on in our planet. I am publishing this paper to inform you of the development of events in the world and to encourage you to read and write in Kurdish (Blau 2006: 106).

These educational and cultural activities also had a political dimension and the first significant Kurdish political organisations were established in this period, during which Kurdish activities, or 'revival' in the late nineteenth century, transformed into an 'organised political movement'

(Bajalan 2013: 5). Kurdish Society for Solidarity and Progress (KSSP, *Kürt Teavün ve Terakki Cemiyeti*), established in 1908, was the most significant Kurdish society that emerged in Istanbul after the 1908 revolution. Its founders were Sherif Pasha, Emin Ali Bedirhan and Sayyid Abdulkadir.[3] The KSSP Charter emphasised 'the high esteem of being an Ottoman' (Özoğlu 2004: 78) and included goals such as opening schools, ensuring Kurds' attainment of positions in administration and the judiciary, make Kurdish an official language of the Empire, opening universities in cities in Kurdistan, and publishing newspapers and journals in the Kurdish language.[4] It set up a newspaper called *Kürd Teavün ve Terakki Gazetesi* (Kurdish Newspaper for Solidarity and Progress). The KSSP, its newspaper and other Kurdish organisations established during this time, such as the *Kürd Nesr-i Maarif Cemiyeti* (Kurdish Society for the Diffusion of Learning), sought to educate, modernise and protect the Kurdish people for the good of the empire overall rather than for specifically nationalist goals (Klein 2007: 138–9; Olson 1991: 397). The KSSP and its newspaper were closed by the CUP government in 1909. The CUP, it initially prioritised an Ottomanist ideology over a pan-Islamist one, was against authoritarian rule, and initially allowed a relatively open space for political and cultural activities. However, soon after the 1908 revolution, it began to emphasise the Turkish identity over others and to suppress political debate (Natali 2005: 10–13).

The above-mentioned Kurdish activities, which took place in the last two decades of the Empire, cannot easily be classified as nationalism – defined as a form of politics that connects nationalism to the aims of attaining or using state power (Breuilly 1993: 1). This is for several reasons. The Kurdish organisations formed in this period did not carry out activities similar to other nationalist movements of the time in the Ottoman Empire, such as the Armenians, Greeks or Bulgarians (Klein 2007: 135). These organisations were fragmented and divided, lacked a prominent Kurdish nationalist organisation with a clear agenda, and did not specifically call for secession or autonomy like other movements. Each Kurdish group had different political visions based on

---

[3] Emin Ali Bedirhan is the son of Bedirhan Pasha and Sayyid Abdulkadir is the son of Sheikh Ubeydullah.

[4] Kürt Teavün ve Terakki Cemiyeti Nizamnamesi (The Charter of the Kurdish Society for Solidarity and Progress) was adopted on 19 September 1908 in Istanbul.

their own interests and goals, such as regaining their tribal influence and authority that they lost under the centralisation policies of the nineteenth century.

One of the reasons that made it difficult for Kurdish leaders to mobilise together around Kurdish nationalism was some of these leaders' strategic partnerships with Ottoman rulers in the past. For instance, being an important component of the Hamidiye Cavalry[5] during Abdulhamid II's rule reinforced Kurdish tribes' loyalty to the Empire, and this loyalty certainly influenced some of the Kurdish elites' political activities even after 1908. Kurdish tribes that joined the Hamidiye Cavalry hugely benefited from this. They gained power and authority, they were exempt from paying taxes and some of them were even entitled to collect taxes from Armenian villages (Klein 2007: 141; Olson 1991: 397). Being part of these cavalries sustained and reinforced Kurdish hostility towards non-Muslim populations in the region. It is said that these cavalries were involved in the Armenian massacres in the 1890s and carried out some of the worst abuses (Houston 2008: 56–8). The ascending power of non-Muslim populations, especially the Armenians, in eastern Anatolia and the possibility of the establishment of an Armenian state in the region were key underlying factors that enticed Kurdish tribal leaders to join the Hamidiye forces.[6]

Another reason that made it difficult to organise around specifically nationalist goals was the decisive role of Islam and the Ottoman identity in shaping the Kurdish tribal elite's goals and alliances – even more significant than the Kurdish identity in many cases. For the vast majority of the Kurds, being a Kurd represented being Muslim and according to the Ottoman administrative system based on *millet*s, Kurds were considered as part of the Muslim *millet*. The Ottoman *millet* system did not denote 'nations'; it reflected a form of compartmentalisation based on religious and sectarian divisions. In the era of nationalism, the *millet* system helped to define the identity of emerging

---

[5] Under Abdulhamid II's rule, certain tribal groups and families joined the Hamidiye Cavalry, a military force established in 1891, to organise the Sunni population (some of the Kurdish tribes and Turks) and secure their loyalty against the Armenians and their supporters, particularly the Russians and the British (Van Bruinessen 1992: 268; Olson 1991: 395).

[6] The Hamidiye Cavalry was abolished just before Abdulhamid II's reign came to an end after the 1908 revolution.

nations (Ortaylı 2003: 29–31); but this was harder in the case of non-Turkish Muslim populations. Turks, Kurds and Albanians identified themselves as Muslim and Ottoman (Ortaylı 2003: 20). When the nationalist wave was sweeping through the Ottoman territories in the second half of the nineteenth century and early twentieth century, the Ottoman *millet*s attained their independence one after another. These conditions did not substantially affect the Kurdish urban and provincial elite, and the Islamic affiliation of the Kurds with the Ottoman Porte made it harder for the Kurds to assert their distinct identity. Some scholars even argue that if the Empire had survived and recovered, Kurdish nationalism might not have emerged (Özoğlu 2004: 70).

The internally divided nature of Kurdish tribal elites was another important factor that hindered the emergence of Kurdish nationalism and the mobilisation of the Kurdish tribes as part of one united movement in the late Ottoman era. Maintaining or increasing tribal influence and territorial control was a key driver for each tribal family to engage in political activities. The Kurdish elite was highly divided along tribal and familial lines, and their interest in maintaining their influence and territorial authority took priority over a Kurdish national attainment beyond their interests. Several of these families often saw each other as rivals. These conditions served as impediments for the emergence of Kurdish nationalism, while other peoples of the Ottoman Empire, such as the Armenians and Greeks, had attained their independence.

The Kurdish revolts in the late nineteenth century also exemplified the tension between tribal and national identity. These two identity features, tribe and nation, are not necessarily in conflict with each other; in other words, having tribal characteristics does not prevent a movement from being also nationalist. This is certainly the case for the Kurds. However, even though tribal divisions did not prevent someone from being also nationalist, they delayed or hindered the formation of a unified Kurdish political movement in this period. The Kurdish revolts in the late nineteenth century and the rivalries and activities of Kurdish leaders in the following decades showed that tribal territorial aspirations could not be easily substituted entirely by national aspirations or could not comfortably co-exist with a national identity (Natali 2005: 11; O'Shea 2004: 105). Nationalism gradually became an important ideological force among the Kurds in the course of the twentieth century, but tribal loyalties and territorial affiliations maintained their importance (Van Bruinessen 1992: 268, 275).

The Kurdish elite's relationship with the international community also demonstrates that a nationalist agenda was not to the fore in shaping their interactions and demands. In their attempts to maintain or regain territorial control, some Kurdish leaders tried to gain outside support even if this did not promote their chances of independence or even resulted in dependence on external powers. This was actually a historical practice for Kurdish families; for centuries Kurdish tribal leaders benefited from the rivalries between internal and external powers (such as the one between the Ottomans and Iranians) and offered allegiance to the state that offered them the best deal, defined as the deal that allowed local elites the greatest authority (Van Bruinessen 1992). In the last decades of the Ottoman Empire, tribal leaders lobbied their case in the international arena and sought the support of powers like Britain and Russia and even then, they were ready to compromise nationalist goals of the wider Kurdish community. The predominance of tribal structures 'encouraged Kurdish chiefs to act according to their personal and tribal interests and not on behalf of a larger Kurdish nation' (Natali 2005: 11).

Instability caused by the weakening and collapsing of state power in the region before and during the First World War led different factions of Kurdish tribal elites and their clans to attempt to increase their political power. In this process, although the desire to control tribal dominions began to be increasingly legitimated in nationalist terms, none of the tribal leaders were willing to give up their own control. Klein describes this as an effort 'to reclaim traditional political arrangements for one family through nationalism' (Klein 2007: 148). Therefore, it is hard to talk about a Kurdish nationalism felt as a sentiment or pursued as a goal by most of the Kurdish tribal and urban elite across the board in this period. For the Kurdish tribal elite, territorial control was more important than raising a Kurdish national consciousness. Although the Kurdish intelligentsia in Istanbul, some of whom were from large Kurdish tribal families, promoted a sense of Kurdish national identity and tried to increase awareness, within an Ottoman identity framework, their influence remained limited. The tribal structures in the rural areas were determinant, as a result of which, a tribal territorial mentality weakened or slowed the development of Kurdish nationalist tendencies.

By the end of the First World War, the Kurdish elites and tribal leaders in Istanbul, eastern Anatolia and northern Mesopotamia were still divided. Despite the formation of organisations with clearly nationalist goals, such as the *Kürt Teali Cemiyeti* (Society for the Advancement of the Kurds,

SAK), the divisions continued. SAK was established on 17 December 1918 in Istanbul by Emin Ali Bedirhan and Sayyid Abdulkadir. There were strong disagreements between the two founders. Each had different political and territorial projects for Kurdistan. While Bedirhan wanted a smaller Kurdistan separated from the Ottomans (excluding parts in Iran and Iraq), Abdulkadir had a vision of a larger autonomous Kurdistan under Ottoman rule. What shaped these different visions is the rivalry for authority in a possible future Kurdish entity of any kind. Historical enmities between the families of these individuals played a significant role. There was tension between the Ubeydullahs of the Şemdinan tribe and Bedirhans of the Badinan tribe in the nineteenth century. The Bedirhans had lost their authority after the defeat of the Bedirhan Pasha Revolt (1847). After the defeat, the Şemdinan family emerged as the strongest power in the region and took some of the old territories controlled by the Bedirhans. This caused bitterness between the two families (Özoğlu 2004: 77). Emin Ali Bedirhan was disgruntled by Abdulkadir's leadership of the *Kürt Teali Cemiyeti* as he probably thought this would not bode well for Bedirhan's desire for himself or his son Celadet to be the ruler of a future possible Kurdistan (Özoğlu 2004: 118–19).

While in the Ottoman Empire Kurdish activities were led by an urban nationalist elite, who formed political parties and published journals, Kurdish activities in Iran, ruled by the Qajar dynasty (1796–1925) at the time, were even more limited to the tribal context (Natali 2005: 25). This is partly because the Iranian social order did not go through a substantial change similar to the change the Ottoman system went through as a result of reforms, interactions with the Western world and weakening of the empire. The continuity in Iran enabled tribal elite to maintain their positions in a decentralised system (Natali 2005: 14, 19). This resulted in the tribal system playing a greater role in the way Kurdish nationalism developed in Qajar Iran compared to the Ottoman Empire. In the early twentieth century, Kurds in Iran found themselves in a political atmosphere that was dominated by debates on foreign influence and on the role of Islam. In this atmosphere, the *ulama*,[7] a social category with distinctive religious and occupational functions (Moaddel 1986: 520), was able to galvanise resentment

---

[7] The *ulama* 'were adherents of a particular brand of Shi'ism, Usulism, whose somewhat exclusive domination in society was established in the early nineteenth century ... [they were] tied functionally to the Qajar state, structurally to the "feudalist" class, and instrumentally to the merchants and traditional petty

against foreign penetration among all sections of the population, including the Kurds (Natali 2005: 20–1). In the period after the First World War, the future of the Kurds in Iran was left out of the discussions as the post-War redrawing of the Middle East excluded the Qajar Iran's territories and only dealt with the Ottoman territories.

By the end of the First World War, in the Ottoman territories, a unified Kurdish movement with the aim of forming a Kurdish state had not yet developed. Although the Kurdish elite had begun to embrace the notion of Kurdistan as a 'homeland', their tribal territorial dominions and interests still took priority. However, the changing regional and international conditions during and after the War, the dissemination of Wilson's ideas for a new international order across the world and the serious possibility of the formation of an Armenian state triggered more nationalistic activities and goals among Kurdish leaders. When it was understood that the break-up of the Ottoman Empire was inevitable, the bonds that maintained the loyalty of some of the Kurdish elites to the Ottoman Porte also began to weaken; Ottomanism was no longer a feasible ideal (Klein 2007: 146). The transformation of Kurdish political activism into one with more nationalist undertones was also enabled by some external actors', especially the British officials', tentative plans to create a Kurdish state and promises made by some of the British officers to certain tribal leaders, even though these plans and promises were forgotten even before the peace proceedings ended.

The Post–First World War Settlement, Self-Determination and the Kurds

Tension between Power Politics and the Norm of Self-Determination

The concept of self-determination was more specifically defined in the early twentieth century, but its roots were planted in the late nineteenth century when popular sovereignty and nationalism became defining ideas for political systems in Europe. In the nineteenth century, European powers perceived nationalism as a unifying force because it

bourgeoisie ... [performed] educational, judicial and legitimation functions of the Qajar state' (Moaddel 1986: 522–3).

enabled the integration of people and territories in modern nation-states in Europe. Self-determination, then known as the 'nationality principle', as an idea or a justification for attaining statehood through secession also existed. A number of separatist movements rebelled against the Habsburg and Ottoman Empires in Eastern Europe and established their own states – but it was not defined as 'self-determination'. Western states, who saw themselves as the ideal form of political govern-ance, adopted self-determination as a principle to be implemented beyond western Europe after the First World War. However, their aim to create homogeneous nation-states proved unrealistic.

Self-determination sat at the centre of the international agenda dur-ing the First World War and became a key principle that shaped the post-War international order. It was introduced by United States' President Wilson. During the 1919 Paris Peace Conference where post-War settlements were designed, self-determination came to be seen as a modern democratic entitlement (Castellino 2000: 8–12). Wilson is known as the instigator of the principle, but the concept was initially defined and used as a policy by Lenin. Lenin defined self-determination as 'the right to existence as a separate state' (Lenin 1914: 394), and he supported self-determination movements in colonial and imperial territories against European colonisers. The Soviet system implemented the principle of self-determination internally for admin-istrative purposes, with the intention of this being temporary and to last until socialism was fully achieved and states ceased to exist. This is because from the Soviet perspective socialist class-based rights took precedence over the right to self-determination (Knight 1985: 254).

After the internationalisation of self-determination in the post–First World War order, the principle was eagerly adopted by the peoples of the world from the Americas to Europe and East Asia. Its institutionalisation was part of a newly emerging international order based on self-rule in which the nation-state was the primary legitimate political form. Self-determination, as a pathway to the goal of state-hood for small nations in this period, turned into an international framework for demanding new states out of existing ones (Moore 2015, 2014; Miller 2014; Moynihan 2002), although its implementa-tion remained very limited during this period. Still, Wilson's call for self-determination for small nations internationalised the concept and led to its adoption by separatists to justify their desire for statehood (Manela 2007; Moynihan 2002: 11; Cumings 1999: 228). It was used to justify requests for self-rule in the old Habsburg and Ottoman territories and to promote rival nationalist claims. Some of these groups also used the principle against other nationalist projects rather than directly attempting to free themselves from empires.

Wilson had developed his plans for the post-War world before the war ended and he was successful in convincing other state leaders at the Paris Peace Conference to support their implementation. Wilson and his team had publicly declared plans for a new order as early as 1916. In 1917, Wilson's speech 'Peace without Victory' provided the first clear description of his vision. This speech was disseminated to the world and was extensively discussed throughout the war years (Manela 2007: 16). The idea of national governance made its appearance also in other states' policy documents even before the war ended. For instance, the concept was first mentioned in a British Foreign Office memorandum in 1916 regarding the post-War peace conditions. The memorandum stated that it was essential that national aspirations receive full recognition and the principle of nationality should be key in the consideration of territorial arrangements after the war (Knight 1985: 255 from Lloyd George, 1939).

Wilson's most famous speech, known as the 'Fourteen Points', which he gave on 18 January 1918 at the United States Congress, set out clearly his plans for the post-War peace. Wilson introduced his plan by declaring:

What we demand in this war . . . is nothing peculiar to ourselves. It is that the world be made fit and safe to live in; and particularly that it be made safe for every peace-loving nation which, like our own, wishes to live its own life, determine its own institutions, be assured of justice and fair dealing by the other peoples of the world as against force and selfish aggression.

Wilson's plan for the future international order had three components: 'equality of nations', 'right over might' and 'consent of the governed'. Equality of nations meant that all states – small, big, weak or powerful – would have the same rights. 'Right over might' emphasised the importance of law and voluntary and peaceful means, such as international mechanisms, in resolving problems, and avoiding other methods, such as war or conflict (Manela 2007: 23–5).

'Consent of the governed', which is of particular interest here, was about self-determination. It meant that peoples should be free to determine their type of government and that all international

arrangements should receive the consent of the group of people concerned. According to this principle, in order to ensure the attainment
and maintenance of international peace, no nation should try to
dominate another (Manela 2007: 22). Wilson later started to call
this principle 'self-determination'. Even though his *Fourteen Points*
speech is considered as the official statement of the principle of
self-determination, the term was not actually used in that speech.
Less than a month after the *Fourteen Points* speech, on 11 February
1918, in another speech he gave to the United States Congress, Wilson
used 'the rights of peoples to self-determination' publicly for the first
time (Manela 2007: 24; Knight 1985: 254). In this speech, which is
known as *Four Points*, the President called for respect for national
aspirations and the right of peoples to be dominated and governed
only by their own consent. Wilson also added that only well-defined
national aspirations that did not create conflict would receive serious
consideration, but he did not come up with criteria to delimit claims.
The League of Nations and the mandate system were created to enable
developed powers to observe and support populations that wanted to
reach the stage of self-governance.

Wilson's ideas were not uncritically endorsed by all world leaders.
European leaders in particular found objections (Manela 2007: 24;
Cobban 1945: 57–8; Lansing 1921: 103–4). Actually, even Wilson
himself eventually called the principle into question because, as he
put it, 'nationalities began appearing everywhere' (Knight 1985:
255). The Paris Peace Conference limited the implementation of self-
determination to Europe and the territories related to Europe – such as
Italy, Turkey, Austro-Hungary, Poland, Romania, Montenegro, Serbia
and the Balkan region. But this did not stop the leaders of other
communities and colonised peoples elsewhere from perceiving self-
determination as legitimating their claims for statehood, but their
hopes ended in vain (Manela 2007: 4). Following the overwhelming
amount of demands submitted to the Conference from all around the
world, Wilson declared that the League of Nations would later take up
the un-responded claims (Manela 2007: 5).

The post-War territorial settlement embodied the challenge, and
also naivety, of implementing Wilson's new vision of a world
based on the principle of self-determination. The implementation
of self-determination was constrained by the security interests and
balance of power dynamics of the great powers. These powers did

not want to implement self-determination at the expense of their own imperial and colonial interests. Although the principle was presented and perceived as a universal ideal applicable for all nations, it was not applied universally. Plebiscites were rarely utilised even in territories where self-determination was implemented. The pragmatic necessities of drawing lines for new political entities and the 'unequal sympathies [of Western states] for different nationalities' hindered the fair and consistent implementation of self-determination (Whelan 1994: 101).

Difficulties also derived from the difference between the way the principle was presented and the way it was used. Wilson did not come up with a clear plan on how this principle would be implemented in Europe, let alone throughout the world. The principle was presented as a democratising principle that provided distinct national and cultural groups with the ability to determine their own political future. It implied people's right to select their own *democratic* government, but it also required that the people or the nation were ethnically identifiable (Whelan 1994: 100, 108). This meant specific groups should be identified to be given the right to self-determination. As a result, the principle served as a call for differentiating between groups on the basis of language, culture, race, religion and aspirations. Hence the question that emerged in the post-War period was 'who are the people in question?' Wilson's Secretary of State Robert Lansing wrote in April 1921, 'When the President talks about "self-determination," what has he in mind? Does he mean race, a territorial area, or a community? Without a definite unit which is practical, application of this principle is dangerous to peace and stability' (Lansing quoted in Castellino 1999: 525). In his narrative of the peace negotiations, Lansing argued that while it was a desirable principle in theory, self-determination was almost impossible to implement practically without causing trouble because it legitimated anti-government movements (Lansing 1921: 96–204).[8]

Because of the way self-determination was implemented in this period, members of the same ethno-national group potentially became either members of a nation or a minority in an adjacent state, depending on

---

[8] Sir Ivor Jennings, another critic of the principle, was aware that its implementation required a definition of the 'self': '[o]n the surface it seemed reasonable: let the people decide. It was in fact ridiculous because people cannot decide until someone decides who the people are' (1956: 55–6). Due to this impossibility Jennings was puzzled by self-determination's wide acceptance.

where the line was drawn (Whelan 1994: 103).[9] There was no clear definition of what a nation was, what conditions render a group of people a nation, and what gives them the right to claim self-determination. The ambivalence over who could be defined as a nation and who had the right to claim self-determination led many groups to reimagine their identity and consider internally their status among the nations of the world. This was a crucial process for Kurds and one which forced them to clarify their position vis-à-vis Ottomanism and Islamism, to address their relationship with Turks, and to assert their distinct identity more forcefully through political mobilisation, engagement with Western policymakers in the Middle East and advocacy in regional and international platforms.

Paris Peace Conference and Kurdistan

The Paris Peace Conference hosted many delegations representing different peoples and groups, however, not all these delegations were given official hearings, including the Kurdish delegation. Sherif Pasha,[10] an Ottoman diplomat in Paris, acted as the Kurdish representative to the British Ambassador in Paris and as the head of the Kurdish Delegation to the Paris Peace Conference. The Pasha prepared a Memorandum on the Claims of the Kurd People (Kurdish Memorandum) that included a map of Kurdistan that he produced (Map 3.1). At the Conference, maps were widely used by multiple different delegations as tools to persuade others of the existence of territorially identifiable peoples that should be considered as nations around the world (House and Seymour 1921: 14) and the Kurdish representation was no exception to this. Sherif Pasha's Memorandum demanded a free Kurdish state and its main goal was to show the soundness of Kurdish demands against Armenian claims. It argued that the districts claimed by the Armenians were actually within the boundaries of Turkish Kurdistan (Kurdish Memorandum: 3). While doing this, Sherif Pasha also emphasised Kurds' loyalty to the Ottoman government:

---

[9] For instance, 'Poland's economic and security needs, and France's pride and historic claim, took precedence over the inhabitants' wishes in Danzig and Alsace-Lorraine respectively' (Whelan 1994: 101).

[10] The Pasha was raised in Istanbul and had Kurdish origins.

In virtue of the Wilsonian principle everything pleads in favour of the Kurds for the creation of a Kurd state, entirely free and independent ... Since the Ottoman Government has accepted Mr Wilson's fourteen points without reservation, the Kurds believe that they have every right to demand their independence, and that without any way failing in loyalty towards the Empire under whose sovereignty they have lived for many centuries, keeping intact their customs and tradition ... (Kurdish Memorandum: 14).

The Kurdish Memorandum stated that if contested districts were to be included in the new Armenia, disorder and guerrilla warfare would be inevitable. It defined the ethnographic frontiers of Turkish Kurdistan as follows:

in the North at Ziven, on the Caucasian frontier, and continue westwards to Erzéroum, Erzindjan, Kémah, Arabkir, Benismi, and Divick; in the South they follow the line from Haran, the Sindjihar Hills, Tel Asfar, Erbil. Kerkuk, Suléimanié, Akk-el-man, Sinna; in the East, Ravandiz, Bash-Kalé, Vizir-Kalé, that is to say the frontier of Persia as far as Mount Ararat (Kurdish Memorandum: 12).

The definition of Kurdistan and the map included in the Memorandum were constructed on the basis of early definitions of Kurdistan and maps produced by Western travellers, British and German armies and entrepreneurs in the region. Among these, Major Maunsell's map produced in the 1890s became widely accepted and used by Kurdish nationalists after the First World War (O'Shea 2004).

The Kurdish Delegation led by Sherif Pasha was not considered representative of the Kurds and, despite Pasha's efforts, eventually it was not taken seriously by the British (McDowall 1996a: 122). The Pasha was neither chosen nor supported by Kurdish leaders and came to be seen as disconnected from the Kurdish masses and Kurdish leaders in Istanbul. The Conference received a series of telegrams from Kurdish chieftains stating that they did not recognise Sherif Pasha as a legitimate representative and protested against his map of Kurdistan.

Emin Ali Bedirhan, one of the leaders of the SAK,[11] severely opposed to the Pasha's plans, especially the extent of Kurdistan on his map (Bozarslan 2003: 169). Sherif Pasha's map left the Lake Van area, which was considered as the heart of the Armenian homeland, out of his map of Kurdistan. It is said that the Pasha also made a secret

---

[11] Sayyid Abdulkadir, the other leader of the SAK and rival to Emin Ali Bedirhan, supported Şerif Pasha's efforts at the Paris Peace Conference.

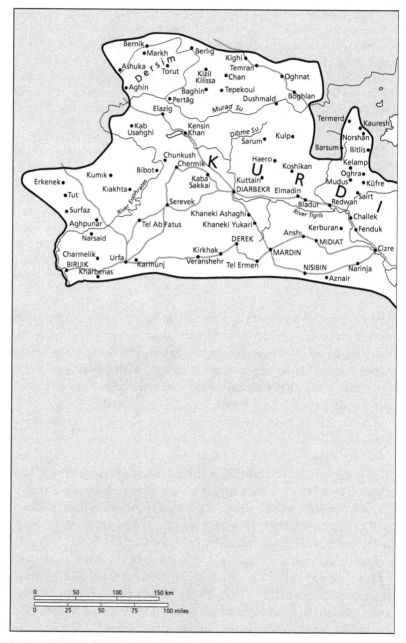

Map 3.1 Map of Kurdistan by Sherif Pasha (1919)
Source: Redrawn based on Memorandum on the Kurd Question submitted to the Paris Peace Conference 1919, Sherif Pasha.

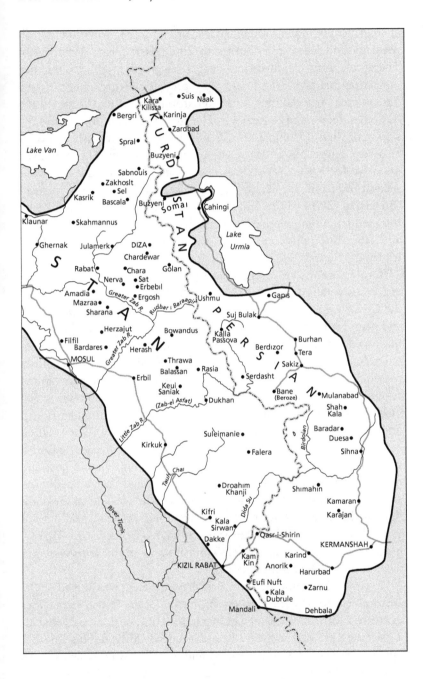

arrangement with the Armenian Delegation for the formation of both Armenia and Kurdistan (Bozarslan 2003: 169; Olson 1991: 399). Therefore, Emin Ali Bedirhan sent a telegraph to the Conference indicating that Sherif Pasha did not represent all Kurds, rejecting the Pasha's map and claiming a new territorial extent that included the 'Ottoman *vilayet*s of Diyarbakır, Harput, Bitlis, Van, Mosul and the *sancak* of Urfa' (Özoğlu 2004: 39–40). Some other Kurdish chieftains also sent telegraphs to the Conference to condemn Sherif Pasha's initiative for a Kurdish state and to assert that they did not want separation from the Turks, emphasising their fraternity instead (Bozarslan 2003: 172; Van Bruinessen 1992: 279). The Pasha resigned from his position as Kurdish representative in April 1920 and from this point on, the British interacted directly with local leaders (O'Shea 2004: 129).

During the Paris Peace Conference, it was decided that the Ottoman territories would be divided between the British, French, Italians and the Greeks. However, these external actors had different expectations and plans for the territories. Rivalries and dynamics within this cohort of countries made it hard to decide the territorial boundaries of potential political entities. Each external actor wanted new political entities to help fulfil their own economic, political and strategic plans in the region. The southeastern territories of the Ottoman Empire, which included Kurdish populated areas, were divided and put under British and French mandates (later Iraq and Syria, respectively). The creation of an Arab Mesopotamian state was seen almost as a given. The British wanted to establish and maintain this state with minimum cost and problem. The idea of forming a unified Kurdistan that included those areas inhabited by Kurds under the Iranian State was out of the question, as the Allies did not want to antagonise Iran. They also did not want this new Mesopotamian state to have a border with Turkey, mainly because of the highly anti-Turkish stance of the British government at this time (O'Shea 2004: 127).

However, that is not to say the British government was unified on the creation of a Kurdistan. The options in front of the British were either to create a Kurdish state, albeit not a unified one, or not create it at all and let the Kurds live in the territories of a newly formed state. Another option that was considered was to find a middle way, which was to form a small autonomous Kurdish zone around Mosul (O'Shea 2004: 139). Initially, this idea of creating a Kurdish buffer zone between the territory under their domination and the future Turkish state appeared appealing to the British. The British government already had contacts on the ground to initiate such a formation.[12] However, the only area where some form of self-determination for Kurds was implemented, albeit in a limited way, was in northern Iraq, the administration of Sulaymaniyah as discussed next.

The Treaty of Sèvres and Its Aftermath

During the Paris Peace Conference proceedings, Wilson became aware of the destabilising influence of his self-determination principle. Eventually, the process through which the new territorial settlements were planned during the Conference did not fully comply with the principle of self-determination. The principle of state sovereignty and the interests of the European powers trumped other counter demands (Knight 1985: 256). As a result, cautious measures were implemented during the arrangements. The concept of self-determination was removed from the Conference document. It was decided that the Conference would only deal with territories and peoples related to Europe because the implementation of the principle proved very difficult beyond European and Ottoman territories. The Conference decided to create an international mechanism to deal with future claims (the League of Nations) after the post-War settlements were finalised (Manela 2007: 60–1). In the end, with regard to the Ottoman territories, the Allied Powers' policy was mainly to draw viable boundaries for new entities rather than fully implement the principle of self-determination.

The future status of the Kurds remained uncertain throughout the post-War process and soon this international support, especially British support, for creating a Kurdish state began to diminish. This was because they realised that maintaining and supporting such a state would be a big undertaking and that an Iraqi state would not be feasible if the areas in question were given independence instead of included within Iraq (Tahiri 2007: 53). They also realised that the multicultural composition of the population in the area rendered the implementation

---

[12] During the War they sent political officers to Mosul to encourage Kurdish uprisings against the Ottoman Empire with promises of an independent Kurdish state in Mosul and Sulaymaniyah (O'Shea 2004: 125).

of self-determination very problematic for all populations because it proved difficult to draw boundaries for viable political entities due to the complex ethnic and confessional distribution (O'Shea 2004: 118). Moreover, given these different groups were living in an integrated way, it was hard to associate one geographic area with one single group identity. In any case, for the British, Kurdistan was not an end in itself, but a potential means to reach the most suitable and favourable political, economic and geostrategic conditions in the region in line with their own interests. The promises made to many Kurdish tribal leaders were left unmet. Needless to say, subsequent Kurdish nationalist discourse often criticises the British state for this inconsistent policy towards the Kurds during this period.

The British gradually became less interested in the idea of creating a Kurdish state also because of the fragmented and inconsistent Kurdish representation. The British considered the fragmentation and multiplicity of Kurdish voices and the rivalries between different leaders as a drawback and an impediment towards the Kurds' ability to form a state (O'Shea 2004: 117–18). Indeed, the Kurds lacked a strong Kurdish leadership that was able to speak effectively on their behalf. Moreover, the Kurds had a negative image in the eyes of the Western powers. Lloyd George, the then British Prime Minister, wrote 'no Kurd seemed to represent anything more than his own particular clan' (quoted in Macmillan, 2002: 458, from Lloyd George's diary). This was seen as a stark contrast to the coherent, stronger and unified Armenian movement supported by an influential and well-organised Armenian representation (Helmreich 1974). The role of the Kurds in the suppression of minorities and treatment of Armenians under Ottoman rule, especially through their involvement in the Hamidiye Cavalry under Abdulhamid II's reign, also tainted the perceptions of Western actors towards the Kurds and weakened the case for a Kurdish state.

Another related factor that led to the failure to create a Kurdish state was the existence of multiple competing claims from other groups inhabiting the region. The Arabs were promised a Mesopotamian state. The Assyrians had territorial claims in the same area and sent delegates to the Paris Peace Conference presenting a large map that projected the location and boundaries of their envisaged state. The Assyrian demands had some support from the French and the Americans, mainly due to these states' missionary work in the region. But the British were not willing to support such a small community, which was also divided among themselves and had no clear leadership. The Armenians were claiming a large part of the territory and there was significant overlap between Kurdish and Armenian territorial demands. However, the European powers felt compelled to consider the Armenian claims, considering the combined 1915 expulsions and massacres, defined as genocide by a large section of the international community today, as well as on political grounds due to the effective Armenian lobbying during the Conference (Helmreich 1974: 38–63). Turkish political aspirations, on the other hand, were opposed to Armenian, Kurdish and Assyrian claims. These were far from ideal circumstances for the implementation of self-determination in the way Wilson envisaged.

The Treaty of Sèvres was signed in August 1920 between the Ottoman Empire and the victorious powers. This treaty set the terms for the partition of the Ottoman territories and its Articles 62–4 dealt with the status of the Kurds. The Ottoman Parliament, and later the Turkish Parliament, did not ratify the Sèvres Treaty, therefore it was never implemented. The new Turkish government established after the Turkish Independence War of 1920–2 instead signed a new treaty, the Treaty of Lausanne, in 1923. The Kurdish nationalist historiography today sees the Treaty of Sèvres as a legal guarantee for the establishment of a Kurdish state and argue that if it was not for the Treaty of Lausanne, their state would have been established. However, a closer look at the Sèvres document shows that the guarantee appears far more elusive than assumed.

The proposals in the Sèvres concerning the Kurds were formalities and a nod to Wilson's self-determination principle. Article 62 provided that:

A Commission sitting at Constantinople and composed of three members appointed by the British, French and Italian Governments respectively shall draft within six months from the coming into force of the present Treaty a scheme of local autonomy for the predominantly Kurdish areas lying east of the Euphrates, south of the southern boundary of Armenia as it may be hereafter determined, and north of the frontier of Turkey with Syria and Mesopotamia ... If unanimity cannot be secured on any question, it will be referred by the members of the Commission to their respective Governments. The scheme shall contain full safeguards for the protection of the Assyro-Chaldeans and other racial or religious minorities within these areas, and with this object a Commission composed of British, French, Italian, Persian and Kurdish representatives shall visit the spot to examine and decide what rectifications, if any, should be made in the Turkish frontier where, under the provisions of the present Treaty, that frontier coincides with that of Persia (Treaty of Sèvres 1920).

Article 64 explained when and how Kurds could apply to the League of Nations to show their desire for independence:

If within one year from the coming into force of the present Treaty the Kurdish peoples within the areas defined in Article 62 shall address themselves to the Council of the League of Nations in such a manner as to show that a majority of the population of these areas desires independence from Turkey, and if the Council then considers that these peoples are capable of such independence and recommends that it should be granted to them, Turkey hereby agrees to execute such a recommendation, and to renounce all rights and title over these areas (Treaty of Sèvres 1920).

For Kurds located in the north of Mesopotamia the situation was different. They realised that the European powers had no real intention of creating a unified Kurdistan and preferred not to influence the future of the areas in eastern and southeastern Anatolia. As a result, some of the Kurdish elite and most of the tribal leaders and sheikhs in the rural areas joined Mustafa Kemal's *Kuvayi Milliye Hareketi* (National Forces Movement). This movement adopted the *Misak-ı Millî* (National Pact),[13] a document passed by the Ottoman Parliament in February 1920 (just before the occupation of Istanbul by the Allies). These parliamentarians later left Istanbul and formed a new representation in Ankara. The *Kuvayi Milliye* rejected the Sèvres provisions and denied the legitimacy of the government in Istanbul. It declared the establishment of a new government in Ankara and aimed to fight against the Allied occupation of Anatolia.

In the southeast and eastern Anatolia and north of Mesopotamia, several Kurdish chieftains supported the *Kuvayi Milliye* since they perceived Mustafa Kemal as the most likely person to protect Kurdish lands from Armenian claims. Some tribal chieftains thought they needed the Turks to consolidate and increase their own power. Their attachment and loyalty to the Ottomanism also played a role, which was exacerbated due to Greek and other forces' occupation of Anatolia

---

[13] The provisions of this document were discussed in the negotiations that led to the signing of the Treaty of Lausanne in 24 July 1923 and were mostly implemented.

and open European support for the desire to establish Armenia (Olson 1991: 401–2). The Kurdish tribal elite's support also derived from the *Kuvayi Milliye*'s aim, at least at the beginning, to defend Islam as part of the 'Turkish-Kurdish Muslim fraternity' (Bozarslan 2003: 169).

The Post-War Middle East: Kurdish Nationalism Emerges

With the emergence of nation-states as the centrepiece of the new world order after the First World War, several Kurdish revolts demanding self-determination or resisting new boundaries took place in the immediate aftermath of the political redrawing of the region. These revolts and demands for self-determination were not isolated phenomena. In the period that followed the First World War until the Second World War, the new nation-state system and the internationalisation of self-determination triggered nationalist demands all over the world. Areas that were particularly affected by secessionism and demands for self-government were in the British and French colonies, in Egypt and India, across North Africa and the Middle East, central America, the Philippines and in the home countries of European states including Britain, France and Spain (Knight 1985: 258). These led many experts to argue that the new system made the world even more unstable than before the First World War (Cobban 1969).

After 1918, the Middle East was practically unrecognisable. New states emerged in the ex-Ottoman territories in Mesopotamia, Anatolia and the Levant: the Republic of Armenia (1918), the Republic of Turkey (1923), the British Mandate of Mesopotamia (1920; Kingdom of Iraq as of 1932) and the French Mandate of Syria (1920; Syrian Republic as of 1946). This new setting not only failed to lead to a Kurdish state, but it also compounded the already divided status of the Kurds in the region. Having lived under Ottoman and Iranian Empires for centuries, Kurds never had a unified territory, and after the First World War, Kurds fell under the jurisdiction of even more states: Iran, Turkey, Syria, Iraq and Armenia.

In the initial years of the formation of the new Middle East, Kurdish political activities, including armed resistance, proliferated. Although initially maps of Kurdistan did not feature very often, in the 1930s Kurdish political activists began to produce maps of Kurdistan. These maps mostly relied on the earlier European maps and atlases produced to study eastern territories of the Ottoman Empire's geography and ethnography in the second half of the nineteenth century and early twentieth century (O'Shea 2004). A good example of such maps was Muhammad Emin Zeki Bey's map of Kurdistan, published in his *History of the Kurds and of Kurdistan* in 1936. Zeki Bey was a Kurdish historian, politician and Transport Minister in the Iraqi government. He was also one of the ex-Ottomanists who became a Kurdish nationalist after realising that the Ottoman Empire would dissolve (Houston 2008: 22). The sources he used to produce his Kurdistan map were Sykes' 1908 Map of Kurdish Tribes of the Ottoman Empire, a map drawn by the Commission of Inquiry of the League of Nations of Iraq and a secret Indian Army map from 1912 (O'Shea 2004: 172). With the maps produced in the 1930s, such as Zeki Bey's, maps representing Kurdistan began to be produced mainly by the Kurds to support their political ambitions.

The only area where self-determination was implemented for Kurds, albeit in quite a procedural form, was north Mesopotamia. In this area, the British created a semi-autonomous regional administration called Sulaymaniyah in 1918, in accordance with the ideals of President Wilson's Point 12[14] (Edmonds 1971: 92). This was done with the aim of complying with the League of Nations' expectations, but it was made clear that this area was Iraqi territory. Sheikh Mahmud Barzanji, a Kurdish tribal leader, was appointed as the governor of Sulaymaniyah, but this semi-autonomous status only lasted until 1932.

The Sheikh rebelled against the British in 1920 because he argued some of the districts did not accept his leadership and the British restrained his freedom. He declared himself the King of Kurdistan and argued that the Kurds of Sulaymaniyah were entitled to a state of their own (Natali 2005: 28–9). Sheikh Mahmud's quest was almost impossible, because the British had no intention of recognising Kurdish independence. After a short military operation, Sheikh Mahmud was defeated, captured, and deported. The areas under his control were

---

[14] Point 12 in Wilson's *Fourteen Points*: 'The Turkish portion of the present Ottoman Empire should be assured a secure sovereignty, but the other nationalities which are now under Turkish rule should be assured an undoubted security of life and an absolutely unmolested opportunity of autonomous development, and the Dardanelles should be permanently opened as a free passage to the ships and commerce of all nations under international guarantees.'

incorporated into the Iraqi administrative organisation. The Sheikh rebelled for a second time in 1924 but his rebellion was defeated in 1932. After this, the British sent a memorandum to the Council of the League of Nations to legitimise their denial of Kurdish right to self-determination (Tahiri 2007: 59).

In the early state formation period in Iraq after the First World War, despite the experience of administrative autonomy, a Kurdish national consciousness across the Kurdish society did not form. Kurds in Iraq had different political positions, and the mandate system had a divisive style of rule leading Erbil, Sulaymaniyah, Mosul and Kirkuk to be administered based on different rules. Kurds in these areas also had different loyalties. For instance, Kurds in Kirkuk did not want to be under Sheikh Mahmud's authority. Two powerful tribal confederations, the Jaf and the Pizhdar, were opposed to the Sheikh's revolts (Jwaideh 2006: 184), and several Kurdish aghas preferred not to revolt against the central government or the British mandate authorities because they benefited from the status quo.

Although the post-War settlements did not affect Iran, changes in the region had an impact on the Kurds of Iran. The Qajar regime was in a state of turmoil in this period. Kurdish discontent and political activism rose initially, however, a strong nationalist consciousness did not emerge among Kurds at this stage. Tribal, local and religious interests prevailed over nationalist tendencies. This was also partly because of the multi-ethnic nature of the Iranian society, which included the Azeris, Kurds, Lurs, Afghans, Arabs, Armenians, Baluchis, and Turkmen. Lack of strong emphasis on a Persian identity in Iran did not give much reason for different ethnic groups to differentiate themselves from the dominant identity (Natali 2005: 22–4). The only notable Kurdish rebellion against the state in this period in Iran was led by Simko Agha, emerged as the most powerful figure in the Kurdish inhabited areas from 1919 to 1922. Simko was reported to have worked on a plan to include the Persian Kurds in an independent Kurdistan. He tried to ally himself with Britain, the United Soviet Socialist Republics (Soviet Union), the United States and France and declared an open rebellion against Iran. However, the tribes that joined his forces deserted him and his expectations of British support for his revolt against the government were not fulfilled. In the end, he was defeated and escaped to Iraq (Jwaideh 2006: 139; Edmonds 1971: 96).

Syria after the First World War was under the French mandate until 1946. Kurds constituted about 10 per cent of the population and were located in the northern part of the country, in the Al-Jazeera Province, Jabal al-Akrad and Ayn al-Arab as well as large cities such as Aleppo, Hama and Damascus (Lazarev and Mihoyan 2001: 246). Kurds in this period did not experience too much suppression under the French mandate and they found opportunities to develop their cultural life. Celadet Bedirhan, son of Emin Ali Bedirhan, who took refuge in Syria after the establishment of the Turkish Republic, took the lead in carrying out cultural activities. The French allowed this because they saw the Kurds as leverage against oppositional Arab groups in Syria. However, some of the Kurds also allied themselves with the Arab nationalists against the French mandate rule. They believed that after removing the French occupiers, Kurds would be given their national rights. These Kurds, especially in the Jazeera and Hasakah regions, rebelled against the French mandate between 1937 and 1939 (Lazarev and Mihoyan 2001: 247).

In Turkey, the first large-scale Kurdish revolt was the 1925 Sheikh Said Revolt. Azadi (meaning freedom), the organisation behind the revolt, was founded as a secret organisation in Erzurum in eastern Turkey in 1923. Its members were Kurdish officers and tribal leaders (Olson 1991). Azadi planned to instigate a general revolt to form an independent Kurdistan. Sheikh Said, a well-known religious authority, was selected as the leader of the revolt because it was thought that his religious character would facilitate mobilisation at a time when Kurdish nationalism was weak among the masses. His main support base was the Zaza-speaking Sunni Kurds. Alevi Kurds of Dersim did not support him and some Sunni Kurds and tribes in Van and some of the tribes and the townspeople of Diyarbakır and Elazığ joined in the suppression of the revolt (Tahiri 2007: 66–9). According to Tahiri, the attempt of Sheikh Said was unsuccessful, similar to the Sheikh Mahmud Barzanji and Simko revolts, because all these leaders undertook actions 'for a society in which its people were at odds with each other' (Tahiri 2007: 69). The revolt was easily defeated after heavy Turkish military response. Sheikh Said and other Kurdish leaders who joined the revolt were executed for the crime of attempting to establish an independent Kurdish state.

Sheikh Said's revolt is the most debated Kurdish rebellion in the literature and there are different arguments about its nature.

According to Jwaideh, there was a strong nationalist sentiment under-lying the revolt and religion was simply manipulated for a nationalist cause (2006: 210). In contrast, Van Bruinessen is sceptical that this was a nationalist revolt and describes it as a traditional tribal rebellion, arguing that the religious component of the revolt was far more sig-nificant than many assumed (Van Bruinessen 2003b). On the other hand, others argued that the abandonment of the Ottoman legacy and the religious authority of the caliphate made the traditional and con-servative Kurdish elite realise that the dominant doctrine of the Turkish Republic was Turkish nationalism, not Muslim fraternity, and this led to Kurdish resistance (Bozarslan 2003: 178; Edmonds 1971: 91). The 1924 Treaty of Lausanne was seen as another reason for the frustration of the Kurds with their situation, leading to the Sheikh Said revolt. According to this view, the Kurdish elite believed that Turkey aban-doned the Kurds by accepting the division of the Kurds between Turkey and Iraq through the Treaty of Lausanne. Therefore, for them, British dominance over Mosul was the result of a betrayal by the Turkish state. A follow-up agreement between Turkey and Britain in 1926 appears to confirm this. Based on this agreement, Britain gained full control of Mosul while Turkey agreed to cede the territory on the condition that Baghdad would control the Kurds and Kurds would not obtain self-government (Bozarslan 2003: 179).

Kurdish revolts continued to take place in Turkey in the 1930s. The Ararat (*Ağrı Dağı*) Revolt is a significant one in this period. The revolt took place during 1930–1 in northeast Turkey and was organised by Khoybun (meaning independence or being one-self). Khoybun was established in Damascus in 1927 by Kurdish activists who escaped or migrated to Syria after the foundation of the Turkish Republic. Kurds in Syria were less numerous than the Kurds in Turkey, Iraq and Iran and they lacked a focal centre. Therefore, Kurds who migrated from Turkey, such as Celadet Bedirhan, Osman Sabri, Nuri Dersimi and Ahmed Nami benefited from several opportunities in Syria. The French patronage in Syria also sanctioned them to engage in nationalist activ-ities. Khoybun's aim was to promote the Kurdish national cause, to form a Kurdish state within the territories of Turkey, the democratisa-tion of the Kurdish social life and to bring together the struggles of the suppressed peoples of the Near East (Lazarev and Mihoyan 2001: 270). The organisation distributed manifestos in Turkey, Iraq and Syria as well as sending them to the League of Nations, to Beirut and to Paris. It later opened Kurdish centres outside Syria, in Cairo, Paris, Detroit and Philadelphia and was particularly active in Paris (Jwaideh 2006: 145).

However, Khoybun, like other Kurdish groups before it, was unable to unify and organise the Kurdish masses. Again, this was due to a familiar reason: Kurdish tribal leaders were more intent on pursuing their own interests and the intellectuals engaged in these activities had no real power over tribal leaders. Moreover, most of the Kurds in Iran and Iraq did not support Khoybun, and Kurds in Turkey were divided. The level of disunity among the Kurds became particularly clear during the course of the Ararat Revolt. Most Kurds in Turkey did not take a side whereas a small number of Kurdish groups supported either the revolt or the government. Meanwhile, most Kurds living outside Turkey saw the revolt as irrelevant to their situation and considered it as a Kurdish revolt in Turkey (Tahiri 2007: 71–2). The Turkish army suppressed the revolt and its leader İhsan Nuri escaped to Iran.

Still, the Ararat Revolt is one of the most significant rebellions where Kurds from Iran, Iraq and Turkey, although limited in number, took part. This was quite interesting because most of the Kurdish nationalist activities at that time were confined within individual states (Olson 1991: 402). İhsan Nuri and former Ottoman officers led the revolt. Although the leaders of the revolt made appeals to the League of Nations and the Great Powers and called for the support of Kurds in Iran and Iraq, they did not receive much help. This was because of the signed treaties and protocols between Iran, Turkey and Britain and the Soviet Union, and also because of the security agreements between Turkey, Iran and Iraq to stop cross-border Kurdish activities (Olson 1991: 402–3; Edmonds 1971: 91).

The second most significant Kurdish revolt in the 1930s was the Dersim Revolt in 1937. This rebellion was organised for similar reasons to the Sheikh Said and Ararat Revolts. Turkish government policy displeased the Kurdish tribal leaders and sheikhs, with the government's continuing confiscations and deportations causing tension. Sayyid Reza, a religious leader, led the revolt. The revolt has been generally characterised as religious and tribal (Edmonds 1971: 91), but there are also arguments that the organisers had nationalist sentiments and goals (Jwaideh 2006: 215). The revolt started in 1937 in the mountains of Dersim and continued until the end of 1938, but the insurgents did not receive support from most Kurds outside Dersim and some Alevi Kurds in Dersim did not support the revolt either (Tahiri

2007: 75). The rebellion was severely suppressed and following this, Kurds in Turkey remained relatively inactive and no Kurdish revolt arose again in Turkey until the 1980s.

In the same period, there were cross-border organisations other than Khoybun such as the Kohestan group and the Kurdish Union. The Kohestan group had a newspaper carrying the same name published in Tehran. It wanted to bring the parts of Kurdistan in different countries together and form a Greater Kurdistan. The Kurdish Union was formed by Kurdish intellectuals, educated in Europe during the Ottoman times, such as Muhammad Emin Zeki Bey, Davut Pasha and Tevfik Vehbi. The Union sought the Kurdish right to self-determination, the establishment of a parliamentary system and the enlightenment, education and westernisation of the Kurdish people (Lazarev and Mihoyan 2001: 269–70).

Kurdish organisations and revolts in Turkey, Syria, Iraq and Iran after the formation of new states in the post–First World War period reflect the level of dissidence and discontent among the Kurdish intelligentsia and the tribal elite. The new state system in the region disenfranchised these groups and alienated them from the political centre. The revolts and organisations also reflect the still developing but increasingly nationalistic goals of the Kurdish political elite and their move away from trying to integrate themselves with other wider political ideologies and movements of the dominant political elite in their states. But several Kurdish groups and leaders also preferred to side with the political elite of the new states they were located in. The revolts highlight the fractionalised nature of Kurds at the time. There were multiple and rival Kurdish movements, and it was not always clear if they had nationalist goals at their core. Nonetheless, they set the Kurds down a nationalist path, especially in the way nationalists subsequently framed and interpreted these revolts and aligned them with the idea of Kurdistan.

Conclusion

The First World War period is significant for Kurdish nationalism and the idea of Kurdistan. It is in this period that Kurdish political activism started to include a nationalist character. The dissolution of the Ottoman Empire and the existence of multiple ideological and political groups and movements led the Ottoman Kurdish elite and intellectuals to affiliate themselves with a variety of positions. Until the beginning of the war, several members of the Kurdish tribal elite were Ottomanists due to their good relations with the Porte and the strong positions they had obtained in the Ottoman administration. Kurdish families who did not benefit from such relations were more critical of the Ottoman Porte under Abdulhamid II and allied themselves with the Young Turk movement and other political groups. However, with the dissolution of the empire and the division of its territories, and the dissemination of the principle of self-determination as a new norm to shape the new world, Kurdish nationalism started to develop with specifically Kurdish political agendas.

The First World War was also a period of rising hopes for a Kurdish state, followed by a dashing of these hopes on the rocks of real politics. Self-determination became an international principle for shaping the post-War period, but the politics on the ground made the implementation of this principle problematic. Internal divisions and rivalries among the Kurds, changing power configurations among the Allied Forces, difficulties in implementing self-determination due to the complex and mixed religious and ethnic composition of the populations in the region, all made it hard for the Allied Forces to help create independent states or autonomous regions for all minorities who demanded self-rule. Eventually, two Arab states, Iraq and Syria, a Turkish state and an Armenian state emerged in the region.

Although a Kurdistan state was not formed, the idea of Kurdistan existed in the minds of Kurds and non-Kurds. Since the First World War period, Kurdistan has become embedded in the political and historical discourse of Kurdish nationalists, regardless of whether they support Kurdish independence or support some form of regional autonomy instead. The map of Kurdistan that was adopted by the Kurds in this period persisted over successive decades until today and constituted the basis for Kurdish nationalist aspirations despite the fragmented status of Kurdish nationalism and different territorial and political aims of each Kurdish political movement.

After the British abandoned the idea of creating a Kurdish state, firstly within Anatolia and then in Iraq, Kurdish movements led by the Kurdish elite and intellectuals continued to emerge and proliferate. However, they never attained the status of a unified Kurdish nationalist movement detached from localised tribal desires for territorial control. Over time, especially in the next historical period, as explained in

Chapter 4, Kurdish nationalists in each state came to limit their territorial goals to within the boundaries of the states in which they reside;
yet, in the long term, the idea of Kurdistan and its maps still became the
most important and defining feature of Kurdish nationalism despite the
continuing fragmentation of Kurdish nationalism and the proliferation
of politico-territorial goals.

4 | *Kurdish Nationalism during Decolonisation and the Cold War*

Introduction

This chapter positions the idea of greater Kurdistan and Kurdish nationalist movements within the societal and political power relations between and among Kurds, states and international actors between the 1940s and late 1980s as well as within the international normative frameworks and global politics of this period. Such a positioning illuminates the relationship between Kurdish self-determination goals and the international normative framework of the time, drawing attention to how these have changed in relation to each other in the context of this long historical period. In the post–Second World War period until the end of the Cold War, the legalisation of the principle of self-determination and its use in territories previously colonised by Western powers dominated the debates and politics around self-determination. During this period self-determination became an officially recognised international principle and a normative ground for state formation. It was enshrined in the UN Charter of 1945 and subsequently included in the UN 1966 Twin International Covenants on 'Economic, Social and Cultural Rights' and 'Civil and Political Rights' (UN 1966 Twin International Covenants) and implemented in ex-colonial territories in 1966.

From the Second World War onwards the world became increasingly defined by a rivalry between Western and Eastern Blocs, respectively constituted of the United States and its allies on one hand and the Soviet Union and its allies on the other. Western liberal democracy and capitalism was placed in stark opposition to Marxist socialism and communism, and these two opposing ideological positions dominated the normative frameworks for politics globally. Throughout the world, including the Middle East, interactions between political actors were shaped through alliance formations around these two blocs. The Soviet

Union formed alliances with anti-imperialist states, leftist organisations and nationalist movements, such as the Kurds, while the Western Bloc relied on Western democratic states, and non-Western conservative and authoritarian regimes.

The two Blocs provided different frameworks of legitimacy for both state and non-state actors based on their ideological positions. When it came to self-determination, the Western Bloc interpreted it in a limited form and saw it applicable to colonial administration-to-state transformations. The Eastern Bloc interpreted the principle more freely, considering it as a principle for the liberation of peoples, state or non-state, from exploitative imperialism. The Soviet Union implemented the principle in its own territory and supported groups seeking liberation elsewhere, considering self-determination as a necessary stage on the road to achieve the socialist ideal. The evolving Western-dominated international legal framework surrounding self-determination came to provide legitimacy only to peoples who were living in administratively and territorially defined colonised territories, leaving groups such as Kurds out.

Kurdish nationalist groups in this period utilised both liberal and leftist frameworks in efforts to advance their claims to autonomy or independence. They utilised the changing geopolitical, political and ideological shifts in the Middle East as a whole and within their states to promote their claims adjusting their position in response to outside developments and in a strategic effort to gain greater traction. Initially they were hopeful about benefiting from the legalisation of self-determination and the re-ordering of the international order right after the Second World War, however, they soon realised the lack of international support for their cause. Most Kurdish organisations in all four states leaned towards leftist ideologies as the Cold War progressed.

On the other hand, although initially there were stronger transnational and cross-border connections between them, Kurdish political actors in each country increasingly focused their goals to the state they were located in. This was partly because they were trying to survive in their own country due to the consolidation of the state authorities and increased pressure on dissident groups. It was also because, despite their disagreements, regional states formed alliances to counter the Kurdish threat. However, the interactions between Kurdish groups began to increase again in the 1980s thanks to advancements in communication technologies, the growing Kurdish diaspora activism and increased international attention on the Kurds.

During this period, especially in the early years of the Cold War period, maps of greater Kurdistan became particularly prominent and were promoted by the Kurds in international platforms. This coincided and overlapped with an ongoing transnational Kurdish political activism as well as with the increased use of maps as propaganda tools by other political actors across the world. Propaganda maps, such as those used by the Germans, were particularly prominent during the Second World War and continued to be used during the Cold War. Kurds used the maps of Kurdistan to show the location and extent of the Kurdish homeland to the world. Kurds themselves produced these maps and they relied on the earlier maps produced by Western actors as well as by other Kurdish individuals such as Sherif Pasha and Muhammad Emin Zeki Bey, who also relied on the earlier Western maps. However, maps produced by Kurds in the 1940s had more expansive territorial extent compared to earlier maps. Although these cartographic promotions of Kurdistan abated in the late 1950s, the maps produced in the 1940s became the most influential versions and were replicated by the Kurds in the 1980s and 1990s.

Self-Determination during Decolonisation

Much as was the case in the First World War period, self-determination once again sat at the centre of the international political agenda in the decolonisation period. As a principle pertaining to state formation, self-determination developed in an *ad hoc* way under the shadow of decolonisation. From 1945 onwards, self-determination transformed into an international principle through its definition in several international covenants and its use as a legal justification for the creation of new states in ex-colonial territories. Its definition and implementation transformed self-determination into a widely recognised international norm. This legal transformation was paralleled by an increased use of self-determination as a political goal. Indeed, the quest for self-determination became a powerful force in territories colonised by Western powers and led to the creation of more than eighty new states, with the UN framework providing the normative basis for their formation.

Despite their rapid and wide acceptance, the UN documents do not actually explain what constitutes a nation nor do they provide clear criteria for defining who has the right to self-determination. However, a look at these definitions and their evolution indicates that from the end of the Second World War until the end of the Cold War, the meaning of self-determination gradually became increasingly encompassing. This meant that the demands for self-determination from contexts outside the ex-colonial territories, such as those of the Kurds, did not abate, but further increased.

Self-determination was used in legal texts as an international principle for the first time after the Second World War. The United States and the United Kingdom were keen to incorporate self-determination as a principle in their design of the post–War world. This design was developed into the Atlantic Charter (1941) and was approved by the rest of the Allies. Self-determination was subsequently included in Article 1 of the UN Charter, which set out the purposes of the UN, one of which was the development of 'friendly relations among nations based on respect for the principle of equal rights and self-determination of peoples'. Self-determination was defined as the right of peoples to 'freely determine their political status and freely pursue their economic, social and cultural development'. However, there was no further explanation beyond this. In the context of that time, this was interpreted as 'internal self-determination' or enshrining people's right to freely fulfil their economic, political and social rights within the state in which they resided. In other words, it was interpreted as the protection of the rights of the people of one state from interference by other states (Higgins 1993: 114). It was not interpreted as 'external self-determination', which means the right to secession or creating new states and changing boundaries of the existing state to accommodate claims (Wolff and Peen Rodt 2013: 808; Castellino 2000: 14). Clearly, in the UN Charter sovereignty and non-interference were seen as paramount and as guarantees for the protection of peoples' right to self-determination.

Until the late 1970s, self-determination legally applied only to peoples colonised by the European powers in Africa and Asia in their desire for independence (Castellino 2000: 22). The principle of *uti-possidetis* (territorial ownership) was strictly followed in its implementation. This meant, self-determination was limited to colonial administrations and the territorial boundaries of these administrations became the boundaries of the newly independent states. The point of this approach was to maintain territorial stability as much as possible (Shaw 1997: 481). The implementation of self-determination in the colonies imagined peoples within each administrative colonial unit as a whole nation.[1]

This interpretation and implementation of self-determination created a tension between the 'universality' of self-determination and its narrow implementation. This tension continued in the three main documents that shaped the implementation of self-determination in the 1960s: the UN General Assembly Resolution 1514 'The Granting of Independence to Colonial Countries and Peoples' in 1960 and UN General Assembly Resolution 1541 'Principles which should guide Members in determining whether or not an obligation exists to transmit the information called for under Article 73e of the Charter' in 1960 (both related to the independence of colonial countries and peoples) and the 1966 Covenants.

Resolution 1514 provided the justification for peoples' right to claim self-determination. Its Article 2 stated: 'All peoples have the right to self-determination. By virtue of their right they freely determine their political status and freely pursue their economic, social and cultural development.' While affirming the norm of self-determination and linking it to 'better standards of life and larger freedom', this Article emphasised stability through its Clause 6: 'Any attempt aimed at the partial or total disruption of the national unity and the territorial integrity of a country is incompatible with the purposes and principles of the Charter.' (Resolution 1514). This is a clear example of the contradictory nature of self-determination, revealing the tension between self-determination of peoples and state sovereignty. Resolution 1541, adopted three days after 1514, offered guidelines on the circumstances in which self-determination could be claimed and by whom. According to this Resolution, only entities that could be defined as 'non-self-governing territories' could claim self-determination but if they met this criterion they could do so through the 'full measure of government', namely free and fair elections. Upon meeting these conditions, they could then vote on one of the following three options: whether to 'constitute themselves as a sovereign independent state; associate freely with an independent state; or, integrate with an independent state already in existence'. (Resolution 1541).[2]

---

[1]   There were some exceptions to this approach, notably Senegal's separation from Mali in 1960, Singapore's secession from Malaysia in 1965 and Bangladesh's secession from Pakistan in 1971 (Knight 1985: 262).

[2]   For other UN resolutions that called for the application of the principle of self-determination for specific territories and the International Court of Justice

The 1966 Covenants, which laid down the foundations of what has subsequently developed as the International Law of Human Rights, followed the same logic. For instance, Article 1 of the Covenants repeats Article 2 of Resolution 1514 about all peoples' right to self-determination. Article 27 of the Covenants permits minorities the right 'to enjoy their own culture, to profess and practice their own religion, or to use their own language' but not to secede (UN 1966 International Covenants). Therefore, the 1966 Covenants can hardly be interpreted as implying that they require governments to readily accept secessionist demands (Franck 1993: 17).

The international documents in the 1970s, while building on the above-discussed previous resolutions and covenants, also presented a gradual expansion in the implications of self-determination. Initially, 'the people' referred to the citizens of a nation-state and self-determination was seen as their right to participate in the governing processes, enabling territorial administrative units to attain self-government in the colonised lands of Africa and Asia.[3] However, with the 1970s, particularly with the 1970 UN General Assembly Resolution 2625 Declaration on Principles of International Law Concerning Friendly Relations (Resolution 2625) and the 1975 Helsinki Final Act (Helsinki Act), the capacity of self-determination to apply to a wider range of cases increased, at least in theory. Self-determination came to be defined as a principle that applies to all types of peoples – people of a state, people within a state and a group of people that reside in multiple states – and it began to make references to both internal and external self-determination.

Resolution 2625 and the Helsinki Act somewhat moved away from the narrow implications of self-determination. Resolution 2625 described specific circumstances that open the way for claimant groups to use the right to external self-determination: 'all peoples have the right to freely determine, without external interference, their political status and to pursue economic, social and cultural development, and every State has the duty to respect this right in accordance with the provisions of the Charter'. The Resolution adds that the territorial

decisions on the applicability of the principle of self-determination for specific cases in this period see Shaw (1997: 480).
[3] A similar usage was adopted in the early 1990s during the dissolution of the communist states when the new states adopted the boundaries of previous administrative divisions or autonomous republics.

integrity of states should be respected but *only* of those states that conduct 'themselves in compliance with the principle of equal rights and self-determination of peoples ... and thus possess a government representing the whole people belonging to the territory without distinction as to race, creed or colour'. By explicitly emphasising the actions and practices of the incumbent state, Resolution 2625 implies that if the state does not fulfil its responsibilities and if it violates its people's internationally enshrined rights, the state's legitimacy to rule its people can be questioned. For instance, the international recognition of Bangladesh in 1971 as an independent state was justified by the severity of human rights violations.

The Helsinki Act also further expanded the applicability of the right to self-determination to wider groups of people beyond colonial territories. It did so by including all peoples – people of a state or peoples without a state – in its definition of eligibility to the right to self-determination and it referred to external self-determination specifically. Principle VIII of the Helsinki Act stated: 'participating States will respect the equal rights of peoples and their right to self-determination ... all peoples have the right, in full freedom, to determine, when and as they wish, their internal and external political status, without external interference, and to pursue as they wish their political, economic, social and cultural development'. Although the Helsinki Act still did not clearly state what was meant with 'people', it made specific references to both internal and external self-determination and to the actions of the incumbent states.

Despite its extension in this period, self-determination as a principle cannot be interpreted as providing a legal framework that encourages sub-state nationalists to seek secession. By the end of the Cold War, it still lacked a set of principles or criteria to identify which people had the right to independence and the way it was framed always prioritised the maintenance of the territorial unit. However, this does not change the fact that political interpretations of self-determination have always been far broader than its legal expressions (Shaw 1997: 481–2). The use of self-determination as an international principle and tool for dismantling colonial empires inspired nationalist groups around the world to see the principle also as a potential device for separating from non-colonial states. Legal restrictions on its implementation did not stop separatist or autonomist efforts to use self-determination as a political goal.

Maps of Kurdistan and Kurdish Nationalism in International Context

Kurdish nationalism went through significant changes in the long period between the Second World War and the end of the Cold War. Kurds initially tried to benefit from the process of re-establishment of the new international order after the Second World War and the legalisation of self-determination. However, they soon realised the nascent legal framework was of no help. Throughout this period, most Kurdish nationalist organisations adopted leftist, anti-colonial and anti-imperialist rhetoric and established good relations with the Soviet Union. On the other hand, the states with Kurdish populations allied themselves with Western states (except Iran after 1979 and Syria since 1946). Kurdish political groups either formed their own leftist parties or affiliated themselves with communist parties in their countries. On this basis, they adopted an anti-imperialist conception of self-determination, defined themselves as liberation movements and demanded autonomy or independence. During this time, leftist ideas and Marxism became dominant among Kurdish movements.

After the inclusion of self-determination into UN documents, Kurds appealed to the UN and powerful states for the recognition of their existence and rights. Although, the international documents re-stated the principle of self-determination, this was not in the way Kurdish nationalists hoped. Self-determination in these documents was defined in a restrictive manner. Therefore, Kurds were not able to use these as legal justifications for their self-determination demands. Later, in the 1970s and 1980s, self-determination in international texts slightly changed to include the actions of the states and the protection of human rights and democratic rights. These seemed to expand the applicability of the principle to wider ranges of groups, such as those living in nation-states whose boundaries were drawn by colonial powers, such as Iraq. Nonetheless, even in such contexts, self-determination was not intended for those minorities and prioritised the maintenance of the existing international boundaries (Knight 1985: 248).

In most of the Cold War period, the goals and ideals of Kurdish nationalist movements and activities were framed within the framework of self-determination as interpreted by the Soviet Union, which was being picked up by liberation movements around the world. Kurdish political groups that demanded self-determination justified their demands by claiming that even though they are not ruled by external colonial states, they are suffering from 'internal colonialism' within the boundaries of the states that emerged after the collapse of empires (Vanly 1993: 189). Internal colonialism is defined as a policy that targets minorities and it entails economic exploitation, lack of development, violation of human rights and centralised oppression leading to severe levels of injustice (Sidaway 2000: 599). In doing this, Kurdish political activists chose to connect their political activism to Marxist and socialist ideologies, because they believed improving the Kurds' situation and their rights would be possible only through changing the system in their states. This strategy was partly also the outcome of a lack of Western support for the Kurds in this period, as will be explained next.

Nonetheless, ambiguities with regard to who can claim self-determination and increased inclusivity in the more recent international documents, and the growing human rights and democracy discourses, especially after the 1970s, chimed with Kurdish nationalist demands and provided them with a wider international framework to justify their demands to the Western as well as the Eastern Bloc. The move to a more Western international normative framework to justify Kurdish demands became more obvious especially after the 1990s as explained in Chapter 5.

The idea of greater Kurdistan was initially central to transnational and pan-Kurdish connections, activities and goals focused on the Kurdish right to self-determination. The increase in the number of territorial nation-states during the decolonisation period reinforced the territorial nation-state ideal and provided further political and ideological impetus for Kurdish nationalists to promote Kurdistan as their national homeland. Kurdish political activists began to produce and promote their own maps of Kurdistan more widely in the 1940s. These maps utilised the earlier Kurdistan maps produced by Western travellers and officials in the late nineteenth and early twentieth centuries. In turn, the maps of the 1940s became the basis of the Kurdistan maps today. Three such examples were produced by the Khoybun, also known as the Kurdish League, established in Syria, the Rizgari Kurd and an unknown Kurdish group in Cairo.

The Khoybun produced a map in 1945 with similar boundaries to Muhammad Emin Zeki Bey's map of Kurdistan. Khoybun was mainly led by Kurdish leaders who were originally from Turkey. Khoybun's

Kurdish League Delegation to the UN San Francisco Conference presented a Kurdistan map on 30 March 1945. The Kurdish League Delegation also presented a letter to the conference, which demanded Kurdish autonomy (Westermann 1991: 50). This demand was limited to Kurdish autonomy in Turkey and excluded the Kurdish enclaves in Syria in an effort to avoid antagonising the authorities in Damascus (Tejel 2008: 86).

In the same year, on 22 March 1945, a young Kurdish officer in the Iraqi Army submitted a *Memorandum on the Kurdish Question* to the American Legation in Baghdad. This memorandum demanded Kurds to be given 'their place among free nations'. The Memorandum did not include a map but provided a description of the ethnographic boundaries of Kurdistan, which more or less replicated the boundaries produced on other Kurdish maps:

To the west: A line starting from the Kurd-Dagh [Syria, running in a northerly direction through the regions of Kilis, Maras, Elbistan, and Divrik to the Kelkit river [Turkey]. South-West of this line, there are scattered Kurdish settlements as far as the Gulf of Iskenderiye. To the North: A line following the Kelkit river, running east through the towns of Bayburt and Oltu to Kars [Turkey]. North of this line scattered Kurdish settlements reach the Black Sea near Trabzon [Turkey]. To the East: A line starting from Kars in a southeasterly direction, then running along the western shore of Lake Urmia, Luristan, the Bakhtiar country to Sehneh and Kermanshah [Iran]. To the South: From Southern Luristan a line running north west through Khanakin and Kifri to the Jebel Hamrin; from there to the west, south of Mount Sinjar to the Euphrates in Jerablus. (Memorandum on the Kurdish Question 1945)

The following year in January 1946, the Rizgari Kurd submitted a formal appeal, the Proclamation of the Kurdish Rizgari Party, to demand Kurdish self-determination to the American Legation in Baghdad. Rizgari Kurd was formed by Kurdish Communists and leftist students in Iraq in 1945. They were against British colonial rule and the dominance of tribal sheikhs. Although Rizgari Kurd was a short-lived party, it had great popular support and had the largest number of members (around 6,000) among Kurdish organisations during this time (Nerwiy 2012: 93–4). Accompanying their submission was a map of Kurdistan, which they requested to be shown to the UN (McDowall 1991: 294; Proclamation from the Rizgari Kurd in Andrews 1982: 83). In its memorandum Rizgari Kurd claims to speak on behalf of all Kurds, citing the Kurds in Iraq, Iran, Turkey and Syria, and makes clear references to the unity of Kurdistan and how totalitarian regimes and imperialism divided the Kurds:

The Peace Treaties after the First World War and the subsequent treaties divided Kurdistan by force and without consulting the Kurds among the four states of Turkey, Iran, Iraq and Syria, in order to safeguard the interests of imperialism and make them durable in the Middle East. ... The Party when offering your organisation this memorandum has a great reason to believe in your good intentions, and in your unshakable will to put an end to the forces of aggression and imperialism. It will be quite useful here to draw your attention to the fact that it will be impossible to establish world peace and rescue humanity from the terrible and distressful grievances of wars as long as some nations are exploited and humiliated by hateful imperialism. Our Party in the name of the Kurdish Nation who has been humiliated and subordinated to foreign rule, demands the extermination of imperialism in our country and the removal of the persecution and injustice of the governments to which it has been subordinated and divided (Proclamation of the Kurdish Rizgari Party 1946).

Clearly wider international developments and the rise of the principle of self-determination as a principle and a political goal for nationalist liberation movements, as promoted by the Soviet Russian state, was central to the Rizgari Kurd's pitch. On the other hand, the Rizgari Kurd also made references to the normative framework that emerged at the end of the Second World War, shaped by the Atlantic Charter, in which the self-determination was a central principle. This also raised Kurdish hopes as exemplified in the excerpt below from the Proclamation of the Rizgari Kurd. This excerpt shows that the Party, in the immediate aftermath of the Second World War, made references to both nascent framings of self-determination as developed in the Western and Eastern Blocs:

When the World War II drew to its end the hope of the oppressed nations revived. This included the Kurdish nation, who was the most prominent among the nations who supported the Allied nations with all its might in the Middle East, against Fascism and its satellite supporters. The Kurdish nation has attached and is attaching great hopes to the promises given by the statesmen of the Allied nations and provisions of the Atlantic Charter and Moscow declaration which provide small nations the right to achieve full freedom and right to decide their own fates and manage their own affairs. If the great nations gave the brilliant promises to the small nations in their hour of distress in order to leave those promises ink on paper and forget them subsequently in the ecstasy of victory, the small nations will not give them up but will take them as a legal concession for claiming their rights (Proclamation of the Kurdish Rizgari Party 1946).

Finally, an unknown Kurdish group in Cairo also produced another map of Kurdistan in 1947 (O'Shea 2004: 172). The territories this map depicted were slightly more expansive than previous maps. The memorandum accompanying this map stated: 'the presence of Kurds in any given area is only indicated where it is expressly stated by a trustworthy authority' (O'Shea 2004: 176). For instance, Lurs were presented as 'dilute' Kurds who would probably wish to become part of a Kurdish state. The map also included the Arabs of Khuzistan near the Persian Gulf and Bakhtiari lands, but these inclusions were not justified. The Cairo Map is important because it has been very influential, possibly due to its clarity and its decisive and expansive borders.

The territories shown on the Rizgari and Cairo maps have become widely accepted by Kurdish nationalists and outsiders as 'Kurdistan' since their production. Almost all Kurdish organisations in the diaspora publish maps depicting the similar borders and geographical coverage in their programmes and leaflets. They use it is as the symbol of Kurdish identity and a territorial basis for future Kurdish aspirations (O'Shea 2004: 194).

It is no coincidence that these attempts at drawing the boundaries of greater Kurdistan were made in the 1940s because this was a period in which geopolitical configurations during and after the Second World War took place and during which self-determination became a legal international principle. This envisioning of a greater Kurdistan which ran parallel to the existence of transnational cross-border interactions between different Kurdish groups was substantial during this decade. The Kurdish cross-border interaction, as explained below, was partly because newly formed states with Kurdish populations had not fully consolidated their centralised power.

There was also another interesting temporal coincidence, one between the promotion of the maps of Kurdistan and the changes map making went through in the decade after the Second World War. During and after the end of the War, maps became more functional and, more importantly, they began to be used as a tool through which knowledge is constructed and communicated, turning cartography into a field of power relations (Crampton 2001: 235–6). This transformation had its roots in the German propaganda maps. Since the public greatly believed in the authenticity of maps, geo-politicians thought representing ideas on maps could be an effective tool (Wright 1942), turning them into propaganda maps. The use of propaganda maps became especially common during and after the Second World War and through such maps, false impressions were promoted and facts were denied or exaggerated (Quam 1943: 21–2). The anti-Soviet maps produced by the US media were also such examples, and some of those maps even included Kurdistan. One example is the 'Kurdistan' map published in the *Time* magazine on 22 September 1952. This map represented Kurdistan in the shape of a Soviet sickle and spatially very close to the Soviet Union. The article titled 'Report on the Kurds' that accompanied the map portrayed the Kurds as 'violent fighters and . . . threats to Western democracy and as potential allies to Soviet Communism' (Culcasi 2006: 694).

The idea that maps are tools to convey specific messages rather than scientific communications of reality was further developed by cartographers in the 1970s onwards, who considered maps as representations and sites where power and knowledge interacted (Crampton 2001: 236). Even though maps have an air of scientific authenticity because of their precise appearance, every map is actually a reflection of both objective and subjective elements (Harley 1989; Wright 1942: 527). Maps are not objective depictions of what they represent because the aims, knowledge and thinking of those who produce the maps cannot be separated from the map (Crampton 2001: 240; Harley 1989: 11).

The maps of greater Kurdistan produced in the 1940s and onwards are examples of such maps. These maps have become some of the most influential propaganda tools for the Kurdish nationalist discourse. They depict a territorially exaggerated version of the territory of Kurdistan, extending into areas with no majority Kurdish populations. Despite their production with political aims related to specific claims on the demographic and ethnographic structure of the region, and their questionable methodologies, they have become 'Kurdistan in the minds of Kurds' and the boundaries they indicate have been readily accepted (O'Shea 2004: 168).

Regional Trends in Kurdish Political Activism

For most of the Cold War period, Kurds had limited access to transnational processes and did not engage much in cross-border activities with

Kurds in other countries. Although the domestic context of each state mattered hugely for how Kurdish nationalism developed for most of this period, in the initial decades after the Second World War, Kurdish nationalism was more transnational and cross-border activities and collaborations between Kurds in different countries were more common, such as the Iranian and Iraqi Kurdish leaders' collaboration in the formation of the Kurdish Republic of Mahabad in Iran in 1946.[4] In this early part of the post–Second World War period, the development and evolution of Kurdish nationalism in each individual state took place in a transnational context where ideas, activities, individuals and ideologies crossed borders, despite differences between state policies, institutions and socio-economic dynamics. Some Kurdish groups even aimed for a pan-Kurdish unity. Kurdish groups that restricted their goals to achieving recognition within a particular state still made open references to the Kurds in other states and called for self-rule for all Kurds.

This transnational characteristic weakened in the following decades of the Cold War and Kurdish political activism became more focused in each state, but cross-border political activities began to increase again in the 1980s. Technological advancements (transmitters, radios and satellite TVs) increased communication between Kurds in different countries and raised awareness among the Kurds about developments affecting their brethren in other countries. Moreover, the Iran–Iraq War, the Baghdad regime's campaigns against its Kurds, the conflict between the PKK and the Turkish army, employment or education needs and state pressures led to largescale displacement within the state or displacement to another country. Displacement also facilitated increased cross-border and transnational connections. Growing diaspora in Western states also played a role in enabling different Kurdish groups to become aware of the developments in other regional states.

---

[4] The Hiva Party, established in Iraq in 1939 by both Iraqi and Iranian Kurdish activists, was a key political organisation in this period. When Iraq joined the Axis powers in 1941, Barzani escaped to Iran to organise a rebellion against Iraq with the help of the Hiva Party. This culminated in a collaboration between Barzani and the Kurdish political elite in Mahabad, which led to the formation of the Republic of Mahabad in 1946. Another example is the contract formed between Turkey's Kurds, and the KJ and Hiva Party, despite heavy Turkish military control in the border areas in eastern Turkey. As part of this interaction, in 1944, Kurdish representatives from Iran, Iraq and Turkey met on the border to discuss the issue of collaboration for a free Kurdistan (Lazarev and Mihoyan 2001: 278–9).

Throughout the Cold War period, Kurdish nationalism and political activism went through a significant transformation with some common trends across all the states with Kurdish populations. In this period, Kurds continued to struggle for autonomy, collaborated and clashed with each other, rebelled against the governments of their states, formed several organisations and parties, while also partly integrating into the societies they were in. The number of Kurdish nationalist organisations significantly increased in this period; several new parties emerged with different ideological positions and goals in the four countries, and a complex web of Kurdish parties and movements developed in the Middle East.

The grassroots base of Kurdish political organisations and national awareness among the Kurdish populations grew in all the states with Kurdish populations. While in the first half of the twentieth century peasants or urban craftsmen remained distant from Kurdish nationalist activities, in the latter half of the century grassroots support for Kurdish nationalism expanded and increased in all four states. This was also related to weakening tribal structures (at different levels in each state), the state suppression that created resentment among Kurdish populations, and the drastic changes that societies went through as a result of urbanisation, new education systems and increased levels of literacy. All these factors led to increased mobilisation and politicisation among the Kurds in all four countries. However, the degree of Kurdish popular support was different in each state and remained ideologically heterogeneous, especially in Turkey, and none of the Kurdish parties ever gained the full support of all the Kurds in each state.

Kurdish political activism went through different phases in all the states, fluctuating between clandestine activities, open protests, political party organisations and violent armed activities. Several Kurds joined non-Kurdish leftist organisations in their states or formed their own leftist organisations. By the 1980s, political configurations and ideological affiliations within the Kurdish movement began to change, for instance the distance between the Kurds and the leftists of their countries increased. The emergence of the PKK was the outcome of such a division. This ideological change was reinforced by conflicts in the region, especially the Iran–Iraq War from 1980 to 1988, the conflict between the Kurds and the regime in Iraq, and the conflict between the PKK and Turkey. These contributed to a more assertive Kurdish position in each state and across the region.

Alongside with the substantial changes Kurdish political activism went through in the Cold War period, certain long-term historical characteristics of the Kurdish political activities also remained unchanged. These unchanging or slowly changing characteristics created disadvantageous conditions for the development of a more coherent and powerful Kurdish nationalist movement in this period. First, the geopolitical position of Kurdistan remained a significant impediment. Historically Kurds have always been divided, but with the consolidation of nation-states in the region, they became minorities in the peripheries of the new states that pursued suppressive policies towards minorities. There were also internal characteristics that continued to hinder the coherent development of Kurdish nationalism. Tribal structures and relations, although weakened, continued to shape the traditions and practices of Kurdish actors and maintained the divided nature of Kurdish nationalism, and tribal leaders and sheikhs continued to prioritise their own interests (Halliday 2006: 16). Personalisation of power was another significant common feature and on many occasions the leadership interests took priority over Kurdish interests. Yet despite these differences and existing structures that prevent unity among the Kurdish factions, there is no denying that Kurdish nationalism, in its different and separate forms, consolidated itself in each state and regionally in the Middle East.

Country-Specific Developments

The socioeconomic and political transformations in each state, as well as regional and geopolitics dynamics affected the way Kurdish nationalism evolved and developed in each state. These changes affected each Kurdish community or movement in different ways leading Kurdish nationalism in each state to follow a different trajectory. For instance, while Iraqi Kurds aimed to attain autonomous status, Kurds in Iran, Turkey and Syria continued to struggle for the recognition of their ethno-cultural rights. In this period, unable to harness the international framework in their favour, Kurds retreated into domestic politics. The developments in the domestic sphere in this period were formative in how they subsequently re-engaged in the international sphere in the post–Cold War period, as will be discussed in the next chapter. The rest of this chapter will highlight domestic developments and specific

Kurdish movements in each context to illustrate the lack of or limited international engagement and limited cross-border activities between the Kurds in most of the Cold War period.

Iraq

Having lost their administrative self-rule in the post–First World War period, Kurds in Iraq made self-determination demands again hoping to benefit from the newly emerging international context during the Cold War period. However, their demands were ignored and they did not receive international support until the 1990s, which became only possible due to the Gulf War conditions and the severe human rights violations by the Iraqi regime that drew international attention to the Kurds.

In the period from the 1940s to 1980s the pattern in the relationship between the Kurds and the Iraqi regime was that of the Iraqi government reluctantly making concessions following violent conflict but refusing to follow through on commitments brokered in peace deals. The consequence was mutual distrust. Deals that benefited Kurds were reached only when the central government felt weak or was in crisis, but as soon as the government consolidated its position it returned to business as usual and suppression. Therefore, most pro-Kurdish deals in Iraq were the result of circumstances rather than emerging from a genuine desire by the government to reach accommodation.

In this period, Kurdish nationalism remained tribalistic, but alongside the continuation of tribal characteristics, it also increasingly became a mass movement especially from the 1960s onwards. The tribal structure was particularly dominant in the earlier decades and most Kurds accepted this socioeconomic structure and primarily identified themselves with their tribes rather than their national or religious identity. In the following decades, Kurdish nationalist activities became more diverse. Even though tribal structures continued to shape the contours of Kurdish political activism, uneven modernisation and industrialisation and the growing segments of educated leftist Kurdish leaders made Kurdish political mobilisation yet more complex. On the other hand, while carrying out such suppressive and violent policies, the Iraqi government increased its public spending in order to keep dissent under control. It distributed free monthly food rations and expanded its healthcare and education provisions. Many Kurds took advantage of these new programmes and opportunities and chose to integrate into Iraqi society. This period also witnessed the deepening and crystallising of divisions within the Kurdish movement. KDP and PUK became two pillars of Kurdish nationalism in Iraq for many decades and their divisions became institutionalised and territorialised over time.

Key Kurdish developments in the 1940s in Iraq were the rebellions led by Mustafa Barzani. In 1941, when Iraq joined the war on the British side, Barzani escaped to Iran[5] and organised a rebellion against Iraq with the help of the Hiva Party, a secret Kurdish political party established in Iraq. Hiva aimed to unify Kurdistan and create a Kurdish state (Nerwiy 2012: 90). In its first meeting, the party decided to declare the autonomy of Kurdistan and prepared a programme that aimed to unify the tribes and form a Kurdish army (Jwaideh 2006: 239). Barzani's rebellion led to talks with the Iraqi government and to an agreement. Kurds demanded autonomy in Kirkuk, Sulaymaniyah, Erbil, Khanakin and Duhok. The agreement recognised Kurdish administrative control in the areas Kurds obtained during the fight, but not autonomy, and it provisioned the appointment of a Kurd as minister and the use of Kurdish as an official language. However, the agreement was not implemented which led Barzani to rebel once again in 1944 only to be defeated by 1945 and flee to Iran. Barzani's defeat was partly because of the dividedness of the Kurdish tribal society. Several Kurdish tribes did not join Barzani's revolts because they were not happy with Barzani's growing power.

In addition to tribal rivalries, there was also tension between the tribal components of the Hiva Party and the urban Kurdish members. The differences between them and their goals led to polarisation within Hiva and to its eventual splintering into three different parties, Shurish (Revolution), Azadi and Rizgari Kurd. Rizgari Kurd had pan-Kurdish ideals such as unifying and liberating all the Kurds in greater Kurdistan, and more specifically, it sought to secure administrative independence for Iraqi Kurdistan (Jwaideh 2006: 240–1; Andrews 1982). The party was highly active in international platforms and wanted to benefit from the new international frameworks and platforms that emerged after the Second World War. As mentioned earlier in the chapter, the Rizgari Kurd Party sent several letters to the UN and

---

[5] Mustafa Barzani was kept in Sulaymaniyah since he surrendered in 1933 after the defeat of Barzanji, whose rebellion Barzani had joined.

other international actors, including maps, to explain the Kurdish cause. The dissolution of Hiva also led Mustafa Barzani to form his own party, the KDP. Composed of tribal and traditional groups, it distanced itself from urban leftists. The KDP became a key Kurdish political actor and came to be seen by the Iraqi regime as the representative of the Kurds from the late 1950s onwards.

The 1958 Revolution in Iraq led by General Kasim ended the monarchical rule (1932–58) and established the Republic of Iraq. Initially the new regime established good relations with the Kurds, allowed Barzani to return to Iraq after his exile in 1946, legalised the KDP as a political party, released Kurdish political prisoners and included two Kurdish ministers in the government (Lazarev and Mihoyan 2001: 284). The Provisional Constitution referred to Kurds as equal partners with Arabs, the first official document to do so in Iraq's history. However, these constitutional promises were not to be implemented.

The new regime's initial rhetoric of Iraqi identity and Kurdish-Arab fraternity was replaced by an emphasis on Arab identity in the following years (Natali 2005: 35, 45–6). The regime consolidated its power and no longer needed a conciliatory relationship with the Kurds. As a result, the KDP was declared illegal and the government forces began bombarding rural areas (Edmonds 1971: 100). Barzani again left for Iran. In 1961 he initiated a guerrilla war against the Iraqi government, which lasted until 1970. With the guerrilla warfare in the 1960s and the increased Arabisation policies of the Iraqi regime, nationalist sentiment among the Kurdish populations strengthened. The grassroots support for the Kurdish political parties, especially the KDP, expanded in this period (Edmonds 1971: 101). The KDP also began to receive support from Iran, which enabled it to mobilise more effectively.

Two years into the guerrilla conflict, Kurdish representatives met with Iraqi officials in February 1963. Kurds demanded: an acknowledgement that Iraq is composed of Arabs and Kurds; Kurdish representation in the Iraqi government; and the establishment of autonomous governmental and parliamentary institutions in Sulaymaniyah, Erbil and Kirkuk. However, these talks did not lead to an agreement. In the same year the government declared military rule in the Kurdish areas and began a campaign of aerial bombardment. Negotiations were renewed in November 1964 and an agreement was signed. These negotiations led to the adoption of a transitional constitution, which acknowledged equality between Kurds and Arabs, but fell short of granting Kurdish autonomy (Lazarev and Mihoyan 2001: 299–305). However, Jalal Talabani, a leading member of the KDP, and Barzani came to loggerheads over the terms of the 1964 Agreement and the divisions within the KDP came to the fore. When the KDP went ahead and began to establish its administrative rule in certain areas in line with the 1964 Agreement, the Iraqi regime restarted its attacks on the Kurds. The conflict ended with the 1966 Bazzaz Agreement. Bazzaz is an important agreement for the Kurds because it gave the Kurds significant autonomy rights, but similar to previous agreements, it was not implemented (Lazarev and Mihoyan 2001: 311–18).

Another failed attempt at agreement between the Kurds and Iraqi government, the 1970 Agreement, came after the 1968 Ba'athist military coup. The 1970 Agreement was partly reflected in the 1974 Constitution, which changed the status of the Kurds in Iraq on paper. The new revolutionary regime agreed to the terms of the 1970 Agreement because Kurdish mobilisation had become significantly potent by this stage and the new military regime did not have full control over the Kurds and had not yet fully consolidated its power in Iraq. Therefore, realising a military solution was not available at that time. The 1970 Agreement promised limited Kurdish self-rule and cultural rights and led to the announcement of a Kurdish administration in parts of northern Iraq. However, it left out practical and important issues that affected the implementation of its terms, including forced displacements of the Kurds by the previous regime and their return to Kirkuk and Sinjar (Lazarev and Mihoyan 2001: 324). Moreover, although Kurdish autonomy was officially recognised in the 1974 Constitution, the terms of the autonomy were more limited than what was agreed in the 1970 Agreement.

Despite granting less autonomy than originally hoped by Kurdish nationalists, the 1974 Constitution was an important milestone for Kurds. Law 33 of the Constitution, dealing with the autonomy of the Kurdistan region (*mentika*), included commitments to: a census to identify the areas with Kurdish majorities and the use of data from the 1957 census in this process; allowing Kurdistan its own administration whilst remaining part of Iraq; establishing Erbil as the administrative centre of the region; accepting autonomous bodies as part of the state institutions; the provision of education in Kurdish; protection for Arabs and other minorities living in the new autonomous areas;

granting central government and its representatives authority over the autonomous region. However, Article 20 of Law 33 also gave the government in Baghdad the right to abolish the Kurdish autonomous status (Lazarev and Mihoyan 2001: 324–8).

The KDP rejected the constitutional provisions of 1974 because they were more restrictive than what was agreed in the 1970 Agreement. As a result, military conflict started again between the government and the Kurds. However, this time the KDP was in a much weaker position. Iraq and Iran struck a deal in 1975 after which Iran withdrew its support for Iraqi Kurds, proving a major blow to Kurdish aspirations. The Iraqi government was now in a stronger position. Five years after the 1968 Revolution, the revolutionary government had established its power and authority. Emboldened, the Iraqi government pursued suppressive policies to prevent Kurdish mobilisation. It deported Kurds from northern to southern and central Iraq, and settled Arabs in their place, arrested a large number of dissidents and forged alliances with regional states to contain the Kurds. Between 1974 and 1978, 1,200 villages in Diyala, Sulaymaniyah, Erbil, Kirkuk and Duhok were emptied (Lazarev and Mihoyan 2001: 355). The discovery of oil resources in Kirkuk and the government's desire to control the area played a significant role in these decisions. Increased oil revenues enabled the government to impose its power on dissenters and increase its repressive policies further. The Kurdish forces admitted defeat in April 1975.

KDP's defeat deepened existing divisions within KDP and led to a split in the party.[6] Talabani and his supporters separated from the KDP and established the PUK (Patriotic Union of Kurdistan) which was founded in Damascus in 1975 under Talabani's leadership and established its headquarters on the Iraqi–Iranian border in 1976 (Lazarev and Mihoyan 2001: 329–30). The PUK and KDP had different tribal and intellectual bases. While the PUK was supporting progressive and agrarian reforms, the KDP relied on traditional and tribal support and opposed any reforms that could harm the status quo. Divisions between the two parties deepened and became territorial over time, with PUK having control over the Sulaymaniyah area and KDP having

---

[6] Divisions between Talabani and his supporters go back to the 1964 Agreement. Talabani and his supporters found the agreement too favourable to the government at the expense of Kurdish nationalist goals. They refused to recognise Barzani as a legitimate leader in the struggle for autonomy and were expelled from the Party.

more influence over Erbil and Duhok. Even after the whole Kurdish region became de facto autonomous in 1991, the KDP-PUK division continued.

After the defeat of the Kurds in 1975, their situation continued to deteriorate in the 1980s with increased active presence of the Iraqi army in Kurdish areas and strict border controls. At the beginning of the Iran–Iraq War, Kurdish parties increased their control in the north again and brought people back to the villages that were destroyed by the Iraqi government. However, the government carried out the 1987–8 Anfal Campaigns, which included chemical attacks, to retake the control of this region (Van Bruinessen 1994). During these attacks, 4,000 villages were destroyed, 150,000 people were killed, 180,000 people remain unaccounted for and huge numbers of people were displaced (Natali 2005: 59). The inaction of the international community in the face of this humanitarian crisis was severely criticised and provided the pretext for the creation of a safe zone in northern Iraq after the Iraqi regime's attacks against the Kurds in 1990.

Turkey

During the Cold War period, Kurdish nationalism and political activism in Turkey evolved within a more complex political, social and economic context compared to other regional states with Kurdish populations. Kurdish political activists and organisations, engaged with non-Kurdish political and economic actors extensively, and in many ways, integrated into the system in Turkey in a deeper way. On the other hand, the Turkish state never considered making concessions and always approached the Kurdish issue in a suppressive manner and with a military outlook, leading to the development of a more radical form of Kurdish nationalism. The military coups, especially the 1980 coup led to severe suppression of the Kurds and played a significant role in the radicalisation of the Kurdish political movement in Turkey.

Kurds in Turkey have been hugely stratified between different socio-economic groups, divided between traditional rural dwellers and urban educated leftist intelligentsia (as well as between Alevi and Sunni Kurds). These divisions prevented the emergence of a unified voice among the Kurds. Limited modernisation, poor transport and communication networks and inadequate educational infrastructure in eastern Turkey where most Kurds in Turkey were located in this period, increased the divisions between rural and urban Kurds. The traditional landowning stratum formed good relations with the state, but leftist urban Kurds challenged the state; an opposite process to what was happening in Iraq where urban leftist Kurds formed better relations with the state regime and the landowning tribal strata confronted the state. Moreover, in Turkey, higher levels of industrialisation and economic change created different class groups within the Kurds. These divisions, combined with suppressive state policies, hindered the formation of a strong and representative Kurdish movement. On the other hand, the Kurdish movement throughout this period developed effective ways of grassroots mobilisation, especially in the 1970s. This later enabled organisations, such as the PKK to increase the number of their members.

In the early years of the post–Second World War period, Kurdish political activism still had not recovered from the heavy suppression in the 1930s and it was further pushed out of public life in the 1940s and 1950s. Strong one-party rule continued until 1946, and this combined with a heavy police and army presence, meant that Kurdish political activism became clandestine and small scale in these decades. Even after 1946 when Turkey moved to a multiparty system and political space expanded, the suppression of the Kurds continued and cultural and political concessions, such as speaking Kurdish in public and forming explicitly Kurdish associations, continued to be denied. However, with the multiparty system, a new Kurdish class emerged with ties to centre-right Turkish parties established in this period (Özcan 2006: 89). Newly formed populist parties such as the Democrat Party forged alliances with wealthy Kurdish tribal landowners for electoral purposes, which resulted in the integration of the Kurdish tribal elite into finance and trade in big cities while maintaining their land ownership. Kurdish landowners also began to participate and obtain positions in politics and in municipal councils. This alliance strengthened the Kurdish tribal elite's position and created a long-lasting division between the wealthy Kurdish class and the politically minded and less privileged sections of the Kurdish society.

The 1960s proved to be slightly different; although activism around the issue of identity was still not permissible and the suppression of Kurdish political activism continued, Kurdish actors found alternative channels for political activity. This was because of the changes in the Turkish political system after the 1960 military coup, which was the result of the tensions between the government and the opposition. The 1961 Constitution, adopted after a military coup, introduced protections of freedom of speech and association and installed checks and balances on the executive to protect the autonomy of the judiciary and the parliament (Aksin 2007: 268–72). However, even though it is considered the most democratic constitution in Turkey's history, it certainly did not have a permissive approach to the issue of identity. Using the term 'Kurd' in public remained illegal as well as the use of Kurdish in public spaces. Based on a new Law 105, Kurdish families seen as potentially problematic were forced to migrate to cities in western Turkey and academics suspected of trying to form an independent Kurdistan were expelled from their jobs (Lazarev and Mihoyan 2001: 289).

Nonetheless, the more open political space created by the new 1961 Constitution led to the formation of several organisations and political parties with a variety of views. Turkish leftist parties held an appeal for the urban and educated Kurdish nationalists thanks to their inclusive approach towards minorities and because they sought land reform and socio-economic change in favour of disadvantaged sections of society. Several Kurds joined the Turkey Labour Party (TİP, *Türkiye İşçi Partisi*). Within TİP, Kurds formed a Kurdish section, which later established the Revolutionary Eastern Culture Units (*Devrimci Doğu Kültür Ocakları*), that played a significant role in raising political awareness and encouraging mobilisation among the Kurds. TİP was shut down in 1971 after the military memorandum in the same year. The party returned to political life in 1975 but was closed again after the 1980 military coup.

Some of the urbanised and leftist Kurds also formed clandestine leftist organisations, such as the Kurdistan Democratic Party of Turkey (KDP-T) in 1965 that sought the social, political and economic development of the Kurdish people and Kurdistan. These organisations linked their nationalism to leftist revolutionary ideologies, arguing that the situation of the Kurds could be improved and their cultural and political rights could be realised through changing the socioeconomic system (Lazarev and Mihoyan 2001: 333). They secretly published books and journals in Kurdish and Turkish. Their communist and socialist tendencies meant that Kurdish organisations at this time did not receive international support from Western countries and were targeted by the state.

The indirectly permissive space for Kurdish political activism significantly narrowed in the 1970s. By the latter years of the 1960s the Turkish elite were already pursuing a deeper assimilation policy that put more emphasis on Turkish identity. Increased Kurdish activism in Turkey was concerning the government. The potential impact of the 1966 Bazzaz Agreement and the 1970 Agreement between Kurds and the regime in Iraq worried the Turkish political elite (Lazarev and Mihoyan 2001: 334). The control measures on the Kurds (and on all parties critical of the political elite) further increased after the 1971 Military Memorandum. The Turkish gendarmerie and commandos attacked several Kurdish populated areas in eastern Turkey. By 1971 several Kurds were arrested and imprisoned with the claim that they were attempting to create a Kurdish state. The government passed several restrictive laws limiting freedom of speech and association.

In the second half of the 1970s political space in Turkey began to expand again. The government implemented a general pardon in 1974 for all political prisoners. This revitalised political activism, including the Kurds. Several new organisations formed by the Kurds emerged and organisations that already existed became more active. However, Turkey was a very tense place politically in the second half of the 1970s. The political and ideological contexts became highly polarised. Several right- and left-wing groups and youth organisations emerged, with the state allowing and even encouraging right-wing groups' activities. This tension was followed by the 1980 military coup, which brought a temporary abrupt end to dissident activities.

The period just before the coup is crucial for the direction Kurdish political activism took in the following decades. The number of secret organisations with a specific focus on the Kurdish issue increased in this period. Among the secret parties, the KDP-T sought self-determination for the Kurdish people and believed that this could be achieved only through a national-democratic revolution and armed struggle, but the party could not reach out to the grassroots because of its highly idealised programme (Lazarev and Mihoyan 2001: 338). In this period, the divisions between the Kurdish and Turkish left deepened and eventually the Kurdish left separated itself from the former. The PKK was the outcome of this separation. It emerged in 1978 with the aim of liberating Kurdistan and establishing an independent, united and socialist Kurdish state (Van Bruinessen 2003c). It asserted itself among other Kurdish parties and emerged as the strongest Kurdish political party in the following decades.

The two-year transitionary military government after the 1980 military coup restricted individual liberties and press freedom, purged hundreds of academics from universities and introduced a 10 per cent threshold in elections to parliament which greatly hindered the prospects of small parties (Arat 1991: 91). It heavily suppressed and punished members of any opposition group and carried out terrible atrocities against suspects in police detention and in prisons. A much less democratic constitution was designed by the transitionary regime and adopted through a referendum in 1982. Kenan Evren, the leader of the coup, famously declared that they had to design a new constitution because the 1961 Constitution was like a dress too large for the Turkish society (BBC Turkce 2017).

After the coup, in the 1980s, Kurdish groups attempted to continue their activities but were met with heavy suppression by the state, which in turn led to the radicalisation of several Kurdish organisations. In 1983 the PKK began its guerrilla campaign against the Turkish army and the police and duly established itself as the strongest Kurdish organisation in Turkey. It proved effective in mobilising the Kurdish people. Its tactics involved terrorism, including attacks on civilians, which led the party to be listed as a terrorist organisation by Turkey and several Western countries. It engaged in huge propaganda activities in Turkey, the wider region and in Europe, claiming that the PKK's methods were the only viable way to advance Kurdish rights, including the right to self-determination. The party's propaganda was widely disseminated through visual and audio broadcasting, such as MED-TV. Throughout the conflict, several villages were destroyed by the Turkish army and by the PKK militia, and many Kurds migrated or were forcefully deported to other parts of Turkey or abroad (Bose 2003: 24–25). Since then PKK has gone through significant transformations, as will be explained in the next chapter, and the conflict between the PKK and the Turkish security forces has become a deeply entrenched conflict until today.

Iran

The development of Kurdish nationalism in Iran followed a slightly different trajectory compared to Iraq and Turkey during the Cold War period. The Iranian state allowed the expression of Kurdish identity in its cultural form and at specific historical junctures the state deliberately moved away from the idea of a strictly Persian identity. For instance, the head of the Pahlavi regime, Reza Shah, used myths that were inclusive of Kurds, which promoted the idea of a shared ancestry and linguistic and cultural commonality. Unlike Turkey and Iraq, the Iranian regime maintained the privileged positions of the traditional stratum and did not remove Islam as a determinant of public life. As a result, Kurdish nationalism in Iran developed into a more accommodating movement than in Turkey and Iraq. Despite being hostile to the government, most of the Kurdish political groups did not engage in violent methods (Vali 2003: 162). As a result, a more culturally adaptive Kurdish identity than in other countries emerged in Iran.

On the other hand, Iran is also the only context in which an independent Kurdish state was unilaterally established – the Republic of Mahabad in 1946. The entry of the Soviet and British armed forces in Iran and the removal of the Shah regime in 1941 led to a weakening of central control in Kurdish areas. A large part of the Mahabad region was in the neutral area, outside the zones under the Soviet or British control and free of the Iranian gendarmerie and army (Elphinston 1946: 98). The Kurdistan Resurrection Organisation (KJ, *Komalay Jiyanaway Kurd*), a clandestine organisation was established with Soviet backing in 1942, which later became the Democratic Party of Iranian Kurdistan (PDK-I, *Partiya Dêmukratî Kurdistanî Iran*) in 1945. The KJ sought to mobilise Kurds in the struggle for democratic and national rights and had pan-Kurdish goals including establishing an independent Kurdish state comprised of all parts of Kurdistan (Lazarev and Mihoyan 2001: 253–4). In 1945 a rebellion erupted in Mahabad in protest against the Iranian government and arbitrary actions by the army. In a mass meeting organised in January 1946 in Mahabad, which was attended by representatives from different Kurdish areas in Iran, the PDK-I announced the establishment of the Kurdish Republic of Mahabad, with Qadi Muhammad, a well-known local judge, as its leader. Barzani, who had escaped from Iraq, became the foreign minister of the new state and the general commander of its army. Given Kurds received no support from the Soviets in their efforts to gain self-determination, Barzani's military and political support was essential (Olson 1991: 404).

The Republic of Mahabad only lasted eleven months. The most important reason for its short life was the withdrawal of the Soviet army in 1946 under the terms agreed by the Iranians, the British and the Soviets. Even though the Soviets did not directly support the Kurds, their presence was a form of guarantee and protection against the Iranian regime (Lazarev and Mihoyan 2001: 274). Another factor that contributed to Mahabad's short life was disagreements among the Iranian Kurds. Several Kurdish regions and cities were not part of Mahabad anyway and some of the Kurdish tribes opposed to its formation and helped Iranian troops in taking control of Mahabad.[7] Moreover, some of the Iranian Kurdish groups were disturbed by the intrusion of Iraqi Kurds in their affairs and urban and leftist Kurds disliked the traditional and tribalistic approach of Barzani (Olson 1991: 404). By the end of 1946, Iranian troops took over Mahabad and executed its leaders. Barzani and his fighters escaped and Barzani found refuge in the Soviet Union. Despite its short life, the Republic implemented important cultural reforms, in language, education, literacy, publishing and literature. Women played an active role such as forming and joining women's organisations and working in hospitals and health centres (Lazarev and Mihoyan 2001: 274).

After the collapse of the Mahabad Republic, Kurdish activists left Iran or began to organise secretly within the country. Among these, the PDK-I continued to be active. Some Kurdish nationalists, especially among urban intellectuals, joined the Iranian Communist Party (Tudeh), which had a Kurdish committee. Tudeh recognised minority rights and saw these rights as an important component of its democratic struggle (Entessar 2009: 47). In the late 1950s, however, as a result of the weakening of Tudeh due to internal ideological divisions and defections (Abrahamian 1979: 5), most Kurdish nationalists turned to the PDK-I.

In the 1960s and 1970s, the Iranian Pahlavi regime increased its emphasis on the Persian identity, heightening ethnic distinctions. Militaristic, centralised and authoritarian policies of the regime significantly narrowed the political space for Kurds and other dissidents. The economic policies of the regime also alienated rural Kurds and those

---

[7] The Republic's territory included Mahabad, Usnu, Mergaver, Tergaver, Serdest and Bane, but excluded Saqqez, Sanandaj and Kermanshah, the three largest Kurdish-populated cities (Lazarev and Mihoyan 2001: 273).

who migrated from rural areas to urban cities with no relevant skills. On the other hand, drawing on US assistance along with significant oil revenues, the government invested in infrastructure, economy and education. As a result, a Kurdish educated and urban class grew and began to integrate into Iranian society but 'as Iranians first' then Kurds (Natali 2005: 136).

From the mid-1960s onwards, both the visibility of Kurdish political activism and government suppression of their activities increased, most notably, the Kurdish guerrilla campaigns of 1967–8 in Iran. The guerrilla war that started in the early 1960s and the Kurdish developments in Iraq and the concessions Iraqi Kurds gained through the 1966 and 1970 agreements led to increase in Kurdish political activism in Iran (Lazarev and Mihoyan 2001: 340). However, the Kurds in Iran lacked a strong party leadership, professional staff and military experience, and were easily defeated by Iranian forces. After the defeat, Kurdish political leaders reorganised themselves. In 1969 the Komala Party of Iranian Kurdistan (Komala) was established, which became one of the key Kurdish organisations in Iran. The PDK-I recommenced publishing the journal *Kurdistan* and insisted on continuing with its activities despite the imprisonment and execution of several of its members. The Party adopted a new programme in 1973, which demanded democracy in Iran and autonomy in Kurdistan (Lazerev and Mihoyan 2001: 340).

The protest environment in the 1970s, which led to the Islamic Revolution in 1979, brought a different dynamic to the Kurdish movement in Iran. Kurdish activism continued to grow amidst other oppositional groups. In response, the regime's pressure on Kurds further increased. It banned Kurdish books, prohibited students and teachers from speaking Kurdish and expelled Iraqi Kurdish political refugees (Lazarev and Mihoyan 2001: 340–1). Some of the Kurds had joined the large social-political movement driven by the opposition against the Shah regime. Even though the movement increasingly turned into a Islamic one, Kurds continued to utilise this platform to mobilise. The revolutionary regime of Khomeini initially appeared to be conciliatory towards the Kurds and Iranian officials even met with Kurdish leaders. However, soon it became clear that the regime had no interest in negotiating or giving concessions to the Kurds. Khomeini terminated the talks with Kurdish leaders, rejected PDK-I's demands for autonomy, abolished the party's local offices and soughtto disarm Kurdish fighters (Entessar 2009). The new regime followed the same minority policy as before, which confirmed the rights of minorities, but only religious minorities, not ethnic or linguistic. These policies led to military resistance by the Kurds, which was not strong, and by the mid-1980s all Kurdish areas were under the control of the regime.

Kurdish mobilisation in the 1980s in Iran was weak because of the narrowing of political space in Iran after the 1979 Revolution and domination of right-wing Islamic discourse. The Iran–Iraq War in 1980–8, during which several Kurds fought against Iraq with other Iranians, further narrowed the political space for Kurdish political activism. The war had disastrous economic and military effects on all of the country creating a sense of collective loss and hardship and bringing the Kurds closer to adopting an Iranian identity (Natali 2005: 152). Another reason for the weakness of Kurdish mobilisation in the 1980s is related to divisions between competing Kurdish parties. Some Kurdish groups wanted to continue to seek accommodation while others did not. There were also disagreements over methods and tactics; Komala was using violent methods, whereas PDK-I was against violence (Lazarev and Mihoyan 2001: 343). As explained in the next chapter, a strong or unified Kurdish organisation did not emerge in Iran in this period and later, and Kurdish activism became increasingly clandestine in Iran and pushed to the border areas to carry out their activities.

Syria

Until the end of the French mandate in Syria, there were some limited opportunities for Kurdish political and cultural activities, which disappeared with Arab nationalists coming to power in 1946. Initially, the new Syrian government, feeling weak, tried to gain the support of the population in rural Kurdish areas by promising land reforms, investment and protection for peasants against exploitative landowners (Lazarev and Mihoyan 2001: 268). However, reforms were largely ineffective and the poor conditions in Kurdish areas – lack of basic health, education services, malnourishment and other issues – did not improve significantly. Moreover, Kurds did not gain much benefit from having joined the Syrian Arab movement against the French. Kurds were given positions in the government but then even this inclusion was used as an argument against Kurdish dissidents to prove that Kurds should not have issues with the way the government treats them. Kurdish areas continued to be neglected, and the government did not allow any Kurdish political activism that would criticise the government and challenge its policies.

Kurdish political actors were under government pressure in the 1950s, but in the 1960s, especially with the Ba'athists coming to power in 1963, the degree of suppression further increased. The first Syrian Kurdish political organisation, the Kurdistan Democratic Party of Syria (KDP-S), established in 1957, was able to carry out its activities to demand the recognition of the Kurdish identity and traditions, and the involvement of the Kurds in political and social institutions (Lazarev and Mihoyan 2001: 349). Kurdish rights temporarily improved under the United Arab Republic, a union formed by Egypt and Syria in 1958–61, and Kurds obtained the right to publish and broadcast in Kurdish and to open Kurdish schools in areas with a Kurdish majority. After the dissolution of the Republic, the rights Kurds gained were reversed. Using Kurdish in public was banned and the pressure on Kurdish activities increased once again. The leaders of KDP-S were arrested and were asked to leave Syria. In 1962, the government undertook a census in Jazira and stripped 120,000 Kurds of Syrian citizenship (Tejel 2008). These Kurds were forcefully displaced from their villages and replaced by Arab Syrians. The Ba'athist regime labelled Kurdish political groups as the agents of imperialists and entered into an alliance with the regime in Baghdad against the Kurds in Syria and Iraq.

The political context in the 1960s led to factionalism among Kurdish political actors and this factionalism continued until the end of the Cold War and later. The KDP-S was divided between those wanting to focus on gaining cultural and social rights and those that wanted to focus on the political struggle. By 1965 the division became starker and the party divided into leftist and rightist groups (Halhalli 2018: 35). Other new parties also emerged at this time and in the following years, including the Kurdistan Democratic Progressive Party of Syria and Kurdish Democratic Leftist Party. After Hafiz Assad came to power in 1966, Damascus slightly softened its policy of political discrimination against the Kurds.

In general, Syrian Kurdish activists and parties did not forcefully and directly challenge the regime, did not seek autonomy or independence. They carried out political activities that would not hugely antagonise the government, such as seeking cultural and linguistic rights, sought to maintain their position and were hugely divided due to personal rivalries and interests. A very factionalised Kurdish political field emerged and no Kurdish party was able to unify a majority of the Kurds under one political agenda. The entry of the PKK into the Syrian Kurdish political field politicised the Kurds in Syria but also further divided them as some Syrian Kurds joined the PKK and its militia. The Ba'ath regime allowed this as part of its policy of supporting Kurds against the Turkish government.

The situation of Kurds in Syria in the period during the Cold War has not been explored much by researchers. In short, in this period, Kurds did not generate a nationalist movement similar to that in Iraq or Turkey. They lacked strong leadership and the Kurdish parties that were formed were quickly dissolved or splintered due to internal disagreements. The heavy control of the Ba'ath regime also played a role in the relatively underdeveloped and quiet Kurdish political activism in Syria. Kurdish political actors in Syria often drew support from external Kurdish political movements, such as the PUK or the KDP (Allsopp 2017: 292). Later in the Cold War period, the PKK also entered the Syrian Kurdish political field creating itself a space for mobilisation and activism.

Conclusion

The Kurdish nationalist movement can best be understood by looking at the historical and political contexts that defined its emergence, development and evolution. This chapter provided an overview of the interactions between Kurdish movements and their host states and other regional states, and Kurdish attempts at seeking international support for their cause immediately after the Second World War and into the Cold War era. The legalisation of the principle of self-determination gave the Kurds hope and international dynamics influenced the formation and development of Kurdish nationalist organisations. However, the implementation of the self-determination principle only to the colonial context and lack of support for Kurdish demands for statehood, autonomy or international recognition as a distinct group led the Kurds to somewhat retreat from the international realm over time. This dynamic interacted with domestic political developments and increased state control, leading to increased focus among the Kurds on the domestic and regional context.

Despite the lack of Western support, in the early stages of this period, Kurds in Iran established a short-lived self-proclaimed republic in Mahabad. By the end of this period, in Iraq, Kurds managed to obtain approval for their de facto autonomy. The international normative context continued to influence Kurds in the Middle East as well but Marxist and leftist ideologies, rather than Western liberalism, had more influence on the thinking of the Kurdish political actors under the conditions of the Cold War. Western political frameworks such as the UN principles did not provide the expected support for their goals. The history of Western imperialist mandate or indirect rule in the region until the mid-twentieth century led to an anti-imperialist sentiment in the political thinking in the region. This found resonance in the Marxist and Communist anti-imperialist ideological frameworks that focus on the suppressed sections of the society and generate an inclusive political platform for minorities and the protection of their identities. Therefore, leftist frameworks found strong support among the Kurdish populations in the Middle East and led them to describe themselves as internally colonialised. However, under the circumstances of the Cold War, adhering to leftist ideologies further weakened Kurdish political actors' chances of receiving legitimacy and support for their goals from Western actors and their normative frameworks that were being increasingly internationalised.

Another significant characteristic of the Kurdish movement in this period was that initially cross-border connections between the Kurds were stronger but they abated after the 1950s. This was partly because of the consolidation of authority in each state and the different socio-economic and political contexts leading to different outcomes and pathways for Kurds. The last section of this chapter showed the unique nature of the political and societal context in each state, the different government policies and different responses from the Kurdish groups in each context. In Turkey from the 1950s onwards Kurds became either co-opted to the system through socio-economic incentives, or were severely suppressed, forcefully displaced or became involved in leftist movements. In Iraq, a somewhat strong Kurdish leadership emerged that confronted the Baghdad regime throughout this period, but deep internal divisions emerged within the Kurdish movement. In Iran, Kurds integrated into the society while maintaining their cultural rights but small-scale radical Kurdish political activism continued to exist. This was made possible by the perceived ethnic affinity between Kurds and Persians, and by the relatively multicultural state policies. In Syria, with the departure of the French, Syrian state apparatus became consolidated around one identity and similar to Turkey, Kurds either became part of the system or maintained their marginalised position. These internal dynamics became stronger over decades and hindered the formation of strong cross-border links and pan-Kurdish organisations in the Cold War period.

The decrease in cross-border connections between Kurds from the 1950s was also due to regional collaborations between the states. The states with Kurdish populations were acutely aware of the transnational and cross-border links between the Kurds and Kurdish organisations. They took precautions to stop this or block the spillover effects of the developments in a neighbouring country on their own Kurdish issue. In order to contain the Kurdish threat, regional states formed alliances and strategies despite their disagreements on several other issues. For instance, the 1955 Baghdad Pact between Turkey, Iran, Iraq, Pakistan and the United Kingdom allowed alliance members to make dual agreements, which was mainly used to contain Kurdish activities. The states also forged good relations with some Kurdish groups against other states. Iran provided logistical and military support for Iraqi Kurds, particularly the KDP, to gain leverage against the Iraqi government with regards to its strategic goals in the Gulf. The Syrian government had good relations with the PUK in Iraq, allowed the PKK to use its territory for mobilisation and training and used this as a political leverage against Turkey.

Throughout this abating transnational and cross-border interaction, and the increasing disassociation with the Western international norms and actors, the idea of greater Kurdistan remained ambivalent but present. In the 1940s, when transnational connections were strong and the post–Second World War international order was still forming, the map of greater Kurdistan was mapped and promoted in international platforms by various Kurdish groups but fell away in prominence over time partly due to the introverted nature of Kurdish politics and decreasing cross-border activities among the Kurds. Even though it was not systematically pursued as a political goal by a pan-Kurdish nationalist organisation, the idea of a united or greater Kurdistan remained live in the minds of political actors as a potential political capital and source. The greater Kurdistan maps produced early in this period became influential later in the 1990s and were replicated by various Kurdish actors, especially in the diaspora.

5 | Kurds and the International Society after the Cold War

Introduction

This chapter examines the wider normative context from the end of the Cold War to the present day that informed the meaning of self-determination, how Kurdish political actors in the Middle East used this to frame their self-determination claims. In this period, self-determination in state discourses and non-state nationalists' rhetoric was quite often framed in the context of justice, human rights and democracy norms. International legal documents also made references to these norms with regard to the justification for self-determination.

The post-Cold War context witnessed the return of a Wilsonian conception of self-determination as an innate right of peoples (usually ethnically defined) to decide their future. The formation of new states and autonomous regions based on ethnic identity gained a new momentum following the collapse of the Soviet Union and the Socialist Federal Republic of Yugoslavia (SFR). The legitimacy of states was questioned as never before and several states were labelled failed, weak, authoritarian or dictatorial. Demands for statehood or autonomy, such as the Kurdish demands, and their realisation gained a new momentum. The world witnessed a series of demands for independence or autonomy across cases as diverse as the Kurds, the Tamils, the Sudanese, East Eritreans, the Chechens, the Catalans, the Basques, East Timorians, the Abkhazians, South Sudanese, the Sikhs and others. Some of these secessionists and autonomists frequently used the denial of their right to self-determination and their dissatisfaction with their political and cultural status in the country in which they reside as justification for their engagement in armed conflict.

As such, this was a very active time for Kurdish nationalism: the de facto autonomous Kurdish region of Iraq emerged in 1991 and became official in 2005; the PKK shifted its ideological ground but continued to demand autonomy or democratic self-rule; the Democratic Union Party (PYD, *Partiya Yekîtiya Demokrat*) unilaterally declared autonomous rule in the Kurdish areas in Syria in 2017. This increasing Kurdish assertiveness drew heavily on international norms that justified and strengthened demands for self-determination in this period, including norms around issues like the violation of human rights, denial of cultural rights, lack of democracy, experience of genocide and displacement. Since the 1990s, the international framework around legitimacy has been dominated by liberal democratic rights and human rights and the Kurdish political actors have certainly integrated these norms into their rhetoric, demands and goals.

As has been argued, the more norms, ideas and rules are adopted and expressed in official or political statements and declarations, the more they become reified and institutionalised (Adler 1997: 340), and thus it was the case with self-determination. These formal rules and informal norms are reproduced and disseminated within international society, thus creating normative frameworks. Normative frameworks are not static; they change over time depending on the political context and power relations as well as dominant ideologies. They become part of political decisions and interactions between international actors during negotiations, conferences and treaties and, thus, come to define legitimate and illegitimate actions in international society (Philpott 2001). Despite not being official and recognised members of international society, nationalist separatist and autonomist groups align their aims and strategies with relevant international norms and engage with the values widely accepted by international society. In doing this, they do not necessarily follow the same route; they adopt some norms, ignore others, or they transform and reinterpret some norms in a way that fits their own goals.

Kurdish nationalist groups adjusted to the post–Cold War context and utilised certain norms to justify their goals and actions, and to criticise the behaviour of the states they were challenging. Kurdish nationalist claims have become further territorialised through demands for self-rule in the form of autonomy or independence and each Kurdish nationalist party became focused on their territoriality within the states rather than seeking cross-border claims, similar to the Cold War period. However, the idea of greater Kurdistan and its map came to be used more explicitly as a reference point to show the homeland of the Kurds, giving resonance to their nationalist goals. In the post–Cold War era the map of greater Kurdistan has had huge traction among the Kurdish diaspora and made its way into the international media, as the next chapter shows. This chapter focuses on the same period but looks at the regional Kurdish movements, their evolution and their engagement with the international normative framework.

Wilsonian Self-Determination

Self-Determination in the Legal and Political International Context of the Post–Cold War Era

The legal and historical transformation of self-determination in the late twentieth century shows that there is an increasing tendency to emphasise cultural and human rights of communities in relation to demands for self-determination over a specific territory. For most separatist nationalists and their supporters, self-determination is about the protection and maintenance of cultural identity through political and democratic freedom. Liberal democratic principles combined with the existing division of the world into nation-states underpin this perspective. The idea of a national identity distinct from the identity of the majority, which was a prerequisite of Wilsonian self-determination, once again became a prominent idea in the post-Cold War world. Separatist and autonomist nationalists came to see this as a tool for breaking from existing states with no colonial or communist antecedents (Shaw 1997: 481–2). Even though a legal definition of the norm of self-determination was restrictive in encouraging secession, the aftermath of the Cold War led to a further increase in separatists' use of the principle in framing political demands. The implementation of self-determination in the ex-communist territories was based on existing administrative divisions, quite similar to the way self-determination was implemented in the decolonisation context. This time, the administrative boundaries that were taken to be the boundaries of the new state were, for instance, that of the republics of the Soviet Union or of the SFR. These republics were defined in ethnonational terms in the first place and they were 'nominally autonomous ethnic homelands' (Roeder 1991: 197). The question that remained was whether self-determination was applicable to cases that were not part of a decolonisation process or dismemberment of the ex-communist states (Shaw 1997: 481).

In the post–Cold War period, internal self-determination became directly associated with the transition of the communist republics but also with democracy. In this context, the transition of the communist republics into states was framed within Western-style democratic norms (Moynihan 2002: 11). As discussed in the previous chapter, the Helsinki Act already presented a slight change in the interpretation of self-determination and the conditions under which the principle was applicable. It declared that states should respect peoples' right to self-determination and act in conformity with international norms set out by the UN. This idea was further emphasised in the post–Cold War summits, documents and declarations. The Organisation for Security and Co-operation in Europe (OSCE) at its summit in 1990, where the Charter of Paris was adopted, 'explicitly associated internal self-determination with Western-style democracy' (Miller 2003: 624–7). The European Commission declared that they would recognise the new republics emerging in the SFR and in the Soviet Union territories as long as their peoples enjoyed the right to internal self-determination and their governments followed the rule of international law, human rights and democracy. The United States declared its expectation that self-determination claims should be based on a democratic political process (Halperin, Sheffer and Small 1992: 25–39). As a result, in the re-ordering of the ex-socialist territories, the implementation of self-determination became a method for realising democratisation, promoting peace building, and for reinforcing human rights and electoral processes.

Several nationalist leaders since the 1990s used the human rights and democracy rhetoric to legitimise their demands and mobilise support from Western countries to attain democracy through secession (Lynch 2002: 421). Their use of the concept of self-determination affirms the idea that if a group of people shares distinct social bonds and has a clear geographic location, it has a right to establish its own government and alter the jurisdictional borders of a state (Fabry 2010: 10; Barkin and Cronin 1994: 111). In most cases, Western states still prioritise state sovereignty and stability over self-determination demands but there are notable exceptions. The support provided by some states, international organisations, lobbies, media and scholars to the humanitarian interventions in northern Iraq, Bosnia, Kosovo, and East Timor and the formation of autonomous or independent self-rule in these contexts are examples of this. In these contexts, the Wilsonian paradigm and humanitarian liberal and democratic principles were invoked to justify these interventions (Mann 2004: 632). Western states' support for Kosovo's unilateral declaration of independence in 2008 is another example. The political governance systems established after interventions also follow a similar principle. For instance, in Iraq, an identity-based power-sharing system was introduced to stabilise and democratise the country. The assumption that dividing territorial control into different identity groups helps create and maintain democratic institutions and regimes in multi-ethnic societies underlined such systems (Stansfield 2005; Horowitz 2000).

In short, self-determination in the post–Cold War era is akin to a contemporary version of Wilson's formulation of the principle. However, the protection of state sovereignty is still a priority for most of the international community and secessionist or autonomist self-determination has certainly not become the norm. The lack of international support for the 2017 Kurdish independence referendum in Iraq clearly showed this. Still, self-determination claims, if connected to human rights and democracy discourses, now appear to have a wider international audience, even if they do not receive open political support.

Territorial Identity, Liberal Democracy and Self-Determination

The democratic right to self-determination is usually seen related to communities with a distinct identity; indeed, nationalists struggle for democracy because they desire recognition for their identity and the rights that ensue from this identity (Halliday 1994: 118; Brownlie 1988). This recognition can be associated with territorial control, either in the form of administrative autonomy, political autonomy or independence. For Kurdish nationalists, their democratic struggle is presented as necessary for their national, as well as individual, dignity as human beings. It is necessary because it will enable the recognition of the idea that Kurds have been resident in the territories of these states in Kurdistan, that it is their homeland, and that their political demands have been ignored and their rights have been violated by the states they live in.

Franck defines the demands for autonomy or secession based on identity in the post–Cold War period based on distinct identities as 'postmodern tribalism' (Franck 1993: 15). Postmodern tribalism aims to breakup states 'along the lines of dominant or exclusive mutually compatible ethno-national communities', such as the Quebecois, the Ashanti, the Sikhs, the Bavarians, the Serbs, the Hutus, the Scots, the Welsh, the Karen and the Basques (Franck 1997: 162–6, 1993: 15). Tamir's liberal nationalism in some ways, especially in terms of outcome, is similar to the processes Franck describes as tribal nationalism, although Tamir has different underlying arguments. According to Tamir (2003: 58–62), a cultural community rather than a homogeneous nation-state is more equipped to face the political and social challenges of the twenty-first century, such as social and economic upheavals, and migration. Community, defined in cultural terms, offers a sense of belonging, loyalty and solidarity to individuals within a cultural space whose borders are defined by members of a society. It nurtures the capabilities of autonomous and free individuals, and such a cultural space is crucial for self-determination (Tamir 2003: 5–9). Civic nation-states, in most cases, according to Tamir, ignore the existence of different national groups within their jurisdictions. However, in a political space relevant to their communal identity, individuals are more likely to enjoy a meaningful life and to secure their communal identity (Tamir 2003: 57, 72–4).

The aim here is not to argue that Franck's description of postmodern tribalism is accurate or the views Tamir purports are commonly accepted. But these views show that debates around the right to self-determination are certainly complicated. Indeed, at the other end of the spectrum is prioritising states' right to their sovereignty when they deprive sections of their populations of their democratic and human rights because of their identity. This complexity is perpetuated by the view that the coexistence of nationalism and liberal democracy has worked best in countries where the dominant culture is more or less racially and culturally homogeneous (Fukuyama 1994: 26–7). 'Collective forms of particularity' in the form of communities, nations, cultures and ethnic groups is seen as the source of democracy (Williams 2002: 1–3). There seems to be an elusive synthesis between cultural nationalism and liberal values (Gerson and Rubin 2015). On the other hand, nationalism, by prioritising identity-based characteristics, can also create divisions, exclusions and hinder people from coming together around civic ideals, as is the case today in several east European countries and Turkey. The tension between different views on nationalism reflects the long tension between collectivist nationalism and individual freedom and democracy.

Clearly, this long-standing debate will not be resolved here, but the debate does shed important light on nationalists' conception of their territoriality and identity. For nationalists, nationalism is a means for resolving ethnic conflict and promoting democracy, cultural creativity and diversity. Nationalism is a doctrine hinging on several key assumptions: humankind is divided into nations and this division is natural; the denial of the right of self-determination to a nation can mean the denial of fundamental human rights; and a group's self-determination claim derives its justification from universal human rights and political and cultural rights (Mayall 1990: 41). However, the right to determine the political future of a people and attain self-rule comes with the whole baggage of territoriality. Nationalists want to enforce their laws and policies, and protect the national/cultural identities of peoples, and that often is done in a specific territory where their people constitute the majority. Nationalists perceive a strong link between their national identity and territory. For them, sovereignty over a defined territory should be exercised by the people that 'owns' it.

Indeed, the historical development of popular sovereignty and the idea of international recognition together highlight the link between people and territory. Within this historical evolution, a state's absolute control transformed from control over a specific territory to control over a specific territory filled with national meaning, which directly associated people with that territory (Krasner 2001; James 1999: 469–70).[1] Nationalist groups claiming their right to statehood or autonomy through self-determination pitch the territory they claim as an ethnic territory, as a space to which they attach their identity and they desire full or semi-control over it. The territory and its past are central to nationalism because it sees territory as the holder of the past (Anderson 1988: 24) and past memories, events, sites come to define 'ethnospaces' (Smith 1996: 454). Kurdish nationalist historiography considers the Kurds as inhabitants of the same land for thousands of years and nurtures an ethnic conception of nationhood rendering the political claims of

---

[1] In that sense, by demanding self-rule and territorial control, separatist and autonomist nationalists are not challenging the idea of sovereignty, they are actually perpetuating it, because they are demanding their own sovereignty. What they challenge is the sovereignty of a state, not sovereignty as an idea.

Kurdish nationalists as a historical 'national will' (Vali 2003: 61). Although liberal nationalist thinking or postmodern tribalism do not seek to justify such claims, the rhetoric on which they are based appears useful for separatist and autonomist nationalists. The wider human rights and democracy discourses and normative frameworks since the end of the Cold War further embolden their claims especially because of the human rights and minority rights violations and political discriminations they have experienced in their states.

The international normative framework and the wider political understandings of self-determination as a political right since the end of the Cold War did not give full resonance to the claims of the Kurdish nationalists. However, this international context surely facilitated the Kurds' access to the international platforms more easily and to make their claims, demands and complaints heard. Kurdish political parties have not explicitly used the map of greater Kurdistan in their party propaganda and publications but used the idea of greater Kurdistan as a form of reference to show the divided nature of Kurdistan by four countries and the idea of being under occupation or being deprived of their own state. In that sense, the territoriality of the Kurds and their ideal homeland, the greater Kurdistan was a source that gave resonance to each Kurdish nationalist movement and the nationalist sentiments of their supporters.

More explicitly, for instance, the PKK used the idea of four Kurdistans constituting one greater Kurdistan in its rhetoric. The Party labelled the different parts of Kurdistan as 'North Kurdistan' in Turkey (*Bakur*), 'West Kurdistan' in Syria (*Rojava*), 'South Kurdistan' in Iraq (*Bashur*) and 'East Kurdistan' in Iran (*Rojhilat*). The map became an everyday symbol among Kurdish nationalists in this period, being used on the walls of the houses and on jewellery such as brooches, and, became particularly visible on online platforms or publications of Kurdish activists in the diaspora. In this chapter, the focus is not on the maps of Kurdistan per se, but on the increase in international connections Kurdish actors forged and their use of the international normative frameworks to increase their visibility and to gain support from outsiders. This internationalisation was key in the increase in the use of the map of greater Kurdistan by Kurds themselves as well as outsiders for various reasons, nationalist or not.

Kurdistan and Kurdish Nationalism

The most significant characteristic of Kurdish nationalism in the post–Cold War period was its internationalisation. Interactions between different Kurdish groups and international actors including states, non-governmental organisations and transnational platforms increased. This was partly the result of globalisation, increased communication between Kurds across borders and the Kurdish diaspora. Events in the region that affected the Kurds also played a significant role in this internationalisation. For instance, Saddam Hussein's treatment of the Kurds increased international awareness of the Kurdish plight and eventually led to the creation of a safe zone by the US-led international coalition in 1991. The struggle in Iraq for autonomy and the attainment of the de facto autonomous status, the relatively quiet but continuous Kurdish struggle in Iran, the conflict between the PKK and Turkish army, the activities of the Kurdish parties, the formation of a de facto Kurdish autonomy and the Kurdish fighters' role in the fight against the Islamic State of Iraq and Syria (ISIS), the activities of the Kurdish diaspora in the United States and Europe – all these contributed to the internationalisation of the Kurdish issue in the last three decades.

Kurdish movements needed to adjust and change their ideological positions, goals and strategies in recognition of changes in the international circumstances and normative frameworks after the end of the Cold War. Circumstances in each state continued to shape Kurdish movements but the policy frameworks and norms that became available internationally became more influential than in the Cold War era and affected each Kurdish movement in different ways. Kurdish nationalists found access to a larger legal and political arena and became increasingly engaged with international actors and norms. Another significant characteristic of Kurdish politics across the region in this period was increase in Kurdish political assertiveness and in military conflict between Kurdish groups and their states. Although in this process none of the Kurdish groups aimed for the unification of the Kurds in the territories of greater Kurdistan, they adhered to the idea that this map showed the divided homeland of the Kurdish nation. Demands for autonomy within a state rather than secession became the norm for most Kurdish parties.

Iraq

The Kurds in Iraq went through the most profound transformation relative to other Kurds in this period. Their goal for de facto autonomy was achieved in 1991 after the Gulf War, and their autonomous status became official in 2005 after the intervention in Iraq in 2003 (although they certainly have not abandoned the idea of forming their own state). The Kurdistan Regional Government (KRG) in many ways resembles a state government, manages its internal affairs and has its own legislative institution and armed forces. Kurdish society in Iraq and its politics have gone through substantial changes since autonomy. The tribalistic nature of the Kurdish nationalist parties remained and has led to a patronage system. The two main parties, the KDP and the PUK, established their own economic, territorial and military control areas. Nonetheless, the governance institutions developed, electoral politics became consolidated, several universities opened, and platforms for political discussion, such as newspapers, have expanded and diversified. More recently, the two-party system has been challenged by the emergence of strong opposition parties, such as the Gorran Party, which made anti-corruption its main focus and became the third biggest party electorally. Though Gorran has become a mainstream party and recently allied with the KDP in the formation of the new government after the elections in 2018.

The violation of Kurds' human rights and the atrocities committed against them by the Iraqi regime were central to the decision of the US-led coalition to create a safe zone for the Kurds in northern Iraq. During the intervention to oust Iraqi forces from Kuwait in the Gulf War in 1990–1, the United States encouraged Kurdish groups to rebel against Baghdad. As a result, Kurdish rebels took control of most of Iraqi Kurdistan. However, after the war, the Coalition preferred to keep Hussein in power for fear of unleashing increased Iranian influence over Iraq. Indeed, Iran was ready to exploit the Shi'a dimension in Iraq and a weak Baghdad would not be able to counter this. As a result, the Coalition withdrew support from the Kurds and left northern Iraq to the behest of Baghdad. Baghdad's subsequent attacks on the Kurds resulted in large number of deaths and injuries and the flight of thousands of Kurds to Turkey and Iran (Entessar 2009: 200–1), leading to a huge humanitarian crisis, which created international uproar. The

George H. Bush administration and its allies were severely criticised for letting this atrocity happen.

Eventually, the United States and some of its European allies created a 'safe haven' in Sulaymaniyah and Erbil to the north of the 36th parallel under international protection for displaced Kurds to return. After this, in 1992, a Kurdistan National Parliament was formed. The first elections took place on 19 May 1992 and representatives from the KDP and the PUK entered the parliament. Four seats were allocated to Assyrians and one for Christians. Initially, there were disagreements whether Talabani, the leader of the PUK, or Masoud Barzani, the leader of the KDP, would become president. Neither was able to receive the majority vote they needed. A joint committee was formed and the first Kurdish government was created in October 1992. In the first two years, the government carried out significant development work, with international support, in agriculture, rebuilding and education. However, the PUK–KDP tension did not disappear and resulted in a four-year civil war between the two parties and their support base. The civil war ended after a deal that divided control between the two parties was reached in 1998 with the help of United States officials.

The period between 1992 and 2003 is most notable for the way in which Iraqi Kurdistan and Kurdish nationalism in Iraq transformed. The struggle for Kurdish national recognition and autonomy transformed into state-building underpinned by the principles of democracy. The regional government allowed the formation of women's, youth and development organisations, and undertook and encouraged collaborations with international actors including UN agencies, states and human rights organisations. This created a vibrant humanitarian, developmental as well as political platform. The increasing dominance of norms related to democracy, human rights, power sharing and civil society in the international arena and the Iraqi Kurds' ability to tap into this international framework increased their legitimacy and facilitated the continuation of the international political, economic and military support, from the creation of the 'safe haven' in 1991 to the UN-led humanitarian and development initiatives, the setting up of a separate UN Assistance Mission for Iraq office in Erbil after the 2003 intervention, military support in terms of equipment and training for the Kurdish peshmerga, funding from state donors or international organisations to develop and support civil society.

Iraqi Kurds' interactions with international political, economic and security actors, and their engagement with their normative frameworks through international and transnational platforms continued to increase after the United States- and British-led intervention in Iraq in 2003. In fact, the intervention further reinforced international connections and engagement (Natali 2010). This engagement overlapped with strong international support for Kurds in Iraq. Kurds living in the diaspora, who had escaped from the Ba'ath regime's pressures and attacks, returned to Iraqi Kurdistan bringing with them ideas, skills and resources. With the formalisation of the autonomous status for the Kurdistan Region of Iraq (KRI) in the new Iraqi Constitution of 2005 and the international support, Kurdish institutions and humanitarian and developmental organisations further expanded. The economic boom until 2011 and the relative stability and safety in the KRI in contrast to sectarian violence in the rest of Iraq further reinforced the sense of being in a Kurdish state-building process (O'Leary et al. 2005).

Yet international support since 1991 also created dependency issues and other forms of vulnerabilities for the KRI (Natali 2010). International aid made the region dependent on donor funding. After 2003, the situation improved with the allocation of a percentage of the Iraqi budget to the KRG and an increase in international investments (mostly in the oil and construction industries). These economic benefits, combined with the continuing but reduced international aid, led to a financial boom in the region, but the opportunities this generated were not utilised to develop sustained growth and political stability. Instead, KDP and PUK deepened the patronage system and sought to strengthen their positions against political opposition. Relations with the Turkish state also created dependency issues and vulnerabilities for the KRG. Although not initially recognising Kurdish autonomy in Iraq, Turkey came to an agreement with the KRG, mainly with the KDP. Ankara allowed the flow of crude oil extracted from oil fields in the region through the newly built pipelines in its territory and via land routes, which made the KRG dependent on Turkey for selling oil to international markets. Turkish investment and construction companies also became heavily involved in the Kurdish economic marketplace.

Acutely aware of their vulnerabilities and dependencies, Iraqi Kurdish political leaders wanted to ensure the continuation of the international support. In order to resonate with the international

community, they embedded commitments to democracy and emphasised the rhetoric of democracy, human rights, minority rights and
gender equality in their statements and policies.[2] By strengthening
their democratic credentials and adopting the international normative
discourses, Kurdish leaders wanted to show to the international community that they are better off managing their internal affairs without
interference from Baghdad. They projected such a vision using the
contrast between the KRI and the political instability, sectarian violence and increased conservatism in the rest of Iraq. In this context,
Kurdish nationalist goals became defined in terms of state-building and
nation-building rather than simply struggle for autonomy (O'Leary
and Salih 2005). However, lacking political will and institutional
capacity continued to be a problem. Corruption and tribal patronage,
and a political system that is designed to maintain the position of two
main political parties limit the region's democratisation.

The achievement of significant autonomy, and even 'quasi statehood'
(Natali 2010) or 'de facto statehood' (Voller 2014), did not mean the
abandonment of a desire for independence within some sectors of the
Kurdish political elite, especially the KDP. Not all political parties and
all sections of the Kurdish community gave full support to the idea of
independence, and several of them continue to have reservations about
when and how independence should be pursued. Nonetheless, the idea
of an independent Kurdistan at some point in the future, when the
circumstances allow, resonates with most Kurds in Iraq. International
support for Kurdish self-governance in the form of autonomy within
a federal Iraq continues and Iraqi Kurds have benefited from significant
international and transnational opportunities. However, this does not
mean that the international community is ready to support Kurdish
secession from Iraq. Neither the United States, the United Kingdom nor
the regional countries consider Kurdish secession from Iraq as an
acceptable option (United Kingdom Parliamentary Inquiry on
Kurdish Aspirations 2018). The lack of international support for the

---

[2] Although there is no denying that Kurdish political leaders used this normative
framework in an instrumental fashion, this does not preclude a prior perspective that
is prone to similar principles among the Kurdish population. Therefore, it is not fair
to say that the integration of international norms around democracy, human rights
and minority rights was simply instrumental and a top-down process. There is
considerable and long-term pressure for the adoption or development of such
policies and frameworks among the Kurdish public (Watts 2014: 151), especially in
urban areas.

Kurdish independence referendum in October 2017 clearly showed this.

Turkey

The Kurdish issue in Turkey internationalised in the post–Cold War period and the Kurds' interactions with the international community and international frameworks have increased significantly. Since the 1990s the Kurdish movement in Turkey has gone through profound changes. Here, the Kurdish movement in Turkey will be mainly explained through focus on the PKK. Surely, the PKK is not the only Kurdish actor and certainly does not represent all the Kurds in Turkey. Turkey's complex electoral space has fragmented the Kurdish political mobilisation and political choices of its Kurdish citizens. Several Kurdish political organisations emerged with different ideological and political positions, including Islamist ones (Kurt 2017). Kurdish society and Kurdish political thinking are diffused along complex socioeconomic, religious and political lines which enables the Kurds in Turkey to identify with civic, religious and localist identities in addition to their Kurdish identity (Natali 2005: 116). Nonetheless, the PKK has a large support base in Turkey and has been the primary actor shaping debates around Kurdish nationalism in Turkey since the 1980s.

The PKK went through substantial changes in its goals, ideology and organisation in the post–Cold War period. What is interesting in this transformation is that while the movement has remained radical, it has also become more integrated internationally. In a symbiotic relationship with the PKK, a non-violent Kurdish political movement also developed in this process (Yanarocak 2014). The co-existence of these different directions is interesting, but not an anomaly. It is the result of the Kurdish movement's efforts to adapt to changes in Turkey, in the region and internationally, as well as the changing internal dynamics within the PKK, while trying to maintain its radical ideological position. The PKK realised that a Kurdish nation-state would not be possible in the near future given the Turkish state's response and gave up on its goal of independence, switching to autonomist demands. It sought to stay true to its ideal of self-determination and the leftist ideology while changing the way it defined and understood self-determination. In the meantime, the Turkish government continued to suppress Kurdish political activism and clamped down on Kurdish activities, introduced restrictive legal measures, imprisoned, tortured and tried several people, depopulated certain areas and deported thousands of people, especially in the 1990s (Entessar 2009: 135–40). In the late 2000s, the Turkish government also initiated secret then open talks with the PKK and its leader Öcalan, but these talks did not result in an agreement and the conflict between the PKK and the Turkish army, and the government pressure on Kurdish political activism continues.

The PKK was established in 1978 but did not emerge as a violent movement until the 1980s, the era of coup politics and heightened state clampdowns on groups who were seen as threats to the Turkish nation. After the 1980 military coup in Turkey, the regime again adopted a militarised approach to the Kurdish issue. In the 1980s and 1990s, the PKK expanded its support base within Turkey as well as in the neighbouring countries, especially Syria and Iran. The conflict and the Turkish military's inability to control Kurdish guerrillas increased confidence among Kurdish activists and expanded the movement's support base (Lazarev and Mihoyan 2001: 360). Industrialisation and rural-to-urban migration in Turkey also benefited the PKK because these processes changed the tribal economic relations among Kurdish communities and led some of the pro-state Kurdish communities to turn away from mainstream political parties and look towards Kurdish ones instead. Kurdish political activists on the left began to engage in national and local elections while continuing clandestine activities such as publishing nationalist and Marxist journals critical of the state (Natali 2005: 110–11). The People's Labour Party (*Halkın Emek Partisi*, HEP) was formed in 1990 under the PKK's influence, and entered the general elections the following year. The party was subsequently closed by the Constitutional Court in 1993, with some of its MPs imprisoned. The HEP was replaced with new incarnations and a pattern of state bans of a Kurdish party emerged. The latest and most electorally successful incarnation, Peoples' Democratic Party (*Halkların Demokratik Partisi*, HDP), was founded in 2012.

Since the 1990s, Kurdish political actors (affiliated with PKK or not) have increased their engagement with international platforms such as the European Union and its institutions, non-governmental organisations and states. In their engagement, they have sought to raise awareness of the Kurds' situation in Turkey, solicit international support and generate international pressure on the Turkish government. In doing this, they situated their rhetoric and claims within international human rights and democracy frameworks. Kurdish political actors in Turkey tapped into this available and continuously strengthening international normative agenda, and effectively forged a link between their rights as an ethnic community and identity-based discrimination on the one hand, and the human rights frameworks and democracy on the other.

Kurds in Turkey were able to access the European Parliament and bring the violation of their cultural and political rights as a community to the agenda of the European states (Natali 2005: 169). Several Kurdish individuals who believed they were unfairly incarcerated by the Turkish state applied to the European Court of Human Rights (ECHR) against the Turkish government. Kurdish claims that their human and democratic rights were being violated resonated with Western governments, all the more strongly, given Turkey's long-standing ratification of the European Convention on Human Rights and its more recent desire to join the European Union, which was throwing close scrutiny on its human rights and political rights record. Local and international non-governmental organisations in Turkey and Europe provided legal and political platforms for Kurdish activists. International non-governmental organisations, such as the Helsinki Watch and Amnesty International also played significant roles in raising the profile of the Kurds by bringing violations to the attention of international bodies. These organisations criticised the Turkish government's violation of its Kurdish populations' human rights, the closure of Kurdish parties, the pressure on freedom of expression and the right to form associations, the arrest and arbitrary detention of Kurdish political actors, random disappearances, torture and questions around the independence of the judiciary. Kurdish political actors also brought up the violation of their cultural rights, especially their right to speak Kurdish publicly, use Kurdish names, receive education and broadcast in their own language.

In the early 2000s, the Kurdish movement in Turkey entered a new phase. The Kurds continued with their legal and political engagement in Turkey and outside but under very different circumstances. The PKK leader, Öcalan, had been captured in Kenya in 1999, having been ejected from his hiding place in Syria after Turkey put pressure on the Assad regime. After this, the PKK went through a significant transformation, changed its goals, ideology and structure. Between 1999 and

2004, during a PKK-declared ceasefire following Öcalan's capture, the PKK reorganised itself and identified new goals and a new ideological direction. The PKK's initial aim of independence for Kurds in Turkey and unification with Kurds in other countries had a traditional conception of self-determination. It referred to the right to form national governance, which was endorsed in the Leninist thinking of the Soviet Union in its goal to attract anti-state nationalist movements in the context of the Cold War rivalry. With the end of the Cold War, the party ditched this Leninist conception of self-determination and adopted a new interpretation of the principle that referred to deepening democratic processes through decentralisation and local administration, and increased connectedness between localised democracies.

With this new interpretation of self-determination in play, the PKK declared that it no longer sought separation from Turkey, or a separate nation-state called Kurdistan. Instead it now aimed for a solution based on extensive decentralisation within the borders of Turkey. Öcalan, who continued to be the leader of the PKK from prison, envisioned this solution in the form of 'democratic confederalism', a governance model with 'radical democracy' at its centre (Öcalan 2011). Radical democracy, originally a socialist idea, referred to the rejection of existing democratic models in favour of a more pluralistic and direct democracy (Laclau and Mouffe 2001). For Öcalan, democratic confederalism and radical democracy went beyond simply increasing people's democratic rights and it also implied a revolutionary systemic transformation that would give power directly to people (Küpeli 2014). In order to achieve this, the PKK aimed to form councils at all levels, from village to the regional, and challenged the nation-state format that they claimed led to authoritarianism and diminished real democracy (Jongerden 2017: 246). This conception of radical democracy does not challenge existing borders because it does not seek to establish a new nation-state. But at the same time, it requires a substantial governance change which would potentially render state borders obsolete. In fact, the (unrealistically utopian) idea actually offers a much deeper and revolutionary challenge to the existing state-system.

In order to realise these new goals and implement its new ideology and ideals, the PKK transformed from a communist party into a complex network of military and political organisations with both legal and illegal outlets (Jongerden 2017). It created sister parties in Iraq, Syria and Iran, each with their own guerrilla groups and political parties. An umbrella organisation, the Association of Communities in Kurdistan (*Koma Civakên Kurdistan*, KCK), was created to facilitate coordination and communication.[3] The KCK is important within PKK ideology given it represents the embodiment of democratic confederalism, but it is not very well known by the international community and even by the Kurds themselves due to its complex and ambivalent working structure as an umbrella organisation.

The idea of radical democracy, in a slightly adapted form, also manifested in Kurdish political parties with a leftist and radical democratic approach. For example, in the 2015 general election, the Kurdish-affiliated HDP argued that Turkey needed 'real democracy to be able to build a new life where the whole of society is guaranteed the circumstances that each of its elements needs for its existence and life' (HDP June 2015 General Election Manifesto). The HDP aimed to challenge the long-standing 'one-nation mentality' dominating Turkey and instead sought to promote a multi-identity and multicultural vision (such a vision would of course drastically improve the rights of Kurds within Turkey as well as Turks overall, according to the HDP). The HDP aspired for a more inclusive, non-ethnicity based, civic form of democracy with gender equality at its core. It was able to tap into general frustrations among a sizeable proportion of the Turkish population. Its presentation of itself as a political party of Turkey (*Türkiyeli* – country-based identity not ethnic Turkish), not just as a Kurdish party, paid dividends in elections since 2011 and helped the party pass the 10 per cent electoral threshold in the last three general elections (Kaya and Whiting 2019).

What accompanied the rise of the HDP was the reopening of talks between the PKK and the Turkish government. The political context with regard to the Kurdish issue had been highly securitised in Turkey and the total rejection of even Kurdish cultural rights and identity made any compromise between Kurds and the state decidedly unlikely. The PKK had announced ceasefires and declared they were open to exploratory talks with the government several times in their history. However, successive Turkish governments publicly declared that they would not sit at the negotiation table with a terrorist organisation. Still, since the

---

[3] The KCK today is a network of local councils at village, city and regional levels. The PKK and its three sister parties are KCK members but the organisation is clearly dominated by the PKK. The KCK also has a parliament called Kongra-Gel.

capture of Öcalan notable attempts to resolve the Kurdish issue in Turkey have been pursued.[4]

The Justice and Development Party (*Adalet ve Kalkınma Partisi*, AKP), the newly elected government party in 2002, in its effort to challenge the tutelary state which dominated Turkey until then, initially sought to reach out to the PKK representatives and pursue potential solutions. The AKP's popularity in the Kurdish constituencies and its position as a one-party government raised hopes about the possibility to reach a solution (Çandar 2009: 13–14). This took the form of two sets of talks – first between 2005 and 2011 in highly secret circumstances in Oslo followed by a somewhat more public effort between 2012 and 2014. However, this policy proved unsustainable for both sides and ended with return to conflict in 2014 against the backdrop of increased tensions from the war in neighbouring Syria. The talks could not bridge the gap between the demands and expectations of the PKK and the Turkish government (Tezcür 2014: 171). The lack of willingness by the government to extend the concessions the Kurds aspired for and the lack of willingness by the Kurdish leadership to support initiatives that might threaten its position within the community led the talks to fail.

Following the collapse of the talks, violent conflict resumed with renewed vigour on both sides. The Turkish security forces undertook operations in the southeast and the PKK carried out bomb attacks across the country. The AKP, feeling threatened by the HDP's rise in the last three general elections and the loss of its parliamentary majority, portrayed Kurdish political activities as threats to the nation to justify the armed conflict against the PKK and increase pressures on Kurdish activists. The ability of the HDP to campaign in elections was restricted and arrests started again. After the failed coup of July 2016, the government undertook a widespread purge against its supposed organisers, followers of the exiled cleric and former AKP ally Fethullah Gülen. The purge however also served as cover for the AKP to move against all those against the government, and in particular Recep Tayyip Erdoğan, saw as threats and opponents, including HDP co-leaders Selahattin Demirtaş and Figen Yüksekdağ, the Kurdish civil

---

[4] Some efforts to open up space were also made in the 1990s. In 1992 Prime Minister Turgut Özal allowed limited language opportunities for Kurds and attempted to negotiate a cease-fire with the PKK.

society and journalists even mildly critical of the government's stance on the Kurdish issue. Today, the space for Kurdish political activism is heavily securitised and most activists are labelled as PKK-affiliates and duly criminalised or purged. The HDP leaders have been tried and imprisoned and several civil society actors and journalists have also been arrested, tried or imprisoned.

Today, the relationship between the Turkish government and Kurdish nationalists is stuck in a situation with no possibility of a resolution in sight. The HDP's electoral success and its pro-democracy party programme gained it positive publicity; and the Turkish government's treatment of the HDP and its supporters led to criticism in the Western media, but ultimately the space for Kurdish political activity is close to non-existent. On the other hand, the PKK's move to use urban areas as fighting ground did not pay the dividends it hoped for and lost it some popularity among the Kurds. It also jeopardised HDP's electoral achievements, reinforced the perception that HDP and PKK are connected, and led to the political and legal clamp down against the HDP. A compromise between the PKK and the Turkish government is unlikely due to differences between their political ideologies and the nationalist- and security-focused approach of the government, similar to previous governments in Turkey's history. In a sense both the PKK and the Turkish government are utopian. The government sticks to a utopian ideal of a uniform Turkish identity in a conservative Muslim one-nation state. This actually does not resonate with large sections of the society, not because of identity but because for many people in Turkey religion or ethnic identity should not be what defines the management of the political and economic machine, the provision of state services or income generation. On the other hand, the PKK has a utopian ideal that nation-states and their boundaries will become obsolete and a new more egalitarian and democratic system will emerge in the future. This goal is at least as utopian and possibly even more unrealistic than the goal to secede.

To conclude, in the post–Cold War period, Turkey's Kurds tapped international normative frameworks by communicating their issues and demands within a human rights and democracy framework. The PKK grew significantly while staying on a leftist ideological line but transforming its ideology into a more environmentalist, anarchist and feminist approach than a traditional socialist one. The HDP, competing in elections, changed its party programme to appeal to the wider sections of the Kurdish and Turkish communities by making references to a radical democracy, the rights of individuals, gender equality, LGBTQI rights and social equality. The PKK, even while adopting norms and principles that are widely adopted in the western world, moved away from the mainstream conception of self-determination to a more radical form which envisions direct and decentralised democracy. Its idea of 'democratic confederalism' challenged the nation-state ideal. But this idea actually potentially challenges the existing state-system in the Middle East more so than secessionist or autonomist demands.

Syria

In most of the post–Cold War period, Syrian Kurdish politics remained unchanged. Kurdish parties demanded improved economic opportunities, better services, citizenship for all Kurds, and equal cultural and linguistic rights. The desire to form a devolved authority in Kurdish areas was not voiced publicly, only rarely in private, and there were no plans for autonomy. However, the Syrian war that started in 2011 marked a sharp turn in the Syrian Kurdish community's history. With the war, Kurdish nationalism in Syria transformed from a small, fractured and quiet political presence into a de facto autonomous region. Previously overlooked and understudied, Syrian Kurds began to receive more international attention due to their increasing military and political presence. The PYD, the biggest Syrian Kurdish party, established its de facto administrative rule in northern Syria, which was initially called Rojava but in 2016 named as the Democratic Federation of Northern Syria (DFNS). The PYD has promoted the rhetoric of democracy and gender equality, with women constituting a large proportion of the party officials and military fighters. These characteristics combined with their effectiveness in the fight against ISIS have given the de facto region led by the PYD a positive international image.

After the Cold War ended, in the 1990s, the Kurdish political movement in Syria was fractured and was of limited influence. By this time, the Kurdish political field had splintered into several parties (Allsopp 2014). In the period until the 2000s, the space for Kurdish political activism was restricted by the state but Kurds were politically active through their engagement with non-Syrian parties such as the KDP or the PUK. The PKK too rose in influence in Syria. Between 1980 and

1998, the Syrian regime allowed the PKK to use Syrian territories as a base from which to conduct its armed campaigns against the Turkish state. The PKK developed cross-border links for decades while in Syria and mobilised the Syrian Kurds (Tezcür 2016). Syrian Kurds constitute a sizable part of the members of the PKK to the present day.[5]

Also in this period, a vocal and influential group with a strong base among the Kurdish youth emerged from the leftist strand of Kurdish political movement in Syria. This group, the Kurdish Union Party of Syria (Yekiti, *Partiya Yekitya li Suriye*) organised campaigns and public demonstrations, which were important in the lead up to a Kurdish uprising in Qamishli in 2004 (Lowe 2010: 168). The 2004 Qamishli uprising served as an important catalyst that brought important changes in the Kurdish political scene in Syria. In the 1990s, Kurds were frustrated with the Syrian government's refusal to carry out reforms, notably its refusal to grant stateless Kurds citizenship and they were aware of the emergence of a de facto Kurdish autonomy in neighbouring northern Iraq (Lowe 2010: 167). The 2004 events broke out after a clash between Kurds and Arabs at a football match. The Syrian security forces intervened, killing a number of Kurds and sparking a series of protests and demonstrations primarily in Qamishli but also spreading to other Kurdish cities and Damascus. After these events, relations between the Kurds and the government further deteriorated, leading to more killings and arrests (Lowe 2010: 168).

The PYD was established in this period, in 2003, and rose to prominence very quickly, especially so with the onset of the Syrian civil war. The PYD's affiliation to the PKK is a well-known and debated issue. Following Syria's expulsion of the PKK in 1998 and the arrest of Öcalan, the PKK decided to widen its activities in the region and supported the establishment of sister parties in other states, including the PYD in Syria. Different interpretations about PYD's origin, such as being either set up by the PKK to maintain its support base in Syria or by Kurds in Syria who agreed with the PKK ideology, probably reflect parts of the truth (Kaya and Lowe 2017).

The PYD sat apart from the mainstream Syrian Kurdish movement and numerous other Kurdish parties due to its closeness to the PKK. The party drew on the same symbolism and narrative of the PKK,

---

[5] Including senior figures such as Bahoz Erdal, a PKK military commander until 2004 and one of three individuals on the PKK's Executive Committee.

idealising Öcalan and the cult of martyrdom. Its military structure emulated that of the PKK. Technically, the PKK is a political party and its military activities are conducted by the People's Defence Forces (*Hêzên Parastina Gel*, HPG). Similarly, in Syria, the PYD is the political party while armed defence is conducted by the People's Protection Units (*Yekîneyên Parastina Gel*, YPG) and Women's Defence Units (*Yekîneyên Parastina Jin*, YPJ). The PKK's ideas about women's participation are also evident in PYD thinking and the PYD officially ensures co-representation of women in all positions and 40 per cent representation in its armed forces.

The vacuum created by the war in Syria since 2012, the physical threat to the Kurdish population and the disciplined opportunism of the PYD combined to create an unprecedented experiment in autonomous government in northern Syria. In 2012 when the civil war engulfed Syria and the Bashar Assad regime's authority was weakened, the PYD was ready to act thanks to its better discipline and clearer goals than other Syrian Kurdish parties. It also had the support of the experienced PKK. The PKK supported the development of YPG's military capability through the supply of personnel and training from its veteran forces. Syrian Kurds noted an increasing presence of fighters and commanders from Turkey and Iran during this time (Allsopp 2014; International Crisis Group 2014). The PYD openly admitted that ex-PKK fighters are serving with the YPG but stressed that they became YPG fighters who are answerable to the YPG command (Kaya and Lowe 2017). The PYD established its de facto autonomy in 2012, covering the area called Rojava (DFNS since 2016), including the Afrin, Jazeera and Kobane (now called Euphrates regions). Although the DFNS is composed of multiple groups from different backgrounds, the main political party that leads the region is the PYD.

Emerging in part out of the Rojava experiment was the establishment of the Syrian Democratic Forces (SDF), which is led by the PYD, in 2015 with the support of the United States to help the international coalition in the fight against ISIS due to YPG and YPJ's military effectiveness in the fight. Initially, the SDF were heavily composed of the Kurds but since 2017 several other factions with different ethnic and political backgrounds, such as Arabs, Assyrians and other communities, joined (Hassan 2017: 2–3). The Turkish government has strong objections to the United States' support for the PYD and YPG and to the de facto Kurdish autonomy in northern Syria because of the connections between the PYD and PKK. It does not want the PYD to increase its influence or gain legitimacy over fears of the threat it may pose to Turkey's future.

The DFNS has not received international recognition so far but it has developed international connections. The United States, while acknowledging the complexities of the YPG's regional position and role (*Hurriyet Daily News* 2016), has provided military support to the SDF in the fight against ISIS. In 2016, the DFNS opened official representations in several European capital cities including Moscow, Prague, Stockholm, Paris, Berlin and the Hague. The PYD and DFNS have strong relations with Russia in particular. Although the PYD has been consistently excluded from UN-led peace talks on Syria, mainly due to Turkish objections, Russia included the PYD in the regular Syria talks it held in Astana. The DFNS has not received much humanitarian or developmental support from international organisations and states. UN agencies chose not to operate in areas under the control of the PYD[6] except for the UNHCR's involvement in some Syrian displacement camps and Iraqi refugee camps. The presence of international non-governmental organisations in the region has also been limited, mainly due to an embargo policy by the Turkish government.

The DFNS has been putting emphasis on complying with international norms and regulations. The Social Contract of the DFNS opens with a statement that the nation-state regime in Syria is the underlying cause for the chaos in the Middle East because it generates inequality, leads to destruction and fragmentation, and suggests a democratic federal system as the optimal solution (The Preamble of the Social Contract of the DFNS). The Social Contract has ecological, democratic and feminist principles as its defining principles and prioritises women's freedom, free and democratic elections, and cultural and linguistic rights for all communities. The DFNS's governance system has received interest in the international media with praises of its policy on women's rights, minorities and democratic rights (Sheppard 2016; Tax 2016). Although YPG forces have been criticised for committing war crimes, such as arbitrary arrests, torture and recruiting child soldiers (Amnesty International 2015; Human Rights Watch 2014a and 2014b), the PYD declared that they are working on

---

[6] Conversations with the UNICEF and other UN regional managers November 2016, Amman.

improving their human rights records. Perhaps the PYD is concerned about these violations because they are still gaining favour with the West due to fighting ISIS.[7]

Although it is clear that the PYD is positioning itself for the long term by emphasising its democratic and egalitarian credentials, probably hoping recognition and legitimacy will help them in the future in attaining autonomy or independence through self-determination. There is a limit to how much international support DFNS or the PYD can attract in an international society that considers maintaining the status quo as priority. While neither the PKK nor the PYD officially seeks independence or a united greater Kurdistan, the endgame of democratic autonomy involves increased cross-border unity in a horizontally non-hierarchical system. The border between Turkey and Syria is therefore irrelevant in the purist's view of this theory. This could be seen as a threat from Turkish and Syrian states' perspectives. In addition, there is an inherent tension between the PYD's official position on multi-party politics and tolerance and its actions on the ground. The authoritarian nature of the PKK could be seen in the PYD (Savelsberg 2014). While the party insists that it is committed to pluralism, it has effectively imposed a one-party rule in Rojava. For example, a PYD law announced in 2014 forbids the existence of political parties which do not recognise its administration (Van Wildenberg 2014). Such parties were placed in a similar position of illegality under Ba'ath rule. There are accusations of PYD harassment of political opponents, kidnapping, arbitrary arrest, restrictions on political activities and the use of violence to quash domestic unrest (International Crisis Group 2014).

In the post–Cold War period, the Kurdish politics in Syria went through the biggest transformation, especially since the start of the civil war in the country. The PYD emerged as the strongest party in the power vacuum created by the war and was able to organise quickly to create a defence force against Islamist militant groups and others. It carved a de facto autonomous region that adopted principles of harmony with the principles of the international normative framework

---

[7] For instance, it announced that 21 minors in the YPG forces were demobilised and the military forces began to receive human rights training from Geneva Call, a neutral non-governmental organisation in Syria: New measures taken by the Kurdish People's Protection Units to stop recruiting children under 18. Geneva Call, Website, 22 June 2018.

that makes reference to self-determination through the implementation of direct democracy. The non-democratic policies of the PYD may have been criticised and the human rights violations carried out by its armed forces have been brought to attention by international agencies, but the PYD has declared they are taking steps towards tackling these issues and given their role in fighting ISIS, this has not hugely damaged their cachet with Western states.

Iran

In the period after the end of the Cold War, the opportunities for Iranian Kurds to engage with international actors and platforms were greatly restricted compared to Kurds in Iraq and Turkey. This is mainly because of the isolation of the Iranian state from the Western world and its authoritarian nature. The Iranian regime does not have a legal or institutional procedure in a place like Iraq for international organisations to carry out activities in its territory and it is suspicious of international involvement in any case (Natali 2005: 174). The Iranian Kurds have not had the political processes, conflict and channels that were present in Turkey, Iraq and Syria to enable them to connect with the international community and find spaces of lobbying or being active in international platforms. This could be because of two reasons. First is the authoritarian nature of the state preventing or hindering political mobilisation and interaction with the international community. Second, it is also for strategic reasons. Even though they can make appeals for self-determination on the grounds of democracy and human rights violations, they are probably aware these efforts will not give them leverage in the Iranian domestic context, therefore they chose to allocate their resources elsewhere, such as clandestine activities in border areas and others.

One notable interaction in the international support given to Iranian Kurds since the end of the Cold War has been with regard to the refugee issue. Kurdish refugees from Iran received support from the UNHCR and local and international humanitarian organisations in Iraq. The Iranian government has collaborated with the UNHCR to arrange the return of the refugees (Kessler 2002). Apart from this, interactions remained limited or non-existent. For instance, during the 1990s the Kurdish regions in Iran were under attack and martial law was imposed, but this was not brought to the agenda of international actors

as there were no international organisations associated with or lobbying on behalf of Iranian Kurds. Additionally, no strong Iranian Kurdish
diaspora networks were established in European or American cities
either. Most Iranian Kurdish migration has been to large cities in Iran,
especially Tehran and to the regional states. This has been a very
different migration experience compared to the Europeanised
Kurdish diaspora communities.

In the post–Cold War period, the relationship between Kurdish
nationalists and the government remained uncompromising. The position of hard-line ruling clerics became entrenched during the 1980s and
their approach to the Kurdish issue did not change much in the following decades. In the early 1990s, the regime, led by Rafsanjani, initially
reached out to the Kurds but being dependent on conservative constituencies and the right-wing ulama for his political survival, he ultimately increased pressure on Kurdish parties (Natali 2005: 156). The
moderate Khatami regime also made efforts to reach out to Kurds but
again these efforts did not lead to any substantial change in their
position or in relations between the two in the long term. Khatami,
while emphasising the similarities between the Persian and Kurdish
identities, permitted Kurdish publications, a radio station and cultural
centres. However, these did not last long. Khatami returned to the
position of the previous regimes and their hard-line stance towards
the Kurds (Entessar 2009: 55–7).

However, after the end of the Cold War, an increased awareness of
Kurdish nationalism can be observed among the Kurds in Iran. The
pressures on Kurdish cultural and political activities, a lack of sustained
dialogue and open space, the suppression they experienced at the hands
of the Islamic Republic regime as well as a deteriorating economic
situation increased hostility among the Kurds towards the regime. As
a result, critical Kurdish voices against the regime increased (Natali
2005: 157). However, the lack of political space, the nature of the
Iranian regime and its isolation from the international community
restricted Kurds' ability to have political influence. Moreover, the
Kurdish parties remained divided, and Iranian Kurds lacked a large
representative party.

In this process, Kurdish political parties in Iran further radicalised
and moved away from the idea of a compromise with the regime.
Today, Komala seeks to overthrow the Islamic regime in Iran and
engages in military activities in the border areas (Natali 2005: 156).

Kurdish political parties have offices in the Sulaymaniyah province in the KRI from where they coordinate activities with their supporters inside Iran. Despite having representations in European cities, the KDP-I and Komala lack any influential international transnational networks (Natali 2005: 176). The net result is that their nationalist goals are not framed or adjusted to international normative frameworks.

Conclusion

Kurdish nationalist movements across the Middle East adjusted their discourse, framing, goals and strategies to the increasingly stronger international human rights and democracy frameworks after the end of the Cold War. In the post–Cold War era, the world experienced a rise in ethno-territorial demands for autonomy and self-determination. The trajectory of Kurdish nationalist movements is no exception to this. Indeed, the demands and activities of the Kurdish movements illustrate the rise of the Wilsonian self-determination since the Cold War. All four Kurdish movements in Iraq, Turkey, Syria and Iran became more assertive in their demands for recognition of their identity, territorial autonomy and self-determination. The PKK in Turkey sought secession for Kurdistan but later changed its demands to autonomy and democratic confederalism within territorially demarcated areas. Kurds in Iraq struggled for autonomy in northern Iraq for decades and obtained this in 1991 as de facto and in 2005 as de jure. The PYD in Syria, since the beginning of civil war created a de facto autonomous zone and are now trying to maintain this position. In doing this, Kurds integrated international norms (an exception being the Iranian Kurds' case due to the isolation of the regime), related to human rights and democracy, but in different forms and at different levels. Their different routes were defined by the internal circumstances of their states, domestic politics, the political history of each movement and the nature of their interactions with international actors.

As their demands became more assertive, Kurdish parties' goals narrowed and focused on the smaller Kurdistans in each country, moving away from seeking independence for greater Kurdistan. Since the end of the Cold War, none of the main Kurdish political parties have explicitly used the map of greater Kurdistan in their party propaganda and publications. Still, the map remained as a form of reference to show the divided nature of Kurdistan by four countries and the idea of being under occupation. They used the idea of the greater Kurdistan and the dividedness of its people in their rhetoric, pamphlets and in their references to Kurds in other countries. The map of greater Kurdistan was a source that gave resonance to each Kurdish nationalist movement and the nationalist sentiments of their supporters. The Kurdish diaspora used the map of greater Kurdistan extensively in the period after the Cold War. The map, in its different forms, as a political map, or as a map that shows the demographic distribution of the Kurds, also began to appear in international platforms such as the media. Examination of this is what the next chapter turns to.

6 | *Kurdish Diaspora*
Kurdistan Map Goes Global

Introduction

The Kurdish diaspora has had a vital role in the promotion of the Kurdish identity and Kurdish homeland within the international political and normative context of the post-1990 era. Their efforts in this promotion, in deploying the idea of a unified Kurdistan and widely using the map of greater Kurdistan have globalised this map. The Kurdish diaspora, although directly linked to home-grown nationalisms and domestic Kurdish movements, has had a separate and significant role in promoting the Kurdish cause and in raising awareness of the issues Kurds face in their home countries, especially since the early 1990s. Activists in the Kurdish diaspora framed their arguments about the territoriality of the Kurdish nation and the dividedness of Kurdistan within a human rights, and collective cultural and democratic agenda. This was done in line with dominant international norms on ethnic, linguistic and cultural rights and the responsibilities of states to ensure these rights, as indicated at the UN and European Union levels. Using such frameworks, Kurdish activists publicised the rightfulness of the Kurdish demand for self-determination by showing the Kurds as one people and Kurdistan as one territory unfairly divided among different states and by emphasising the violation of their rights by these states.

The transnational activities of the Kurds in the diaspora played a hugely important role in giving impetus to Kurdish demands for statehood or democratic autonomy, in some respects more so than regional political movements. Kurds in the diaspora promoted the idea that the history of the region was identical to the history of the Kurdish nation, implying that Kurdistan was an ethnic territory throughout history that had been continuously inhabited by Kurdish people. They promoted the idea that the map of greater

Kurdistan represents this territory, making reference to the existence of Kurdish territoriality going back to the thirteenth century, as promoted by Kurdish nationalist historiographers. In this period, the use of the map of greater Kurdistan by outsiders and Kurds themselves increased. Indeed, the legacy of this is evident today in that it remains very common to see this map in written and visual media.

The location of the Kurdish diaspora outside the homeland gives them the ability to carry out activities in a transnational space and make an impact on international actors, in a way that would not be possible for those in the homeland. Moreover, they are able to communicate with co-ethnics at home and abroad, which helps diaspora activists mobilise grassroots, nurture and support a 'Kurdish consciousness', and seek to influence host-states' foreign policies. Similar to the Armenian, Palestinian, Kosovar Albanian, Tamil and Irish diasporas, Kurdish diaspora activists try to influence the perceptions and attitudes of their host-states and international organisations towards their people and their home countries.

This chapter offers an overview of Kurdish migrations from the twentieth century until today, and discusses the Kurdish diaspora's efforts in awareness-raising activities among co-ethnics both inside and outside their homeland, defining their nationalism as a 'long-distance nationalism' (Anderson 2001). It offers an analysis of the Kurdish diaspora's use of the available international rights discourse to promote the idea that Kurds are a nation whose territory is wrongfully divided. Although the Kurdish diaspora is treated as a unit of analysis in the chapter, it is in reality a heterogeneous entity composed of different political and ideological groups with separate goals. The origin of each diaspora community, and their relations with the state and their co-ethnics in that state define their identity and activities. The nature of the host-state in which they are located also leads to a variety of Kurdish organisations with different strategies and goals. The focus here is not on Kurdish migrants in general, but a component of this group that is politically active. Therefore, the notion of a Kurdish diaspora used in this chapter only refers to this politically active group with its several separate actors, political goals and areas of activities.

The Kurdish Diaspora and Migration

The notion of diaspora refers to peoples, relations and processes out-side the confines of established territorial political realms. It originates from *dispersion* and *to sow* or *scatter*, and has evolved to refer to the dispersion of any people from their original homeland (Cohen 1997). Diasporas are typically seen as distinct from state and non-state actors as they adopt strategies and activities in the transnational realm. They establish cross-border interactions away from their original territorial homeland with co-ethnics at home and in their host countries, with other states and international organisations (Waldinger and Fitzgerald 2004: 1181; Clifford 1994). However, despite operating outside their institutionalised state territory, diasporas frame their political activities in national homeland terms – real or ideal – making their activities territorial. If anything, they are more attached to the idea of a national territory than their co-nationals in the homeland (Shain and Barth 2003: 459). The notion of a homeland, actual or imagined, has a key role in characterising the diaspora consciousness. Diasporas maintain a memory or myth of the homeland, and are committed to maintaining, restoring or returning to this homeland (Safran 1991: 83–4).

Here, a narrow definition of diaspora is adopted: active political actors who engage in promoting rival identities to that of the sovereign state in which they reside or to the state from which they come (Adamson and Demetriou 2007: 499–501), or who are 'entangled in homeland-related affairs' (Shain and Barth 2003: 452), or have 'home-land orientation' whether it is a real or imagined homeland (Brubaker 2005: 5). An increase in transnational activities, and faster and cheaper ways of communication facilitated carrying out homeland-related activities as it enabled migrants to remain in contact with each other and their country of origin. It also enabled them to sustain and dis-seminate ideas of common identity and homeland (Adamson and Demetriou 2007: 497; Adamson 2006: 192).

Migration is not a new phenomenon for the Kurds. During the last decades of the Ottoman Empire, Kurdish migration was mainly volun-tary. Most of the Kurdish migrants in Istanbul in this period were from peasant backgrounds and worked in low-skilled manual labour occu-pations (mainly as porters – *hammal*). Many members of Kurdish tribal families went to Istanbul for education or to serve as Ottoman bureau-crats. They were the most active Kurdish community in Istanbul in the late nineteenth and early twentieth centuries. Some members of these families went, usually temporarily, to Europe for educational purposes, or as Ottoman diplomats or political dissidents (some of them as part of the *Young Turks*). They took up leading roles in planting the seeds of Kurdish nationalism during the First World War.

After the collapse of the Ottoman Empire and the establishment of new states in the former Ottoman territories, many Kurds dispersed from their original location. Kurdish tribal leaders and elites who sought Kurdish independence or a foreign mandate system after the end of the First World War and those who supported the Turkish independence war but were excluded when the new Turkish Republic was established, escaped to Syria and Europe. Some of them engaged in militant and political activities against Turkey. They formed Kurdish societies and provided direct economic, military and political support to Kurdish rebellions in Turkey. After the French mandate ended in Syria, these Kurdish intellectuals and nationalists went to Europe and continued their activities there.

Further waves of Kurdish migration were seen during the post–Second World War period. From the 1960s to the 1990s Kurds emigrated to different parts of the world, particularly to Western Europe, North America and Australia, both for economic and political reasons. Most of the Kurdish migration in the 1960s took place from Turkey to Europe as part of the guest-workers under inter-governmental agreements between Turkey and European countries such as Germany, Austria, Switzerland and France, with Germany being the largest recipient.

The biggest flows of Kurdish migration from Turkey occurred in the 1970s, 1980s and 1990s as a result of several political events that took place (Aslan 1988). After the 1971 military intervention and the 1980 military coup, the Kurds, together with the leftists and the Islamists, were subjected to strict and violent state measures (Heper 2007; Sirkeci 2006; Yeğen 1996). These purges led to a large number of Kurds from Turkey seeking refuge in European countries and, what is more, these refugees were highly politicised. Some of them fled to neighbouring countries, particularly to Iran, and from there went to Iraq and then to Europe, and some others lived in Kurdish villages and guerrilla camps in Iran, Iraq and Syria, joined the PKK or took part in political conflicts in these countries.

In Iraq, the main source of Kurdish migration was the conflict between the Iraqi government and the Kurds, especially in mid-1975 when the conflict escalated. The Iraqi Kurds' alliance with the Iranian Shah against the Iraqi regime collapsed with the 1975 agreement between Iran and Iraq. This led to the withdrawal of Iranian support for the Kurds and the latter's defeat by the Iraqi regime. 50,000 Iraqi Kurds fled to Iran and some of them were given political asylum in Western European countries (Van Bruinessen 2003c). The largest Kurdish emigration from Iran took place after the 1979 Iranian revolution and the civil war that followed it, which greatly affected areas where Kurds live. Many Kurds escaped from Iran to Turkey and then sought a way of going to America, Europe or Australia (Van Bruinessen 2003c).

The largest amount of Kurdish emigration from Iraq took place after the 1980–8 Iran–Iraq War. Hussein's policies towards the Kurds and violent attacks during and after the war (Hiltermann 2007) caused a significant flow of Kurdish refugees into neighbouring countries and into Western Europe. Following the 1988 Anfal Campaigns, 60,000 refugees entered Turkey and only half of these refugees returned to Iraq. Another Kurdish flow from Iraq occurred after Iraq's invasion of Kuwait in 1990 and the regime attacks on the Kurds resulting in over one million Kurdish villagers fleeing to Turkey and Iran in April 1991. Some of these refugees ended up in western Europe, northern Iraq and Australia.

Most of the Kurdish migrants today are constituted by Kurds from Turkey who migrated in the second half of the twentieth century and they are mainly located in Europe, the United States and Australia. Kurdish emigration from Turkey, Iraq and Iran continues in smaller numbers today. The largest recent wave of Kurdish migration took place as part of the wider displacement of millions of people due to the Syrian War since 2011. The most recent estimate of the number of Kurds living outside Turkey, Iran, Iraq and Syria is about 1.2 million (The Kurdish Project website).

Kurdish Diaspora and Awareness Raising

From the formation of the first Kurdish diaspora organisations in the 1950s until today, Kurdish political activism in the diaspora went through a massive transformation. Initially, Kurdish activities in the diaspora aimed at cultivating and protecting Kurdish culture and language, but they later started to adopt explicit political aims. This had an important role in raising national awareness among the Kurds in the diaspora as well as increased organisation around political issues Kurds experienced back home. In doing this, they made use of increasingly advanced communication technologies and dissemination methods.

The oldest Kurdish organisation, the Centre d'Etudes Kurdes of Paris, was founded by Kamuran Bedirhan in 1949 in Paris after Kurdish intellectuals began to migrate to France following French withdrawal from Syria. Other Kurdish organisations were established in the 1950s and 1960s such as the Kurdish Students Society and the National Union of Kurdish Students in Berlin, the Netherlands Kurdistan Society and the International Society of Kurdistan in Amsterdam and the Society for the Advancement of Kurdistan in the United Kingdom (Van Bruinessen 2003c; Edmonds 1971: 105–6). These were small organisations and some of them were founded and supported by non-Kurdish students and intellectuals who were 'friends of Kurdistan' (Edmonds 1971: 106).

More politicised Kurdish organisations began to emerge later in the 1970s and 1980s and it was during this period that Kurdish ethnic consciousness became more prominent among Kurdish immigrants in Europe. This was mainly due to the arrival of politically minded dissidents and asylum seekers from Turkey, who were acutely aware of the fragmented status of the Kurdish identity and encouraged the politicisation of second-generation Kurdish labour migrants who had arrived in Europe in the previous decades. The organisations they established – such as Kurdish Institutes in Paris (1983), Stockholm (1989), Brussels (1989), Berlin (1994), Moscow (1996) and Washington DC (1996) – had both cultural and political concerns and played important roles in politicising Kurdish migrants (Başer 2014; Khayati 2008).

Kurdish activists in the diaspora believed that presenting the Kurdish identity as homogeneous was necessary to obtain international support for the Kurdish cause. Therefore, their activities were heavily focused on creating a unified Kurdish language to prove the homogeneity and distinctiveness of the Kurdish nation. They did not have access to the instruments of an existing state apparatus, so they operated through Kurdish organisations and the print media to undertake a project that resembled an elite-led top-down nation-building process (Van

Bruinessen 2003c). For instance, Kurdish intellectuals and political dissidents, who escaped to Europe from Turkey, particularly those in Sweden, played a crucial role in standardising Kurmanji. They organised language conferences, published, held Kurdish language courses and campaigned for mother tongue education at schools. These efforts increased the number of Kurmanji speakers greatly over the decades and spread its use among the intellectual Kurdish community and the grassroots. Later, the writings produced by diaspora intellectuals in Kurmanji, as well as Sorani, were disseminated back home (Van Bruinessen 2003c), and this had a huge impact on raising awareness of national identity among Kurds at home.

Kurdish diaspora activists used radio transmitters, satellite TV and the internet to disseminate Kurdish language, culture and nationalist propaganda. MED-TV, a Kurdish satellite television station, established in 1995 in the United Kingdom and broadcast to the Middle East, Europe and most of Asia, was an important medium. Although it was initiated by the PKK, Kurds from all backgrounds with different political views were included in the production of its programmes (Hassanpour 1998). Today, news, information and propaganda are disseminated through several websites, news agencies, TV and radio stations, publishing houses based in Europe and the United States – such as ANF News in Amsterdam, Newroz TV in Stockholm, the Kurdish Project in San Francisco, Peace in Kurdistan in London, Ekurd Daily in New York, and others. In addition, the PKK's effective mobilisation among migrant Kurds in Europe, especially in Germany, further contributed to the increased politicisation and ethnicisation among second- and third-generation Kurdish immigrants (Adamson and Demetriou 2007: 512).

These nation-building, awareness-raising and mobilisation activities contributed to the integration of Kurdish society both at home and within the diaspora and enabled them to connect to the idea of a Kurdish identity beyond their local or tribal realities. However, divisions within the diaspora continued despite the nation-building and linguistic and cultural homogenisation efforts. This is partly because, like any other people, Kurds at home or in the diaspora are a heterogeneous entity with multiple political views, religions, ideologies and organisations with different goals and strategies related to their host and home countries. Although the idea that Kurdistan represents the national territory of the Kurds is very strong in the diaspora, and its map has become an internationally used visual tool, there is no coherent adherence to this idea.

A prominent division between Kurds in the diaspora is their different countries of origin. Kurdish nationalist groups attempt to influence policies in relation to their own home country rather than in the wider Kurdistan. The existence of separate Kurdish political factions in each home country has implications as most Kurds associate themselves with Kurdish movements in the states from which they come (O'Shea 2004: 13). Their ability to stay in contact with their home country thanks to modern forms of communication and transport helps maintain their ties with their fellow Kurds and maintain their distinct identity within the general Kurdish identity (Van Bruinessen 2003c). For instance, while the PKK has its own members and associations in Europe, the supporters of Barzani's KDP constituted separate diaspora groups (King 2008). Kurds coming from different countries tend not to interact with each other but rather integrate with Kurds from their own country.

Moreover, efforts in cultural homogenisation led to the emergence of new divisions or the crystallisation of existing ones. The efforts to develop a standardised Kurdish language, which led Kurmanji and Sorani to become the two main dominant dialects, triggered micro-dissident nationalisms. For instance, increased Kurmanji education in European schools and Sorani or Kurmanji publications alienated other ethnic communities and increased their awareness of their own distinct identity (Van Bruinessen 2006: 40; Smith 2000: 8–9). The Zazas, although generally assumed to be Kurdish, increasingly disassociated themselves from the Kurdish movement, began to consider Zazaki as a separate language and even started to call their homeland 'Zazaistan' (Van Bruinessen 2006: 41). This emergent Zaza nationalism in Europe was then transferred to Turkey. The Alevis, for mainly religious reasons, also distanced themselves from the Kurdish nationalist organisations and began to see themselves as a distinct nation with their own homeland 'Alevistan' (Van Bruinessen 2006: 39).

Despite these divisions, Kurdish activists in the diaspora have had a significant impact on the advancement of Kurdish nationalism and the promotion of Kurds as a state-deserving nation on a historical, ethnically homogeneous but divided homeland. There is a stronger attachment to the idea of one Kurdish nation and one Kurdish territory. Several diaspora organisations adhere to the idea that the territory indicated on the map of greater Kurdistan represents the Kurdish national homeland more strongly than Kurdish nationalists back in the region.

Kurdish Diaspora Activities in the International Context: Post-1990 and Human Rights Framework

The post-Cold War era witnessed the emergence of a new form of self-determination similar to the way Wilson defined the concept. But, this form of self-determination was explicitly and directly linked to democracy, human rights and cultural rights. In this version of self-determination, the identity and culture of a group and their treatment at the hands of states combined to open a new avenue for separatist groups to justify their claims. Diaspora nationalists have been particularly effective in using this rhetoric especially if they are located in western liberal democratic states that provide ethnic groups the freedom to pursue a cultural and political life (Anderson 1994). Ideas of plural societies and identity-based rights prevalent in the political discourse of these states facilitate these groups' ability to engage in 'long-distance nationalism', meaning carrying out activities related to politics at home from outside (Anderson 2001: 42, 1994: 326).

Many western recipient states provide suitable conditions and opportunities for immigrant societies to raise ethnic and cultural awareness, to mobilise, to develop and reinforce cultural identities and to establish cultural and political organisations. Political activists in the diaspora use this political space to influence host-state policies towards their communities and towards their home countries. The democratic participation principle and mechanisms available to interest groups to influence state policies increases the chances of these groups to make an impact (Smith 2000: 1–2; Shain 1999). The political institutions and prevalent values based on cultural rights in host-states also increase the chances of diaspora activities to be perceived as legitimate. This facilitates seeking support and sympathy in host-states, among international society and would-be nationals for their cause, and against the home-state of whose policies they criticise.

Diasporas seek to influence the foreign policies of their host countries and other states in relation to their home country, or the political groups there, through several methods. They lobby to convince members of parliaments to represent their goals, denounce the policies of their home government and contribute money to the campaigns of the candidates (Smith 2000: 28–9). They publicise the perceived or real sufferings and injustices of their ethnic community at conferences and interact with international human rights organisations and with powerful individuals. They draw up petitions and organise campaigns to encourage local or national governmental authorities to take a stance on the issues they are raising and carry out protests and demonstrations to draw attention to their cause. They may also support the boycotts and measures taken by their host-states or international organisations against their home-country regimes (Sheffer 2002: 216). Of course, the effectiveness of such activities relies on the foreign policy agendas of the host-state governments.

The Kurdish diaspora started to carry out such lobbying activities increasingly more in the 1980s, and especially with the beginning of the 1990s. They developed relations with influential organisations and individuals, especially politicians, to increase awareness on the Kurdish issue or to pressure states to recognise Kurdish as a mother tongue for children at school. With the 1990s, the nature of this interaction expanded to include attempts to increase the Kurdish issue's profile internationally and influence host-states' foreign policies. Through utilising transnational links, they connected with other host countries and established contacts with journalists and politicians. They eventually became part of the European and United States political landscapes (Van Bruinessen 2003c), somewhat less effectively in the United States due to the strategic alliance between the United States and Turkey (Gunter 2011b).

The 1990s also coincided with important events in Kurdish politics that increased international attention to the Kurds. The Iraqi regime's Anfal Campaigns in late 1980s, the Halabja chemical attack in 1988 and the brutal attacks it carried out during the 1990–1 Gulf War killed, injured and displaced thousands of Kurds. These resulted in the creation of a safe zone in northern Iraq which turned into a de facto autonomous Kurdish area. Humanitarian and development work carried out by international actors in the region increased international attention on the Kurds. Another event that raised international interest in Kurdish politics was the capture of the PKK leader Öcalan. These and many other events raised the profile of the Kurdish issue in the eyes of policymakers, the media and scholars in host countries and enabled Kurdish diaspora groups to make their voices heard.

In this new international political and normative context, Kurdish groups in the diaspora began to use the human and democratic rights framework to advance their goals. Activities such as violent protests or incidents such as hunger strikes and self-immolation abated (Başer 2013: 41–8, 13–14), and the emphasis on the military dimensions of the struggle decreased as did drug trafficking, recruiting fighters, financial extortion and tax collection to raise money for the PKK (Eccarius-Kelly 2008: 10). The Kurdish actors started to situate their strategies and rhetoric within human rights and democracy discourses and began to gradually move away from violent and criminal activities.

This shift in strategy to use the framework of human and minority rights certainly contributed to increasing the legitimacy of the Kurdish cause among the international community. The Kurdish diaspora drew attention to the mistreatment of the Kurds at the hands of their home countries and tried to influence Western states' relations with their home states. They brought cases of individual human rights abuses to the agenda of the international community, applied to the ECHR and opened cases against states, especially Turkey, for torture, illegal detention and executions committed by the regime, and security forces destroying Kurdish villages (Lupu and Voeten 2012: 424; Çelik and Rumelili 2006; Reidy, Hampson and Boyle 1997). Diaspora activists also lobbied using complaints about restrictions on their ability to exercise their cultural, linguistic and political rights in their home countries.

The Kurdish Human Rights Project (KHRP), established in 1992 in London, collaborated with Turkish human rights organisations to submit appeals to the ECHR, the Organisation for Security and Co-operation in Europe and UN bodies. The Kurdish Institutes in Paris and Washington have been particularly active in human rights abuses. They have engaged in political activities such as lobbying host countries and organising meetings and discussions between European and American politicians and Kurdish political activists (Van Bruinessen 2003c). Some of the organisations also adjusted their goals and activities to the changing international framework. For instance, the Association of Kurdish Workers for Kurdistan, established in Germany in 1979, shifted its activities from improving Kurdish workers' living standards to a more political agenda framed within the human and democratic rights framework (Başer 2013: 18).

Another group, the Peace in Kurdistan Campaign, established in 1994 in London, organises events and campaigns to bring together

Kurds in the diaspora and in home countries, host-country politicians, journalists and academics. Their events cover topics related to the Kurdish issue, such as Öcalan's proposals for peace in 2012, the Turkish state's policies towards the Kurds, among many others. Speakers at these events usually involve representatives of the Kurdish political party in Turkey, British members of parliament (MPs) and Kurdish or non-Kurdish academics. Events are mainly attended by the members of the Kurdish community. Current UK Labour Party Opposition leader Jeremy Corbyn has openly supported this group and spoke at their events. The Peace in Kurdistan Campaign organises such events to raise awareness among the members' of the Kurdish community in London and influence the UK's policy towards Turkey. For instance, at their events, the organisers encourage attendees to write letters to their local MPs and ask them to put pressure on Turkey to change its Kurdish policy.

The PKK also engaged in diaspora activities directly. In its effort to transform the movement into a political one, the PKK and its supporters established the Kurdish Parliament in Exile on 12 April 1995. The Parliament was established to represent the Kurdish people living abroad and the will of the people of Kurdistan.[1] One of the main reasons behind its formation was the closure of HEP in Turkey in 1993 and the harassment and arrests of its MPs. The Parliament conducted relations with parties and personalities in Europe as the representative of the Kurds (Van Bruinessen 2003c) and played a significant role in drawing the attention of European states and politicians to the Kurdish issue. However, not all Kurdish groups joined the parliament, despite being invited, because they considered it as an effort to widen the PKK's political base. Therefore, the Parliament lacked complete endorsement to speak on behalf of all of Turkey's Kurds' interests and failed to establish itself as a representative and diplomatic body (Ibrahim and Gürbey 2000: 85). The Parliament dissolved itself in 1999.

The Kurdish Conference that is held annually in the European Parliament in Brussels since 2004 is another, relatively new, platform for diaspora Kurds to engage with the international community. This is also mainly led by the Kurdish activists from Turkey. Although it is

---

[1] HEP MPs were elected in 1991. After the party's closure, one MP was murdered, seven of them were arrested and given prison terms ranging from 3 to 15 years. The remaining MPs sought refuge abroad.

widely seen as an event supported by the PKK, the conference is attended by a wide range of international scholars experts, and journalists, as well as Kurdish politicians from Turkey, Iraq and Syria. The topics it covers are also wide ranging covering Kurdish issues in all regional countries, human rights and political participation among many others.

The European states' permission for Kurdish Parliament in Exile to carry out its activities in their countries and for the Kurdish Conference to be held at the premises of the European Parliament could be interpreted as European support for the Kurdish cause. And if this is the case, due to the PKK influence or support in these activities, the European states appear to support the PKK. However, the situation is not as simple as in this interpretation. Providing governmental support for the PKK is not the same as permitting events and platforms for discussions on the Kurds. From the European states' perspective, allowing such events does not mean direct governmental support for the PKK and could mean that these countries prioritise the right to freedom of speech and assembly. For instance, when Turkey and the United States protested against the Netherland's permission to the launch of the Parliament in the Hague, the Dutch Prime Minister dismissed the complaints and emphasised the right to freedom of assembly.

By presenting their national and territorial identity within the rights agenda, in line with the principles in the OSCE's Charter of Paris and UN documents, Kurdish activists in the diaspora have portrayed the Kurdish nationalist struggle as a struggle against repression. In this way, international political norms on human rights and democratisation provided a fruitful arena for advocating the case of the Kurds as a struggle against maltreatment by repressive home countries. In that sense, they link their claim on the abuse by governments due to their distinct cultural identity to the promotion of a nationalist agenda. The Kurdish diaspora has been effective in carrying out these activities and making an impact due to three reasons: (1) as long-distance nationalists, their stronger adherence to the idea of a unified nation than their co-ethnics back home made them assertive in promoting their claims; (2) their location in liberal-democratic host states to organise and engage in cultural and political activities away from the scrutiny of home-country regimes gives them opportunities to mobilise and lobby for their cause; and (3) their use of the discourse of contemporary international politics which puts increasing importance on the democratic and political rights of ethnic communities and criticises the human rights abuses, the violation of socioeconomic rights and any form of identity-based discrimination facilitates the promotion of their cause.

Kurdish Diaspora's Use of the Kurdistan Idea and its Maps

Although there is no strong attachment to the idea of a politically united greater Kurdistan, the idea that Kurdistan represents the national territory of the Kurds is stronger in the diaspora than among the Kurds back home. Representatives of activist groups campaigning for the Kurds avoid, even reject, using terms such as 'Eastern Turkey' or 'Northern Iraq' to refer to the areas where Kurds reside. In their minds those regions are called 'Kurdistan' and there is no question about it. Indeed, most dissident nationalist groups in the diaspora have stronger attachments to their ethnic identity and ideal homeland than their co-ethnics in the region.

Kurdish activists in the diaspora have generated a stronger attachment to the idea of a unified Kurdish identity and been more successful than regional Kurdish nationalists in internationalising and publicising the Kurdish issue. This is partly because such campaigns in the international realm have been driven by activist intellectuals that imagine a Kurdish nation and present the Kurds as a one-nation community, similar to the way Anderson describes in his 'long-distance nationalism' (Anderson 2001). In the region, however, the goals and demands of Kurdish political movements vary according to their social structure and the political conditions within each state. Diasporas feel their distinct identity more acutely in a completely alien cultural environment. They are physically located outside their home states, but they feel mentally located within a specific people, therefore they strongly hold on to an ethnic or kinship identity (Shain and Barth 2003: 473).

Kurdish activists in the diaspora articulated a Kurdish national identity with a common language and a symbolic territory. This articulation was at the core of the discourse they used in their interactions with the international community (Adamson and Demetriou 2007: 509). They claimed that the territory of Kurdistan is occupied and divided by alien nation-states and that this injustice needed to be rectified. The works of Kurdish nationalist scholars articulated Kurdish suffering and mistreatment, and the historical legacy of the Kurdish nation. These activists promoted the territoriality of the Kurdish nation and their homeland Kurdistan. The geographic extent of the maps they used is similar to the maps produced by

Kurdish groups in the 1940s, especially the Cairo Map discussed earlier. The maps showing the location of Kurdistan or the areas inhabited by Kurds in the Middle East were disseminated to provide credibility and raise support to the Kurdish cause. Izady's (1992) work and maps are excellent examples for such maps and are widely used by both Kurds and their supporters in the diaspora (Map 6.1).

Nationalist Kurdish intellectuals who took refuge in Europe were acutely aware of the fragmented status of the Kurdish identity and of the necessity to present Kurdish identities as a single homogeneous entity. Therefore, they focused on creating a Kurdish language and territory and presenting these to the Western community to prove the distinctiveness of the 'Kurdish nation'. They also linked their arguments about territory to the map of greater Kurdistan as the cartographic depiction of their home-land. Several maps listed on the Kurdish Institute in Paris are examples of the use of the Kurdistan map by these groups. A Kurdish student organisa-tion in Sweden called the Kurdish Student Academic Association (Swedish acronym KSAF) includes members originating from all four home states and adopts the rhetoric of 'one Kurdish identity' and 'one Kurdistan'. The idea of a unified homeland, Kurdistan, serves as an umbrella concept to argue for the unity of the Kurdish people and their location in the diaspora enables the promotion of such pan-ideas (Başer 2014: 28).

The Kurdistan National Congress (*Kongra Netewiya Kurdistan*, KNK), formed in Amsterdam in 1999, has explicitly pan-Kurdish goals. The KNK brings Kurds from across Europe together:

to generate moral unity of the Kurdish nation, without ignoring, however, the division of Kurdistan between four states; to bring remedy to disunion and conflict between Kurdish political parties; to elaborate norms of solidar-ity and a concerted strategy for democratic solution to the Kurdish question within the existing states, and, last but not least, to work on the national and international level, for the promotion and the ultimate practice by the people of Kurdistan of their right to self-determination. (KNK Website)

The KNK Convention, endorsed on 26 May 1999, defines the KNK as a nationwide organisation including Kurds from 'four parts of divided Kurdistan' and the Kurdish diaspora across the world. The KNK is very clear about its argument that the Kurds are one nation, and its Convention states that the organisation aims to consolidate Kurds' will of national unity and self-determination. In doing this it makes direct references to the Universal Declaration of Human Rights and

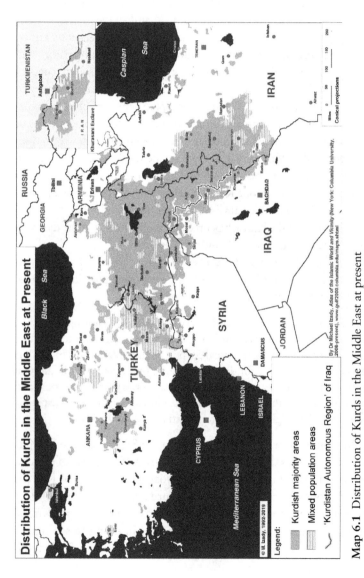

Map 6.1 Distribution of Kurds in the Middle East at present

Source: M Izady, Atlas of the Islamic World and Vicinity (New York, Columbia University, 2006-present).

other international documents that reify the right of peoples to self-determination. The KNK Convention defines Kurdistan as 'the country of all Kurds ... composed of all the contiguous regions where the Kurds form the majority of the populations'. It states that Kurdistan is one country that is divided artificially 'against the will of its people, and against their right to self-determination' (KNK Website).

Another similar umbrella Kurdish diaspora organisation that aims for the unity of the Kurds and establishment of an independent Kurdistan is the Kurdistan National Congress (KNC) (not to be confused with the Kurdistan National Council in Syria), established in London in 1985. The KNC Charter, adopted in 1998, states that the organisation aims to end the 'unfair and artificial borders that cut Kurdistan into five pieces' and to achieve 'Kurdish unity' by bringing the idea of an 'independent Kurdistan' on the agenda of the great powers and international organisations (KNC Charter). The KNC organises conferences in European cities to bring together Kurdish party representatives, Kurdish intellectuals, academics both from the region and the diaspora. It also publishes articles and opinion pieces through its website. The KNC of North America is the branch of the KNC in the United States and mainly involves representatives from Kurdish movements in Turkey. It aims to achieve the formation of a unified Kurdistan or the establishment of four Kurdish nation-states and it has openly called for self-determination for the Kurds (Charountaki 2011: 30).

In recent years, several websites emerged in Kurdish, Turkish and English publicising the plight and nationalist demands of the Kurdish nation, providing information about the Kurdish people, their homeland and culture. For instance, a website based in San Francisco called 'The Kurdish Project: Raising Awareness for Kurds and Kurdistan' defines the Kurds as the 'largest stateless national group in the world' with a unified cultural identity. This website also uses novel techniques to show Kurdistan on the world map, such as using Google Maps to highlight cities that have historically been inhabited by Kurdish populations (Map 6.2). This map, or the combination of yellow dots, looks very similar to the map of greater Kurdistan.

The promotion of the map of greater Kurdistan has reached a new level with the Kurdish diaspora's lobbying. The idea of a unified or greater Kurdistan and its cartographic symbol has become

Map 6.2 Where are the Kurds?
Source: The Kurdish Project website, http://thekurdishproject.org/kurdistan-map

widespread in print and online sources. Even organisations with separate agendas, such as the Kurdistan National Congress and the European Democratic Societies Congress, an organisation based in Brussels that carries out activities in relation to Turkish Kurds, refer to the idea of greater Kurdistan.

The Kurdish political activists in the diaspora drew the attention of international society, including state governments and international organisations, to the situation of Kurdish people in the regional states and their need for justice. They combined these issues with their struggle for self-determination, justice and democracy. In order to justify these demands, they argued that the Kurds and their territory Kurdistan are unfairly divided and that their inability to self-govern is the underlying cause for the injustices they experience. The Kurdish diaspora activists publicised the plight of the Kurds and the nationalist claims of their 'nation' and 'territoriality' as a combined package, therefore, had a crucial role in globalising the map of greater Kurdistan.

The Use of Maps of Greater Kurdistan by Outsiders

The maps of greater Kurdistan have started to appear in the publications of outsiders as well since the end of the Cold War. The developments in the 1990s in Iraq during the Gulf War and later, in 2003, the United States-led intervention in Iraq brought Kurdistan to the attention of the international media. Kurdistan maps produced and used by internationals began to appear in abundance in the 1990s and then especially in the 2000s. While some maps showed only Iraqi Kurdistan, other maps represented a larger Kurdistan that penetrated further to the east and north of Turkey (Culcasi 2006: 698). In the 1990s, the area that was most mapped was northern Iraq and it was labelled as 'Protected Kurdish Zone' or 'Allied Controlled Area', but later such maps began to be labelled as the 'Kurdish Region' (Culcasi 2006: 697). By the mid-1990s, 'Kurdish-inhabited Areas', 'Kurdish lands', 'Kurdish-populated areas' and 'Kurdistan' became common labels used by international actors to show the demographic distribution of the Kurds across Turkey, Iran, Syria and Iraq. Although these are not political or aspirational maps and are mainly produced to show the areas where Kurds live, the cartographic image in demographic and political maps appears almost identical. Political aspirational maps of Kurdistan tend to overlook the heterogeneity of the populations and even include areas where Kurds are not the majority. It is interesting that the demographic maps of Kurdistan also follow the same logic and rely on assumptions made in the political map in producing the Kurdish demographic image.

However, maps of Kurdistan produced by non-Kurds are used for illustrative purposes rather than political reasons and they are usually used in relation to an event that made it to the news. The extent of these maps and what they cover also vary. Nonetheless, whichever purpose they are used for and whatever their extent is, these maps recognised Kurds with varied place names and borders. A Central Intelligence Agency (CIA) map in 1992 represented the whole of Kurdistan, almost identical to the map used by Kurdish nationalists themselves, labelled 'Map of Kurdish Lands' (Map 6.3). Books and encyclopaedias on the Kurds also began to include maps to show the location of the Kurds, such as the map titled 'Distribution of Kurds across Turkey, Iran and Iraq' in McDowall's 1996 book (Map 6.4) and the 1998 Encyclopaedia Britannica map titled 'Areas of majority Kurdish settlement' (not included due to copyright).

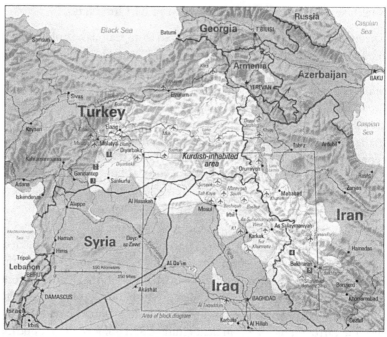

Map 6.3 CIA map of Kurdish lands (1992)
Source: University of Texas Libraries.

The international media has used the map of greater Kurdistan extensively. Some of these examples are *The Washington Post* maps in 1999 'Kurdish Inhabited Areas' and 2007 'Kurdish Populated Areas' (Map 6.5), and *The Economist* map in 2012 titled 'Kurdish-populated area'. Think-tanks also have used this map. For instance, the United States Congressional Research Service, a think-tank that provides policy and legal analysis to committees and members of both the House of Representatives and the Senate, included the greater Kurdistan map, such as the 2009 map titled 'Kurdish Areas' (Map 6.6)

There is a significant cartographic similarity between the Kurdistan maps produced and used by the internationals, especially the international media, since the mid-1990s, and the political maps produced and disseminated by the Kurdish diaspora and the propaganda maps produced by Kurdish nationalists in the 1940s, such as the Rizgari Kurd Map and Cairo Map. Kurdish nationalists use these

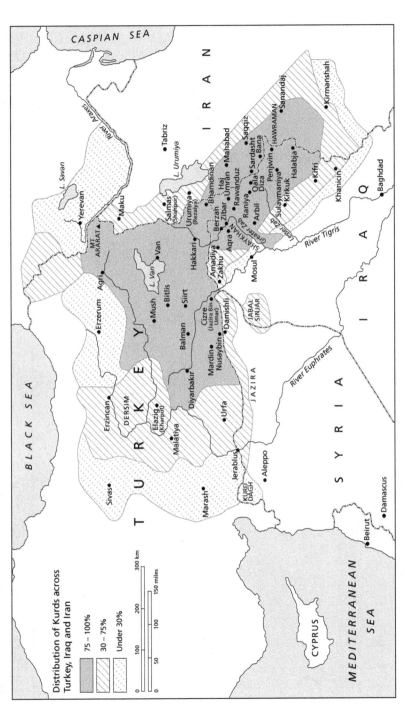

Map 6.4 Distribution of Kurds across Turkey, Iran and Iraq (1996)
Source: Redrawn based on David McDowall, *A Modern History of the Kurds*, 1996, p. xiv.

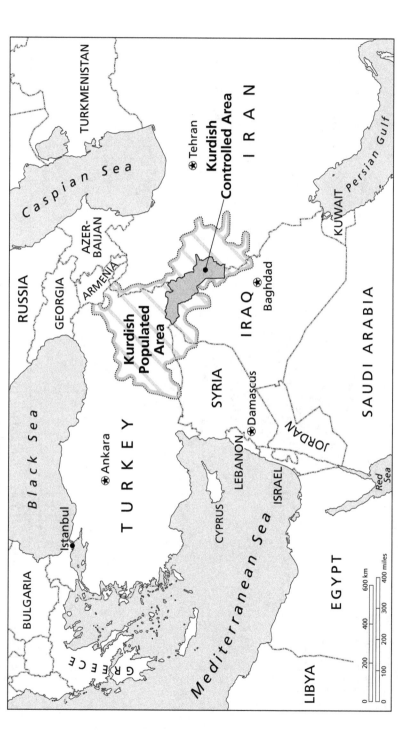

Map 6.5 Kurdish populated areas (1999)
Source: Redrawn based on Laris Karklis, *The Washington Post*, 12 October 2007.

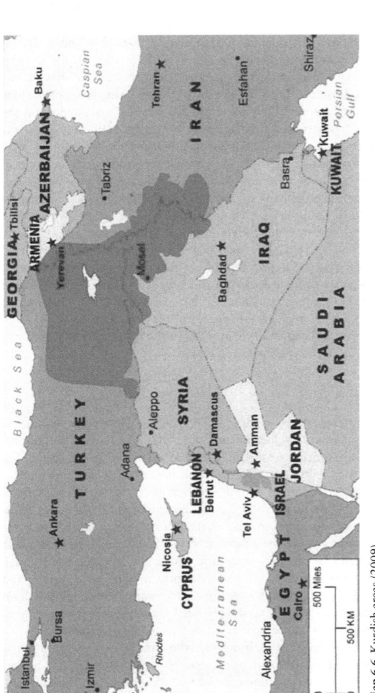

Map 6.6 Kurdish areas (2009)

Source: Katzman, K. The Kurds in Post-Saddam Iraq. *Congressional Research Service*, 3 June 2009. http://fpc.state.gov/documents/organization/125932.pdf, last accessed 9 April 2017.

maps with a particular political agenda, for propaganda purposes and to raise awareness among the Kurds and outsiders on the Kurdish issue. Outsiders may not be using these for reasons as Kurdish nationalists, however, the similarity between these two types of maps is important to note. This does not show international support for the idea of greater Kurdistan and for the Kurdish political goals, but it illustrates the resonance of this image. Maps published in the international media, even if they are used for propaganda or political reasons, can be influential because they are the public's and policymakers' predominant source of source of geographic information (Culcasi 2006: 689). Such maps, especially when available online can be seen by almost everyone who wants to find out about the Kurds. The media has huge power to communicate geographical information and impact perceptions about the world and its peoples. This power combined with the widely held assumption that maps are scientific and factual (Culcasi 2006: 690; Black 2000) facilitate the traction the map of greater Kurdistan has had internationally. However, it also shows that a political claim on territoriality can become everyday information if used unquestioningly.

Conclusion

Like other stateless groups in diaspora, Kurdish nationalists, due to their international location and their ability to interact with institutions and officials at local, national and international levels, have been able to mobilise and publicise the Kurdish case to the international community, more so than their co-ethnics back home. The contemporary international political discourse in relation to self-determination since the end of the Cold War has opened space for separatist and nationalist groups to link their demands to a struggle in the name of human, democratic and cultural rights. The Kurdish diaspora's location in Western democratic states with regimes and institutions facilitating the protection and promotion of ethno-cultural rights and diversity provided a suitable context for them to pursue goals and activities related to identity-related rights. The revival of Wilsonian self-determination and its transformation into a political right (though neither legally nor universally), that further reifies self-determination claims based on cultural identity has facilitated this. If incumbent states are violating a group's human rights and cultural and democratic rights, a self-determination claim of a separatist or autonomist group appears more acceptable to not all but some democratic Western states.

Kurdish nationalists in the diaspora, as long-distance nationalist actors, have played a crucial role in the development of Kurdish nationalism both inside and outside the region. They strongly hold on to a unified Kurdish identity and promote the territoriality of this unified nation. In line with the contemporary international normative framework, they use the rhetoric of suffering, the incidents of human rights abuses and their right to statehood to influence the way host states, other states, international organisations, scholars, journalists and the international media perceive their case and the actions of their home states. They promote the idea that Kurdistan is one country artificially divided among regional states and that this dividedness is the source of Kurdish suffering. Their implication is that if Kurds had self-government, the abuses Kurds experienced would not have happened.

Conclusion

This book told the story of the map of Kurdistan and Kurdish nationalism from an international perspective. On the one hand, existing IR work on territoriality and nationalism overlooks the interesting and important case of the Kurds. Kurdish literature, on the other hand, shows no interest in embedding the Kurdish case within an international analytical level. As this book showed, both sides have a lot to offer each other. The Kurdish case provides important and pertinent insights into debates on the right to self-determination, territorial ownership and national territoriality. Engagement with IR concepts and theories opens the Kurdish case to different analytical lenses and develops our understanding of this case.

The transformation of the justifications Kurds used in their claims for self-determination and Kurdish territoriality is embedded in an international context. Norms around what gives statehood and autonomy claims international legitimacy in different historical periods influenced how the relationship between nation and territory is perceived, which in turn influenced the conception and projection of the Kurdish territorial identity. The transformation of political governance systems from monarchical and imperial systems to republican and democratic rule played the key defining role in this. Most importantly, the rules of legitimate statehood within democratic state systems since the late nineteenth century changed throughout the period in which Kurdish nationalism emerged and developed.

Despite these transformations in what legitimises state rule, the idea that people are connected to a territory has been a constant justification for claims to statehood or autonomy by nationalist movements. Connecting people's identity to a particular territory was embedded in the idea of self-determination offered by Wilson after the First World War. Yet throughout most of the twentieth century, and to a large extent today, this form of self-determination has been considered as

destabilising, and state institutions and boundaries that frame citizenship have been seen as the basis for how people came to own a territory.
However, since the late 1980s, and especially after the end of the Cold
War, democracy, human rights and cultural rights frameworks
attached to ethnic identity have become significant justifications that
separatist nationalists use to make claims to independent rule and
territorial ownership. Underlying this is the idea that if the state does
not respect the cultural identity of part of its citizens or violates their
rights, the legitimacy of its authority weakens, as international documents like the 1975 Helsinki Act states. Of course, this is not
a universally accepted norm, nonetheless, it constitutes a significant
component of separatists' rhetoric and receives sympathy within the
international community.

Over the long term, this constantly transforming and changing international framework shaped the way the map of greater Kurdistan was
projected and received. At the core of this framework is the idea that
people and territory are connected. This is a nationalistic idea, and the
connection between the two notions is constructed, contingent and
historical. However, nationalists, as well as those who believe in the
claims made by a specific group of nationalists, see this link as natural
and intrinsic to people's identity and political demands made based on
this identity. States themselves promote the idea of a homeland inhabited by a specific people over a long course of history. In the same way,
people without a state also promote the idea of historical ownership
over a homeland, but one that is unjustly taken from them. Therefore,
both state and non-state nationalists follow the same logic. Kurdish
territoriality has become a widely promoted and accepted feature of
Kurdish nationalism as the wide usage of the map of greater Kurdistan
shows, both among the Kurds and internationally. The power of maps
in constructing our view of the division of world territory into nations
contributes to the appeal of this map.

Mapping Kurdistan and Kurds

In each historical period, different justifications for the ownership of
territory emerged for separatist groups who wanted to establish their
own state or autonomous rule. These justifications depended on how
the link between territory and people was understood. The way this
link was understood framed how Kurdish leaders and nationalisms

constructed their connection to territory and how they utilised this construction in their strategies of communicating their identity to other 'nations-to-be' and outsiders. The idea of Kurdistan and its maps have been the anchors for such constructions throughout history and served their purpose in a way that fitted with the territory–people link in each historical period and the goals of the nationalist group using the map.

From the time Kurdistan maps began to be used by the Kurds, it is possible to trace shifts in Kurdish claims to statehood as reflecting changes in international norms and developments around state legitimacy. Over time, the Kurdistan map became the core symbol of Kurdishness and came to represent a perceived reality in the minds of many Kurds and outsiders. The idea of Kurdistan also provided a sense of rootedness to the Kurdish past. Kurdish nationalists adopted contemporary conceptions of nation and territory and applied these conceptions to past uses of the notion of Kurdistan, constructing a history of the Kurdish nation around them. This retrospective reading of the past provided the basis for the nationalist imagination of the Kurdish identity.

The Kurdistan maps were not initially created by the Kurds themselves; they were drawn by outsiders in the nineteenth century and were later adopted and used by Kurdish nationalists in the First World War. European travellers, writers and officers who visited the region as agents of the state, scientists, journalists and researchers generated numerous definitions and cartographic depictions of Kurdistan in the latter half of the nineteenth century. These outsiders took the definitions of Kurdistan in historical texts as indicators of the existence of an ethnic territory of Kurds and drew ethnographic maps of Kurdistan. They basically used their orientalist and western conceptions of what constitutes the territory–people link to interpret the territorial identity of the peoples they encountered in the Ottoman territories, including the Kurds.

Kurdish elites did not always frame their claims in line with international trends, but rather this was something they learnt and adopted over time. In the late nineteenth century, Kurdish political activism did not necessarily align its goals and aims with international normative trends. The idea that certain civilisations reach maturity and form states underpinned the ideational aspects of nationalist movements in Europe in the nineteenth century. This idea was defined by Mill as the nationality principle and was dominant in Europe but, of course, not in the overseas colonies. The wave of nationalism based on this principle swept through the Ottoman and Habsburg territories and instigated the formation of several new states in Eastern Europe and the Balkans. On the other hand, the Kurdish tribal elite in this period saw their identity and territoriality as based on the continuation of tribal authorities and territorial dominions. Their territoriality was not nationalistic as defined by European and Balkan separatist nationalists as well as the Armenians in the eastern territories of the Ottoman Empire.

Yet by the beginning of the twentieth century, and especially by the First World War era, the Kurdish political elite began to frame their goals within the generally accepted norms of legitimacy for statehood. These norms were not globally accepted but were resonant with Western states, whom Kurds felt the need to convince and from whom they needed to receive support. This is because these norms of legitimacy emerged in western states and were adopted by multilateral organisations and supra-state entities such as the League of Nations, and later the UN and the European Union. In the First World War period, some Kurdish political actors used Wilson's terminology of self-determination explicitly to make a case for Kurdish statehood. They also joined the frenzy of map-politics in the post-war negotiations and presented their map of Kurdistan, which was actually contested by rival Kurdish leaders. The huge number of self-determination demands across the world and the formation of new states in the ex-Ottoman and ex-Habsburg territories gave newly developing Kurdish nationalism and its representatives the hope of a Kurdish state, especially after the signing of the 1920 Treaty of Sèvres. However, these hopes were not realised, except for the creation of a short-lived Kurdish administrative area in Sulaymaniyah in Iraq under the British mandate.

The post–First World War world showed that Wilsonian self-determination was too ambitious and actually destabilising. From this time on, this form of self-determination was rarely used as a justification for new state formations. The implementation of self-determination was confined to Ottoman and Habsburg territories and dealing with demands elsewhere was left to the League of Nations. Yet, despite its limited usage in the First World War period, self-determination became an international principle enshrined in the UN Charter in 1945. It provided, in a different form, the normative context for the dismantling of western overseas colonial empires. The self-determination principle in this context was different from the Wilsonian version, however. It adopted the principle of *uti-possidetis*, which basically took the territorial boundaries of colonial administrative divisions as the territory of the new states. What defined this form of self-determination was independence from alien occupation and domination.

Following 1945, with the formation of new states in the 'third world', Kurdish demands for self-determination were on the rise again. Maps of Kurdistan were produced and used even more widely in this period by several Kurdish organisations in the region. Most of these maps constituted the basis of the greater map of Kurdistan used today. Kurdish nationalist organisations that emerged in the following decades explicitly framed their demands for independence within the decolonisation rhetoric. They argued that Kurdish people had been dominated by foreign states, which occupied and divided Kurdish territory. Marxist-socialist principles that underpinned anti-colonialist, anti-imperialist and leftist ideologies in the second half of the twentieth century inspired these organisations. These movements received material and political support from the Soviet Union, which even led to the creation of the first (albeit short-lived) Kurdish state, the Mahabad Republic, in 1946. Also, in the Cold War period, Kurds' understanding of territoriality began to transform from a tribal and local one to a nationalist one. However, unsurprisingly, multiple and different Kurdish tribal societies and political visions led to the emergence of disparate and multiple Kurdish territorialities.

Despite the influence of the Marxist ideology in the Cold War period, in the long run, the principles western states and multilateral organisations adopted and propagated provided the main framing context for Kurdish political goals. With the late 1980s and 1990s, a new set of rules of legitimacy emerged around state formation and were picked up on by Kurdish nationalists immediately. International documents started to frame self-determination in connection with the collective human and democratic rights of groups with a distinct identity, state behaviour and treatment of minorities. In line with this framing, Kurdish nationalist rhetoric started to transform from being a territory exploited and dominated by colonisers to a territory whose people are maltreated, and whose democratic and human rights are violated by the incumbent states. This was the rhetoric that was used in the post-1991 Iraq with regard to the Kurds. Kurds' maltreatment at the hands of the Iraqi regime under the Ba'ath Party was used as one of the justifications for gradually decreasing Baghdad's control in the north of Iraq. This process led to the emergence of de facto, and later de jure, autonomous Kurdish rule in northern Iraq.

The rhetoric of violation of human rights and democratic rights of ethnic communities as a justification for autonomy or separation demands was adopted particularly by Kurdish activists in the diaspora and disseminated back in the region. Diaspora Kurdish communities found a suitable environment that enabled them to cultivate their identity and mobilise among co-ethnics away from their homeland in liberal, ethnicity-aware and democratic states. In this period, both Kurdish activists in the diaspora as well as those in the region, combined their claim on the territoriality of the Kurdish people with their ethnic, human and democratic rights. According to this perspective, the dividedness of the territory of Kurdistan and the Kurdish people among regional states is the cause of the problems Kurdish people have faced throughout history and today.

Indeed, despite their divisions and despite not including the goal for greater Kurdistan in their goals, regional Kurdish political parties have not refrained from referring to the idea of greater Kurdistan as a general idea. Kurdish diaspora activists are more insistent on the idea of a unified Kurds and Kurdistan. They widely use the greater map of Kurdistan to represent Kurdish homeland and have been influential in promoting this map. The greater map of Kurdistan has become an effective tool for Kurdish nationalists for arguing that the Kurdish homeland is divided by regional states and this division is the source of Kurds' suffering at the hands of their home-states. Interestingly, these maps were used, most of the time unquestioningly, by non-Kurds as well since the 1990s for illustrative and demographic purposes and have become widely available online, showing the international traction the map has gained.

The continuous use of the map of greater Kurdistan by the Kurdish elite, political parties, nationalists and diaspora activists did not lead to a unification or coordination of the multiple and separate Kurdish political agendas and goals. The expectation that over time a pan-Kurdish movement would emerge has not come to fruition. The connections between different Kurdish factions up until today have been in the form of loose alliances, and in fact, sometimes tensions between them have led to intra-Kurd armed conflict. Only the PKK has forged some degree of transnational connections in the four states where Kurds are located. However, the PKK's transnational connections have led other Kurdish factions in each country to react to this party's activities and mobilisation. These factions have preferred to organise around locally emergent Kurdish parties and movements, rather than follow the PKK, who they believe is only really interested in the situation of the Kurds in Turkey.

The War in Syria and the related advances of Islamist militants in Syria and Iraq, however, instigated a new phase in Kurdish politics in the Middle East and led to the questioning of existing boundaries as never before. The interrogation of the viability of the First World War borders raised the hopes for Kurds to get another chance at independent statehood. Since the start of the Syrian War, there has been a considerable increase in Kurdish political actors' self-assertion as influential actors in Syria and neighbouring countries with Kurdish populations. Kurds in Iraq held an independence referendum in 2017, something Barzani's KDP has been considering since 2007, when it became clear that the Article 140 of the Iraqi Constitution on disputed territories was not to be implemented. Although the referendum received neither national nor international recognition, it showed that 92 per cent of voters (turnout was 72 per cent) supported an independent Kurdish state.

Among the developments in recent years that the Syrian War triggered, the most dramatic change in Kurdish politics has been the emergence of de facto Kurdish rule in northern Syria. The weakening of the Syrian regime's authority provided opportunities to Kurds to pursue their interests. The regime's forces partly withdrew from northern Syria, leading many to believe a tacit agreement not to fight each other had been struck. But as the authority and capacity of the state came under sustained attack, this restricted Damascus's ability to resist Kurdish progress towards self-rule or to strike bargains with the Kurds. By 2012, Kurds led by the PYD began taking control of the territory they call Rojava or western Kurdistan. However, the Syrian regime has not given up its sovereignty in northern Syria. It continues to pay the salaries of its public employees, and many Syrian state structures continue to receive their budgets from the government, weakening the Kurdish authorities' legitimacy (Sary 2016: 14).

Current State of Kurdish Nationalism

Tapping to the International Normative Frameworks

The Syrian War created opportunities for Kurds to push for the recognition of their rights on an international level too. Building on the notion that advancing the autonomy or independence of the Kurds is equivalent to advancing democratic and human rights, Kurds in each state pushed for greater rights in the fall-out from the Syrian conflict. Since the beginning of the uprisings, there have been significant changes in the political position of Kurds in each state. This was initially optimistically labelled as the 'Kurdish spring' (Gunter 2013). The momentum spread throughout the region and was used to frame developments in relations with the governments of Turkey, Syria and Iraq (less so in Iran). Main political parties in these countries increased demands for greater rights and framed their efforts as struggle for democratic rights.

Kurdish party leaders in all three states consciously position themselves as democratic forces in order to attract international support, particularly from the United States and Europe. In Syria, when the war began, and as the authority of the Syrian state collapsed, the PYD presented the administrative rule it established as bottom-up, democratic, inclusive and feminist (Çakır 2014), and its fight against ISIS as an example of resisting authoritarianism. These were used to promote the idea that Kurdish liberation is synonymous with enhancing democratic rights in the Middle East and to increase PYD's legitimacy among the population it controls and within the international community (Middle East Research Institute 2015; Kaya and Lowe 2017: 22).

In Iraq, the KRG has consistently argued that the Kurdish area outperforms the central government of Iraq in ensuring freedoms, democratic governance, minority and religious rights, and gender equality. The KRG adopts policies to show off their democratic credentials and often emphasise that remaining a part of Iraq hinders KRI's democratic, social and economic progress. They believe this legitimises and strengthens Kurds' autonomous status in Iraq, and even possibly justifies their secession from the Iraqi state. They pointed to the Iraqi government's inability to provide peace and stability and increased their demand for independent statehood and plans for holding a referendum, giving further momentum to the discourse of self-determination and its associated rights. In Turkey, the HDP adopted a progressive rhetoric. During its 2015 general election campaign, the party adopted an inclusive political agenda based on democratic and liberal freedoms, gender equality and environmentalism (HDP Election Manifesto 2015), and this expanded their electoral base in the June 2015 election.[1] Their thinking was that an increase in democratic rights for all in Turkey would inevitably improve the position of the Kurds.

Middle East in Crisis: What's Next for Kurdistan?

Kurdish groups, both within Syria and throughout the Middle East, saw the Syrian war as an opportunity to advance their goals. The de facto Kurdish autonomous region of Rojava, now known as DFNS, is held up as proving the viability and necessity of Kurdish self-rule within any future Syria.[2] Some experts interpreted the emergence of Rojava as the first step for the possible unification of Kurds in Iraq and Syria (Spyer 2013). Developments since the war in Syria, it is argued, have transformed greater Kurdistan into a subsystem that co-exists with the regional state system that erodes the regional state dynamic (Bengio 2014). The turmoil and cracks in the Arab societies since 2011 are seen to stand in opposition to a 'growing tendency towards trans-border cooperation and unity' in the Kurdish case (Bengio 2014: 281).

There is no doubt that the state actors in the region felt shaken by the changing dynamics and increased Kurdish assertiveness. The Kurdish actors, especially the PYD, gained some international legitimacy as a Syrian Kurdish actor due to its presence at the forefront of resistance to ISIS. However, the resilience of the state system and international support for the maintenance of the existing borders continues. The PYD's position remains precarious (Lowe 2014: 230–3), as recent years have shown. Already uncomfortable with the de facto Kurdish autonomy across its borders in Syria, the Turkish government became even more disturbed by the US alliance with the PYD and its YPG forces because of the connections between the PYD and the PKK. Eventually, the Turkish army carried out two military operations in Syria in 2016 and 2018 (ongoing as of August 2018) against both

[1]   The talks between the PKK and the Turkish government were ongoing in the two
      years before the election. This contributed to the positive public response to the
      HDP among the Turkish public.
[2]   Al Jazeera, 17 March 2016.

Islamist terrorist groups and the PYD. This put the United States in an awkward position. Donald Trump wishes to withdraw from Syria, and if this is followed through, and if the Syrian government led by Assad further strengthens its power and control, the precariousness of the PYD will further increase.

In many respects, the Syrian War has exposed the heterogeneous and competing perspectives and interests of different Kurdish groups and political parties. Barzani's KDP saw the emergence of another de facto Kurdish region in Syria under the PYD, a party considered as affiliated to the PKK, as a threat rather than a positive development on the way to a larger Kurdistan. The emergence of a new Kurdish rule with a distinct ideology, political disposition, governance structure and different relations with other regional actors to the KRI further deepened existing political and ideological divisions between two of the main Kurdish parties in the Middle East, namely the PKK and the KDP. Rather than binding Kurds into some kind of mythical homogeneous group, the Syrian War added momentum to related but distinct Kurdish political projects in each state, thus increasing competition within and among these groups (Kaya and Whiting 2017).

The two groups have different visions for the future of the Kurds within each state as well as in the region as a whole and for how Kurds should govern themselves. Responses by these two Kurdish factions throughout the Middle East to the emergence of Rojava highlight how the ripples of the Syrian war led to intra-Kurdish discord at the elite level. Rojava disrupted the existing balance between these factions as they tried to influence developments in the region in their own interests.

The main friction between the PKK and KDP after the war in Syria took place over which side Syrian Kurds would take part with. In this sense, Kurds outside Syria tried to extend their influence inside the country. In fact, the Kurdish political scene in Syria until the start of the war was sharply divided into different camps, supported by either the KDP/PUK in Iraq or the PKK in Turkey. In its attempts to shape developments in northern Syria, the PKK drew on its close relationship with the PYD and its armed group the YPG to further increase its influence across the border. The KDP, on the other hand, initiated the formation of the Kurdish National Council in Syria (KNC) in 2011 and argued that Syria's Kurds should join the heterogeneous official opposition against the Syrian regime (Ateş 2012). The PYD initially joined the KNC but later withdrew and emerged with a different understanding of the situation on the ground (Van Wilgenburg 2013), instead coming to be seen as an affiliate of the PKK.

The PYD became the most effective Kurdish party in offering protection to people in northern Syria. This was possible due to the existing cross-border links between the PKK and the Syrian Kurds, which the PKK has been developing for decades. The PYD established de facto control of the area and gradually expanded its territorial control. Throughout this process, the KNC became increasingly side-lined, much to the KDP's and Turkey's disappointment (Bakir 2012). The PYD declared that they chose a third way, not taking part in the opposition or pro-Assad groups, and later pulling various like-minded Kurdish groups around it to build a de facto autonomous zone. In that sense, in terms of controlling the developments in northern Syria, the KDP lost to PKK.

The emergence of Rojava has also revealed the differences, even contradictions, between the KDP's and PKK's vision of a Kurdish future in the Middle East. The Syrian conflict greatly increased the power of the PYD and the PKK to challenge their vision of what Kurdish self-rule should look like. No longer is the Kurdish government in Iraq the automatic rallying point for Kurds looking for a governing figure or ruling spokesperson. Rojava increased the appeal of the PKK's ideology among Kurds and sat uncomfortably next to the KDP model. The playing out of these divisions between the KDP and the PKK can be seen in how both movements tried to influence the debate over Kurdish political parties in Syria during the course of the war.

Rojava's governance style manifested Öcalan's political ideology in practice as opposed to the Iraqi Kurdish model. The PYD tends to share the vision of the PKK, whose leaders strongly endorse the Rojava experiment and whose supporters hold it up as a living example of 'democratic confederalism'. From this perspective, Rojava is seen as the beginning of the adoption and implementation of this governing system in other parts of the Middle East. Before Rojava, Öcalan's ideology and system of democratic confederalism was just an idea that was limited to the way the PKK and its affiliated parties ran their affairs. However, the emergence of Rojava or DFNS, its ability to survive for almost seven years rendered the PKK's ideology a reality. This was in the form of a bottom-up, decentralized and gender-equal, but also quite doctrinaire and radical, model that envisions a post-nation-state system in the Middle East not only for Kurds but for all regional peoples.

The KDP in Iraq, on the other hand, sticks to a more conventional nation-state formation route that emphasises the self-determination of an ethnic community. It is similar to the Middle Eastern state model where authoritarianism, a centralised state, and tribal and economic elites are interlinked with the political elite. While the PKK and PYD both adopt an approach of pursuing democratic confederalism within the existing states' borders (with Syrian Kurds coming much closer to realising this than Turkey's Kurds), Iraqi Kurdish leaders pursue a project of partition and independence (Jongerden and Akkaya 2015: 1–5). Tensions arise when these projects come into opposition with each other.

At the ideological and political levels, the Rojava experiment implemented by the PYD has huge implications for Kurdish politics in Turkey. Developments in Rojava have emboldened the PKK and Kurdish politicians in Turkey. The talks between the government and Öcalan in Turkey, and the surrounding public discussion, often referred to the Rojava experiment as an example of Öcalan's democratic confederalism. However, the Turkish government is deeply reluctant to see a continuous Kurdish belt along its border and has lobbied hard to prevent this emerging in Syria in addition to the already existing one in northern Iraq. In order to prevent this, it has militarily intervened in Syria since January 2018. It sought to shape the Kurdish political landscape in Syria and used its leverage with Kurdish parties in Iraq to limit the possibilities for the PKK. On the other hand, the Turkish government has accepted Kurdish autonomy in Iraq in part because a powerful KRG in Iraq poses a challenge to the PKK's hegemony over Kurdish nationalism by offering an alternative source of leadership (Cagaptay, Fidan and Sacikara 2015; Wood 2015).

Cross-border Opportunities for Kurds

Despite the deep structural, political and ideological divisions explained earlier, there is no doubt that throughout the Syrian War, cross-border interactions between different Kurdish groups have increased. It would indeed be a mistake to claim that the Syrian war did not result in any increased sense of kinship or cooperation whatsoever between Kurdish communities and their leaders in different countries. It is well established that transnational ethnic ties can increase during conflict, even increasing the risk of conflict in neighbouring countries due to a heightened sense of kinship (Cederman, Girardin & Gleditsch 2009). Moreover, sometimes developments in ethnic conflict in one state can influence the conflict in relation to a co-ethnic group across the border in another state and give incentives to the states to address issues within their borders (Gurses 2014: 251). Signs of stronger solidarity among the Kurds at the community level across the region were clearly observable through protests, aid campaigns, the fight against ISIS and others. Solidarity was also evident in the unprecedented and concrete collaboration between different Kurdish political factions.

One of the most significant examples is the siege of Kobane, a city on the Syrian-Turkish border, by the Islamic State in mid-2014. The siege was resisted by militants from the Kurdish YPG and YPJ. The effects reverberated throughout the region, rallying Kurds from other states around the suffering of their co-ethnics, especially Kurds in nearby southeast Turkey. The HDP in Turkey called on international and local actors to help stop the violence and suffering. It also urged people to take to the streets, declaring, 'From now on everywhere is Kobani' (*Hürriyet*, 6 October 2016). The KRG sent Peshmerga forces there with heavy weapons to aid in the fight. The Ankara government reluctantly gave permission for KRG's forces to cross through Turkish territory while carrying arms, having initially denied the request and suggested the Free Syrian Army provide support instead. This was one of the rare occasions where Iraqi and Syrian Kurds (and PKK fighters fighting as YPG militants) took up arms together. The siege was defeated with the support of US air bombardment. The Kobane event led Syrian Kurdish parties, including those close to Barzani's KDP, to sign an agreement to cooperate militarily and politically against ISIS. Barzani welcomed the increased cooperation, declaring: 'This agreement brings us together, and itself is a significant answer to enemies who did not intend the Kurds to be united' (*Rudaw*, 22 October 2014).

Greater Kurdish unity was also on display during efforts to repel ISIS from the Sinjar Mountains. Following a brutal massacre of the Yazidis, declared by the UN as meeting the official definitions of genocide (Wintour 2016), at least 130,000 Yazidis had fled to Duhok and Erbil in the Kurdistan-Iraq. PKK and YPG fighters, as well as some from Iranian Kurdish opposition groups based in the KRI came to the aid of Yazidis, and later fought together with KDP and local Yazidi forces against ISIS. In an acknowledgement of the contribution of these fighters to retaking Makhmour, where ISIS had a stronghold, Barzani visited the PKK camp in August to meet with senior commanders (Salih 2014). These events were optimistically labelled by some Kurdish commentators as the starting point towards unification (Keskin 2014). However, after the defeat of ISIS in Sinjar, Kurdish groups fell into a bitter rivalry over the control of the area, each flying its own battle flag (Salih 2015).

These examples combined with significant geopolitical changes in the Middle East brought to mind the questions of whether the historical tide was turning in favour of the Kurds and whether these developments could be considered stepping stones to new Kurdish autonomous regions or states, or even pan-Kurdistan as illustrated on the map of greater Kurdistan. Opportunities for collaboration as in Kobane and Sinjar discussed, however, were high points that were not sustained. Ethnic communities are indeed not singular entities (Brubaker 2004) and increased transnational solidarity at the grassroots level and some degree of strategic alliance between Kurdish political parties during this period did not automatically translate into greater cooperation and harmony of tactics and goals. Instead, the differences between the main Kurdish political parties in their visions of the rightful future of Kurds in the Middle East and in their political projects and struggles have become increasingly stark (Kaya and Whiting 2017: 79). This renders the idea of greater pan-Kurdish harmony, coordination and the idea of a united Kurdish future on the imagined territory of greater Kurdistan quite slim.

The Idea of Greater Kurdistan vs Fragmented State of the Kurds

Recent developments in the Middle East once again showed the long-existing contradiction between the promotion of Kurdish territoriality as represented on the greater map of Kurdistan and the political reality and heterogeneity on the ground. Indeed, the position of Kurds in the Middle East has changed significantly as a result of the conflict in Syria, such as the emergence of Rojava as an autonomous region of Kurdish self-rule within Syria. Kurds have sought to use the conflict as an opportunity to push for greater rights within the states in which they reside and to frame themselves as being at the forefront of democracy in the Middle East. They have further increased their reference to the normative frameworks around democracy, human and cultural rights, gender equality and environmentalism.

Some commentators in the region also expected (or in some cases feared) that the conflict would engender greater Kurdish unity and lead to a clear harmonisation of Kurds throughout the Middle East around a unified push for self-rule in greater Kurdistan. However, Kurds have always been a remarkably heterogeneous group and claims of the existence of a Kurdish people united by their ethnic identity and territoriality have always been out of step with reality. The fallout from the Syrian war has highlighted the Kurds' diversity and competing interests. It further revealed and deepened the strategic, ideological and political divisions. While increased unity between the PKK and PYD is a by-product of the conflict, the conflict in Syria also resulted in increasing division between Iraqi Kurds and their Turkish counterparts.

It is important to note that the lack of a unified Kurdish nationalism and existence of different perspectives, ideologies and future plans is not necessarily a weakness as usually perceived. Its perceived weakness derives from the embeddedness of the rhetoric of nation-building and national representation in national and international discourses. However, the divided nature of Kurdish nationalism and the particularism that has defined the Kurdish psyche and political activities could also be considered as a strength. This has enabled Kurdish political actors to adapt themselves to different local, regional and international circumstances they found themselves in and benefit from these circumstances, and to maintain and consolidate their particular characteristics. Each Kurdish group have developed increasingly sophisticated relationships with other political groups in their states, with the other state institutions and governments and the international community. The nature of these relationships and interactions were framed and shaped by the wider developments in international politics and normative frameworks. As a result, a rich and dynamic flora of multiple Kurdish existences have emerged.

Nonetheless, the message the map of greater Kurdistan gives – the idea of the Kurdishness of the territory it depicts – does not appear to be hampered by these different visions and divisions on the ground. Quite exceptionally, throughout history, the idea of a greater Kurdistan emerged and sustained itself despite the divisions. The source of the prevalence of the idea of greater Kurdistan comes from separate Kurdish groups promoting it, but not in a united and concerted way, from the efforts of the transnational diaspora networks in promoting a pan-Kurdish idea, and from the international normative framework that is conducive for the reception of such territorial assertions, but maybe not for their realisation. Therefore, even though a greater Kurdistan may take a long time to realise, or may never realise, the idea of greater Kurdistan and its map is unlikely to lose its appeal as long as existing conceptions of the people–territory relationship and the dominant norms of legitimate statehood in international politics remain unchanged.

Bibliography

Abrahamian, Ervand. (1979). Iran in revolution: The opposition forces. *Middle East Research and Information Project*, 75/76, 3–8.

Adamson, Fiona. (2006). Crossing borders: International migration and national security. *International Security*, 31(1), 165–199.

Adamson, Fiona & Demetriou, M. (2007). Remapping the boundaries of 'state' and 'national identity': Incorporating diasporas into IR theorizing. *European Journal of International Relations*, 13(4), 489–526.

Adler, E. (1997). Seizing the middle ground: Constructivism in world politics. *European Journal of International Relations*, 3(3), 319–363.

Agnew, John. (1994). The territorial trap: The geographical assumptions of international relations theory. *Review of International Political Economy*, 1(1), 53–80.

Agnew, John A., Livingstone, David & Rogers, Alisdair (eds.). (1996). *Human Geography: An Essential Anthology*. Oxford: Blackwell Publishers.

Ahmad, Kamal Madhar. (1994). *Kurdistan during the First World War*. London: Saqi.

Aksin, Sina. (2007). *Turkey: From Empire to Revolutionary Republic*. London: Hurst.

Allsopp, Harriet. (2017). Kurdish political parties and the Syrian uprising. In Gareth Stansfield & Mohammed Shareef, eds., *The Kurdish Question Revisited*. London: Hurst, pp. 289–306.

Allsopp, Harriet. (2014). *The Kurds of Syria: Political Parties and Identity in the Middle East*. London: I.B. Tauris.

Anderson, Benedict. (2001). Western nationalism and eastern nationalism: Is there a difference that matters? *New Left Review*, 9(May–June), 31–42.

Anderson, Benedict. (1994). Exodus. *Critical Inquiry*, 20(2), 314–327.

Anderson, Benedict. (1991). *Imagined Communities: Reflections on the Origins and Spread of Nationalism*. London: Verso.

Anderson, James. (1988). Nationalist ideology and territory. In R. J. Johnston, D. B. Knight & E. Kofman, eds., *Nationalism, Self-Determination and Political Geography*. London: Croom Helm, pp.18–39.

Andrews, F. David (ed.). (1982). *The Lost Peoples of the Middle East: Documents of the Struggle for Survival and Independence of the Kurds, Assyrians, and Other Minority Races in the Middle East*. Salisbury: Documentary Publications.

Arat, Zehra F. (1991). *Democracy and Human Rights in Developing Countries*. Lincoln, CO: Lynne Rienner Publishers.

Arfa, H. (1966). *The Kurds: A Historical and Political Study*. London: Oxford University Press.

Aslan, M. A. (1988). *Mülteci Kürtler* [Refugee Kurds]. Ankara: Demokrasi.

Ateş, Sabri. (2014). In the name of the caliph and the nation: The Sheikh Ubeidullah Rebelion of 1880–81. *Iranian Studies*, 47(5), 735–798.

Ateş, Sabri. (2013). *The Ottoman-Iranian Borderlands: Making a Boundary 1843–1914*. New York: Cambridge University Press.

Ateş, Sabri. (2006). Empires at the Margin: Towards a History of the Ottoman-Iranian Borderland and Borderland Peoples (PhD thesis, New York University).

Bajalan, Djene Rhys. (2013). Early Kurdish 'nationalists' and the emergence of modern Kurdish identity politics: 1851–1908. In Fevzi Bilgin & Ali Sarihan, eds., *Understanding Turkey's Kurdish Question*. Lanham, MD: Lexington Books, pp. 3–28.

Bajalan, Djene Rhys. (2012). Şeref Xan's *Sharafnama*: Kurdish ethno-politics in the early modern world, its meaning and its legacy. *Iranian Studies*, 45 (6), 795–818.

Bakir, Ali Hüseyin. 'Türkiye'nin Suriye krizi hesapları ve Kürtler [Turkey's Calculations on the Syrian Crisis and the Kurds]', Al Jazeera Turk, 3 October 2012, www.aljazeera.com.tr/haber-analiz/turkiyenin-suriye-krizi-hesaplari-ve-kurtler.

Banai, A. (2014). The territorial rights of legitimate states: A pluralist interpretation. *International Theory*, 6(1), 140–157.

Banai, A., Moore, M., Miller, D., Nine, C. & Dietrich, F. (2014). Introduction: Theories of territory beyond Westphalia. *International Theory*, 6(1), 98–104.

Barkey, Henry J. & Fuller, G. E. (1998). *Turkey's Kurdish Question*. Lanham, MD: Rowman & Littlefield.

Barkin, J. Samuel & Cronin, Bruce. (1994). The state and the nation: Changing norms and the rules of sovereignty in international relations. *International Organization*, 48(1), 107–130.

Başer, Bahar. (2014). The awakening of a latent diaspora: The political mobilization of first and second generation Turkish migrants in Sweden. *Ethnopolitics*, 13(4), 355–376.

Başer, Bahar. (2013). The Kurdish diaspora in Europe: Identity formation and political activism. Boğaziçi University – TUSIAD Foreign Policy Forum, Research Report.

Bengio, Ofra. (2014). Conclusion: The Kurdish momentum. In O. Bengio, ed., *Kurdish Awakening: Nation Building in a Fragmented Homeland*. Austin, TX: University of Texas Press, pp. 269–282.

Benton, Lauren A. (2010). *A Search for Sovereignty: Law and Geography in European Empires, 1400–1900*. New York: Cambridge University Press.

Bishai, Linda. (2004). *Forgetting Ourselves: Secession and the Impossibility of Territorial Identity*. Maryland, MD: Lexington Books.

Black, Jeremy. (2000). *Maps and Politics*. London: University of Chicago Press.

Blau, Joyce. (2006). Refinement and oppression of Kurdish language. In Faleh A. Jabar & Hosham Dawod, eds., *The Kurds: Nationalism and Politics*. London: Saqi, pp. 103–112.

Bose, Sumantra. (2003). The implications of ethno-national conflict. In *Freedom in the World*. New York: Freedom House, pp. 19–28.

Bozarslan, H. (2003). Kurdish nationalism in Turkey: From tacit contract to rebellion. In A. Vali, ed., *Essays on the Origins of Kurdish Nationalism*. Costa Mesa, CA: Mazda, pp. 163–190.

Breuilly, J. (2001). The state and nationalism. In M. Guibernau & J. Hutchinson, eds., *Understanding Nationalism*. Cambridge: Polity, pp. 32–52.

Breuilly, John. (1993). *Nationalism and the State*. Manchester: Manchester University Press.

Brownlie, I. (1988). The rights of peoples in international law. In J. Crawford, ed., *The Rights of Peoples*. Oxford: Clarendon Press, pp. 1–16.

Brubaker, B. (2004). *Ethnicity without Groups*. London: Harvard University Press.

Brubaker, R. (2005). The 'diaspora' diaspora. *Ethnic and Racial Studies*, 28 (1), 1–19.

Buchanan, A. E. (2003). *Justice, Legitimacy, and Self-Determination: Moral Foundations for International Law*. Oxford: Oxford University Press.

Cagaptay, S., Fidan, C. B. & Sacikara, E. C. (2015). Turkey and the KRG: An undeclared economic commonwealth. *Policy Analysis*, The Washington Institute, www.washingtoninstitute.org/policy-analysis/view/turkey-and-the-krg-an-undeclared-economic-commonwealth

Calhoun, C. (2007). *Nations Matter: Culture, History and the Cosmopolitan Dream*. London: Routledge.

Çandar, Cengiz. (2009). The Kurdish question: The reasons and fortunes of the 'opening'. *Insight Turkey*, 11(4), 13–19.

Castellino, Joshua. (2000). *International Law and Self-Determination: The Integrity of the Politics of Territorial Possession with Formulations of Post-Colonial 'National' Identity*. The Hague: Martinus Nijhoff Publishers.

Castellino, Joshua. (1999). Territory and identity in international law: The struggle for self-determination in the Western Sahara. *Millennium: Journal of International Studies*, 28(3), 523–551.

Cederman, L., Girardin, L. & Gleditsch, K. S. (2009). Ethnonationalist triads: Assessing the influence of kin groups on civil wars. *World Politics*, 61(3), 403–437.

Çelik, A. B. & Rumelili, B. (2006). Necessary but not sufficient: The role of the EU in resolving Turkey's Kurdish question and the Greek-Turkish conflicts. *European Foreign Affairs Review*, 11(2), 203–222.

Chaliand, Gerard. (1994). *The Kurdish Tragedy*. London: Zed.

Charountaki, M. (2011). *The Kurds and US Foreign Policy: International Relations in the Middle East since 1945*. London: Routledge.

Clifford, J. (1994). Diasporas. *Cultural Anthropology*, 9(3), 302–338.

Cobban, A. (1969). *The Nation State and National Self-Determination*. London: Collins.

Cobban, A. (1945). *National Self-Determination*. Oxford: Oxford University Press.

Cohen, R. (1997). *Global Diasporas: An Introduction*. London: UCL Press.

Cohen, R. (1996). Diasporas and the nation-state: From victims to challengers. *International Affairs*, 72(3), 507–520.

Crampton, Jeremy W. (2001). Maps as social constructions: Power, communication and visualization. *Progress in Human Geography*, 25(2), 235–252.

Crampton, Jeremy W. & Krygier, J. (2006). An introduction to critical cartography. *ACME: An International E-Journal for Critical Geographies*, 4(1), 11–33.

Crawford, J. (1979). *The Creation of States in International Law*. Oxford: Clarendon.

Culcasi, K. (2010). Locating Kurdistan: Contextualizing the region's ambiguous boundaries. In A. C. Diener & J. Hagen, eds., *Borderlines and Borderlands: Political Oddities at the Edge of the Nation-State*. Lanham, MD: Rowman & Littlefield Publishers, pp. 107–120.

Culcasi, Karen. (2006). Cartographically constructing Kurdistan within geopolitical and orientalist discourses. *Political Geography*, 25(6), 680–706.

Cumings, B. (1999). Still the American century. *Review of International Studies*, 25(5), 271–299.

Dahl, Robert A. (1971). *Polyarchy: Participation and Opposition*. New Haven, CT: Yale University Press.

Diamond, Larry & Plattner, Marc F. (eds.). (1994). *Nationalism, Ethnic Conflict and Democracy*. Baltimore, MD: John Hopkins University Press.

Dinç, N. K. (2009). Kadim anavatandan bir inkar coğrafyasına [From ancient homeland to the geography of denial]. *Toplum ve Kuram*, 2 (Fall), 151–173.

Eccarius-Kelly, V. (2008). Interpreting the PKK's signals in Europe. *Perspectives on Terrorism*, 2(11), 10–14.

Edmonds, C. J. (1971). Kurdish nationalism. *Journal of Contemporary History*, 6(1), 87–106.

Elden, Stuart. (2013). *The Birth of Territory*. Chicago, IL: University of Chicago Press.

Elden, Stuart. (2010). Land, terrain, territory. *Progress in Human Geography*, 34(6), 799–817.

Elphinston, William G. (1946). The Kurdish questions. *International Affairs*, 22(1), 91–103.

Entessar, Nader. (2009). *Kurdish Politics in the Middle East*. Lanham, MD: Lexington Books.

Entessar, N. (1992). *Kurdish Ethnonationalism*. Boulder, CO: Lynne Rienner.

Eppel, Michael. (2016). *A People without a State: The Kurds from the Rise of Islam to the Dawn of Nationalism*. Austin, TX: University of Texas Press.

Evliya, Çelebi. (2011). *Evliya Çelebi Seyahatnamesi*, 10 Volumes, Translated from Ottoman Turkish by M. Çevik. Istanbul: Üçdal Neşriyat.

Fabry, M. (2010). *Recognizing States: International Society and the Establishment of New States since 1776*. Oxford: Oxford University Press.

Franck, T. M. (1997). Tribe, nation, world: Self-identification in the evolving international system. *Ethics and International Affairs*, 11(1), 151–169.

Franck, T. M. (1993). Postmodern tribalism and the right to secession. In C. Brölmann, R. Lefeber & M. Zieck, eds., *Peoples and Minorities in International Law*. Dordrecht: Martinus Nijhoff, pp. 3–29.

Freeden, Michael. (1998). *Ideologies and Political Theory: A Conceptual Approach*. Oxford: Clarendon Press.

Fukuyama, Francis. (2006). *The End of History and the Last Man*. New York: Free Press.

Fukuyama, Francis. (1994). Comments on nationalism and democracy. In Larry Diamond & Marc F. Plattner, eds., *Nationalism, Ethnic Conflict and Democracy*. Baltimore, MD: John Hopkins University Press, pp. 23–28.

Galip, B. O. (2015). *Imagining Kurdistan: Identity, Culture and Society*. London: I. B. Tauris.

Gellner, E. (2006). *Nations and Nationalism*, 2nd edn. Oxford: Blackwell.

Gellner, E. (2000). Do nations have navels? *Nations and Nationalism*, 2(3), 366–370.

Gerson, G. & Rubin, A. (2015). Cultural nationalism and liberal values: An elusive synthesis. *International Political Science Review*, 36(2), 197–213.

Griffiths, M. (2003). Self-determination, international society and world order. *Macquarie Law Journal*, 3, 29–49.

Griffiths, R. (2014). Secession and the invisible hand of the international system. *Review of International Studies*, 40(3), 559–581.

Gunter, Michael. (2013). The Kurdish spring. *Third World Quarterly*, 34(3), 441–457.

Gunter, Michael. (2011a). *The Kurds Ascending: The Evolving Solution to the Kurdish Problem in Iraq and Turkey*, 2nd edn. Basingstoke: Palgrave Macmillan.

Gunter, Michael. (2011b). The five stages of American foreign policy towards the Kurds. *Insight Turkey*, 13(2), 93–106.

Gurses, Mehmet. (2014). From war to democracy: Transborder Kurdish conflict and democratisation. In D. Romano & M. Gurses, eds., *Conflict, Democratization and the Kurds in the Middle East: Turkey, Iran, Iraq and Syria*. New York: Palgrave Macmillan, pp. 249–265.

Hakan, Sinan. (2007). *Osmanli Arsiv Belgelerinde Kurtler ve Kurt Direnisleri (1817–1867)* [Kurds and Kurdish Rebellions in the Ottoman Archival Documents (1817–1867)]. Istanbul: Doz Yayincilik.

Halhalli, Bekir. (2018). Kurdish political parties in Syria: Past struggles and future expectations. In E. E. Tugdar & S. Al, eds., *Comparative Politics in the Middle East: Actors, Ideas and Interests*. Springer, pp. 27–53.

Halliday, F. (2006). Can we write a modernist history of Kurdish nationalism? In F. A. Jabar & H. Dawod, eds., *The Kurds: Nationalism and Politics*. London: Saqi, pp. 11–20.

Halliday, F. (2000). *Nation and Religion in the Middle East*. London: Saqi.

Halliday, F. (1994). *Rethinking International Relations*. London: MacMillan.

Halperin, M., Sheffer, D. & Small, P. (1992). *Self-Determination in the New World Order*. Washington, DC: Carnegie Endowment for International Peace.

Hani, Ahmedi. (2016). *Mem û Zîn*, Translated to Turkish by I. Sunkur. Ankara: Sitav Yayınevi.

Hannum, H. (1996). *Autonomy, Sovereignty and Self-Determination: The Accommodation of Conflicting Rights*. Philadelphia, PA: University of Pennsylvania Press.

Harley, J. B. (2002). *The New Nature of Maps: Essays in the History of Cartography*. Baltimore, MD: Johns Hopkins University Press.

Harley, J. B. (1989). Historical geography and the cartographic illusion. *Journal of Historical Geography*, 15(1): 80–91.

Harley, J. B. & Woodward, D. (1987). *The History of Cartography*. Chicago: The University of Chicago Press.

Hassan, Hassan. (2017). The battle for Raqqa and the challenges after liberation. *CTC Sentinel*, 10(6), 1–10.

Hassanpour, Amir. (2003). The making of Kurdish identity: Pre-20th century historical and literary sources. In A. Vali, ed., *Essays on the Origins of Kurdish Nationalism*. Costa Mesa, CA: Mazda, pp. 106–162.

Hassanpour, Amir. (1998). Satellite footprints as national borders: MED-TV and the extraterritoriality of state sovereignty. *Journal of Muslim Minority Affairs*, 18(1), 53–72.

Hassanpour, Amir. (1992). *Nation and Language in Kurdistan, 1918–1985*. San Francisco, CA: Mellen Research University Press.

Hechter, M. (1998). *Internal Colonialism: The Celtic Fringe in British National Development*. New York: Routledge.

Held, David, McGrew, A., Goldblatt, D. & Perraton, J. (1999). *Global Transformations: Politics, Economics and Culture*. Cambridge: Polity Press.

Helmreich, Paul C. (1974). *From Paris to Sèvres: The Partition of the Ottoman Empire at the Peace Conference of 1919–1920*. Columbus, OH: Ohio State University Press.

Heper, Metin. (2007). *The State and Kurds in Turkey: The Question of Assimilation*. New York: Palgrave Macmillan.

Heraclides, Alexis. (1997). Ethnicity, secessionist conflict and the international society. *Nations and Nationalism*, 3(4), 493–520.

Higgins, R. (1993). *Problems and Process: International Law and How We Use It*. Oxford: Clarendon Press.

Hiltermann, J. R. (2007). *A Poisonous Affair: America, Iraq, and the Gassing of Halabja*. New York: Cambridge University Press.

Hobsbawm, E. J. & Ranger, T. O. (1983). *The Invention of Tradition*. Cambridge: Cambridge University Press.

Horowitz, D. L. (2000). *Ethnic Groups in Conflict*. Berkeley, CA: University of California Press.

Horowitz, D. L. (1994). Democracy in divided societies. In L. Diamond & M. F. Plattner, eds., *Nationalism, Ethnic Conflict and Democracy*. Baltimore, MD: John Hopkins University Press, pp. 35–55.

House, Edward Mandell & Seymour, Charles (eds.). (1921). *What Really Happened at Paris, the Story of the Peace Conference 1918–19 / by American Delegates*. London.

Houston, C. (2008). *Kurdistan: Crafting of National Selves*. Bloomington, IN: Indiana University Press.

Ibrahim, Ferhad and Gürbey, Gülistan (eds.). (2000). *The Kurdish Conflict in Turkey: Obstacles and Chances for Peace and Democracy*. New York: St. Martin's Press.

İnalcık, H. (2007). *Osmanlı İmparatorluğu Klasik Çağ (1300–1600)*. Istanbul: Yapı Kredi Yayınları.

Izady, M. R. (1992). *The Kurds: A Concise Handbook*. Washington, DC: Taylor and Francis International Publishers.

Jabar, Falah A. & Dawod, Hosham (eds.). (2006). *The Kurds: Nationalism and Politics*. London: Saqi.

James, Alan. (1999).The practice of sovereign statehood in contemporary international society. *Political Studies*, 47(3), 457–473.

Jennings, Ivor. (1956). *The Approach to Self-Government*. Cambridge: Cambridge University Press.

Jongerden, Joost. (2017). The Kurdistan Workers' Party (PKK): Radical democracy and the right to self-determination beyond the nation-state. In Gareth Stansfield & Mohammed Shareef, eds., *The Kurdish Question Revisited*. London: Hurst, pp. 275–600, 245–258.

Jongerden, Joost & Akkaya, A. H. (2015). Kurds and the PKK. *The Wiley Blackwell Encyclopaedia of Race, Ethnicity and Nationalism*, 2015 (online).

Jwaideh, Wadie. (2006). *Kurdish National Movement: Its Origins and Development*. New York: Syracuse University Press.

Kacowicz, Ariel M. (1994). *Peaceful Territorial Change*. Columbia, SC: University of South Carolina.

Kadercan, Burak. (2015). Triangulating territory: A case for pragmatic interaction between political science, political geography, and critical IR. *International Theory*, 7(1), 135–161.

Kaya, Zeynep N. & Lowe, Robert. (2017). The curious question of the PYD-PKK relationship. In Gareth Stansfield & Mohammed Shareef, eds., *The Kurdish Question Revisited*. London: Hurst, pp. 275–600.

Kaya, Zeynep N. & Whiting, Matthew. (2019). The HDP, the AKP and the battle for Turkish democracy. *Ethnopolitics*, 18(1), 92–106.

Kaya, Zeynep N. & Whiting, Matthew. (2017). Sowing division: Kurds in the Syrian War. *Middle East Policy*, 24(1), 79–91.

Keskin, Necat. A Starting Point towards Unification between Kurds: Peshmerga to Kobani, *Ekurd Daily*, 31 October 2014, http://ekurd.net/m ismas/articles/misc2014/10/syriakurd1628.htm.

Kessler, Peter. First Iranian refugees go home under UNHCR auspices. UNHCR News. 16 July 2002. www.unhcr.org/news/latest/2002/7/3d343 a8a4/first-iranian-refugees-iraq-home-under-unhcr-auspices.html

Khayati, K. (2008). From victim diaspora to transborder citizenship? Diaspora formation and transnational relations among Kurds in France and Sweden, PhD Diss., Linköping University.

King, Diane E. (2013). *Kurdistan on the Global Stage: Kinship, Land and Community in Iraq*. New Brunswick, NJ: Rutgers University Press.

King, D. E. (2008). Back from the 'outside': Returnees and diasporic imagining in Iraqi Kurdistan. *International Journal on Multicultural Societies*, 10(2), 208–222.

Kirişçi, Kemal & Winrow, G. M. (1997). *The Kurdish Question and Turkey: An Example of a Trans-state Ethnic Conflict*. London: Frank Cass.

Klein, Janet. (2007). Kurdish nationalists and non-nationalist Kurdists: Rethinking minority nationalism and the dissolution of the Ottoman Empire, 1908–9. *Nations and Nationalism*, 13(1), 135–153.

Knight, David B. (1985). Territory and people or people and territory? Thoughts on postcolonial self-determination. *International Political Science Review*, 6(2), pp. 248–272.

Köhler, W. (1989). *Evliya Çelebi Seyahatnamesinde Bitlis ve Halkı*, Translated from German by H. Işık. Istanbul: Alan Yayıncılık.

Kohn, H. (1929). *A History of Nationalism in the East*, Translated by M. Green. London: Routledge.

Krasner, Stephen D. (2001). Rethinking the sovereign state model. In Michael Cox, Tim Dunne & Ken Booth, eds., *Empires, Systems and States: Great Transformations in International Politics*. Cambridge: Cambridge University Press, pp. 17–42.

Krasner, Stephen D. (1999). *Sovereignty: Organized Hypocrisy*. Princeton, NJ: Princeton University Press.

Kurt, Mehmet. (2017). *Kurdish Hizbullah in Turkey: Islamism, Violence and the State*. London: Pluto Press.

Kymlicka, Will. (1989). *Liberalism, Community and Culture*. Oxford: Clarendon Press.

Laclau, E. & Mouffe, C. (2001). *Hegemony and Socialist Strategy: Towards a Radical Democratic Politics*, 2nd edn. London: Verso.

Lansing, Robert. (1921). *The Peace Negotiations: A Personal Narrative*. Boston: Houghton Miffin.

Laughlin, Jim Mac. (1986). The political geography of 'nation-building and nationalism in social sciences: Structural vs. dialectical accounts. *Political Geography Quarterly*, 5(4), 299–329.

Lazarev, M. S. & Mıhoyan, Ş. X. (2001). *Kürdistan Tarihi* [The History of Kurdistan]. Translated from Russian to Turkish by İ. Kale, Istanbul: Avesta Yayınları.

Lenin, Vladimir I. (1914). The right of nations to self-determination. In *Collected Works. Vol.20. December 1913–August 1914*. Published in 1964. London: Lawrence & Wishart, pp. 393–454.

Limbert, J. (1968). The origins and appearance of the Kurds in pre-Islamic Iran. *Iranian Studies*, 1(2), 41–51.

Lowe, Robert. (2014). The emergence of Western Kurdistan and the future of Syria. In D. Romano & M. Gurses, eds., *Conflict, Democratization and the*

Kurds in the Middle East: Turkey, Iran, Iraq and Syria. New York: Palgrave Macmillan, pp. 225–246.

Lowe, Robert. (2010). The Serhildan and the Kurdish national story in Syria. In Robert Lowe & Gareth Stansfield, eds., *The Kurdish Policy Imperative*. London: Chatham House, pp. 161–179.

Lowe, Robert & Stansfield, Gareth. (2010). *The Kurdish Policy Imperative*. London: Chatham House.

Lupu, Y. & Voeten, E. (2012). Precedent in international courts: A network of analysis of case citations by the European Court of Human Rights.

Lutz, C. A. & Collins, J. L. (2003). *Reading National Geographic*. Chicago: University of Chicago Press.

Lynch, A. (2002). Woodrow Wilson and the principle of 'national self-determination': A reconsideration. *Review of International Studies*, 28 (2), 419–436.

Macmillan, M. (2002). *Peacemakers: The Paris Peace Conference of 1919 and Its Attempt to End War*. London: John Murray.

Manela, Erez. (2007). *The Wilsonian Movement: Self-determination and the International Origins of Anticolonial Nationalism*. New York: Oxford University Press.

Mann, M. (2004). The first failed empire of the 21st century. *Review of International Studies*, 30(4), 631–653.

Mansour, R. (2012). *The role of Iraqi Kurdistan in the Syrian-Kurd pursuit of autonomy*. Al Jazeera Center for Studies, 24 September, available at http://studies.aljazeera.net/en/reports/2012/09/201291910402907471.html

Mardin, Şerif. (2008). *Türk Modernleşmesi Hakkında Makaleler 4* (Articles on Turkish Modernisation 4). Ankara: İletişim Yayınları.

Maxwell, Alexander & Smith, Tim. (2015). Positing 'not-yet-nationalism': Limits to the impact of nationalism theory on Kurdish historiography. *Nationalities Papers*, 43(5), 771–787.

Mayall, J. (1990). *Nationalism and International Society*. Cambridge: Cambridge University Press.

Mazzini, Joseph. (1898). *An Essay on the Duties of Man Addressed to Workingmen*. New York: Funk & Wagnalls.

McDowall, D. (1996a). *A Modern History of the Kurds*. London: I. B. Tauris.

McDowall, D. (1996b). *The Kurds*. London: The Minority Rights Group International.

McDowall, D. (1991). *The Kurds (A Minority Rights Group Report)*, 6th edn, September 1991, No 915. London: Minority Rights Publication.

McEvoy, Joanne & O'Leary, Brendan. (2013). *Power Sharing in Deeply Divided Places*. Philadelphia, PA: University of Pennsylvania Press.

McMurray, Jonathan S. (2001). *Distant Ties: Germany, the Ottoman Empire, and the Construction of the Baghdad Railway*. Westport, CT: Praeger Publishers.

Meiselas, Susan. (2008). *Kurdistan: In the Shadow of History*, 2nd edn. Chicago: The University of Chicago Press.

Meyer, John W. (1980). The world polity and the authority of the nation-state. In Albert Bergesen, ed., *Studies of the Modern World System*. New York: Academic Press, pp. 109–138.

Mill, John Stuart. (1872). *Considerations on Representative Government*. London: Longmans, Green, and Co.

Miller, D. (2014). Debatable lands. *International Theory*, 6(1), 104–120.

Miller, D. (2012). Territorial rights: Concept and justification. *Political Studies*, 60(2), 252–268.

Miller, R. A. (2003). Self-determination in international law and the demise of democracy? *Columbia Journal of Transnational Law*, 41 (3), 601–648.

Moaddel, Mansoor. (1986). The Shi'i Ulama and the state in Iran. *Theory and Society*, 15(4), pp. 519–526.

Moore, M. (2015). *A Political Theory of Territory*. New York: Oxford University Press.

Moore, M. (2014). Which people and what land? Territorial rights-holders and attachment to territory. *International Theory*, 6(1), 121–139.

Moore, M. (1997). On national self-determination. *Political Studies*, 45(5), 900–913.

Moynihan, D. P. (2002). *Pandaemonium: Ethnicity in International Politics*. New York: Oxford University Press.

Nardin, T. (1983). *Law, Morality, and the Relations of Sates*. Princeton, NJ: Princeton University Press.

Natali, Denise. (2010). *The Kurdish Quasi-State: Development and Dependency in Post-Gulf War in Iraq*. New York: Syracuse University Press.

Natali, Denise. (2005). *The Kurds and the State: Evolving National Identity in Iraq, Turkey and Iran*. New York: Syracuse University Press.

Nerwiy, Hawar Khalil Taher. (2012). The Republic of Kurdistan, 1946. Doctoral Thesis. University of Leiden.

Newman, E. & Visoka, G. (2016). The foreign policy of state recognition: Kosovo's diplomatic strategy to join international society. *Foreign Policy Analysis*, 1–21. e-print http://dx.doi.org/10.1093/fpa/orw042

Nezan, K. (1996). The Kurds: Current Position and Historical Background. In P. Kreyenbroek and C. Allison, eds., *Kurdish Culture and identity*. London: Zed Books.

Nodia, G. (1994). Nationalism and democracy. In L. Diamond & M. Plattner, eds., *Nationalism, Ethnic Conflict and Democracy*. Baltimore, MD: John Hopkins University Press, pp. 3–22.

Öcalan, Abdullah. (2011). *Democratic Confederalism*. Translated by International Initiative. London: Transmedia Publishing.

O'Leary, Brendan, McGarry, John & Salih, Khaled. (2005). *The Future of Kurdistan in Iraq*. Philadelphia: University of Pennsylvania Press.

O'Leary, Brendan & Salih, Khaled. (2005). The denial, resurrection, and affirmation of Kurdistan. In Brendan O'Leary, John McGarry & Khaled Salih, eds., *The Future of Kurdistan in Iraq*. Philadelphia, PA: University of Pennsylvania Press, pp. 3–46.

Olson, Robert. (2009). *Blood, Beliefs and Ballots: The Management of Kurdish Nationalism in Turkey, 2007–2009*. Costa Mesa, CA: Mazda.

Olson, Robert. (1991). Five stages of Kurdish nationalism, 1880–1980. *Journal of Muslim Minority Affairs*, 12(2), 391–409.

Orhan, Mehmet. (2014). Transborder violence: The PKK in Turkey, Syria and Iraq. *Dynamics of Asymmetric Conflict*, 7(1), 30–48, 33.

Ortaylı, İ. (2007). *Tanzimat Devrinde Osmanlı Mahalli Idareleri (1840–1880)* [Ottoman Local Administrations during the Tanzimat Period (1840–1880)]. Ankara, Cedit Yayınları.

Ortaylı, İlber. (2003). *Osmanlı Barışı* [Pax Ottomana]. İstanbul: Ufuk Kitapları.

Ortaylı, İ. (2002). Osmanlı İmparatorluğu'nda millet sistemi. In *Türkler* [The Turks], Ankara: Yeni Türkiye Yayınları.

O'Shea, Maria T. (2004). *Trapped between the Map and Reality: Geography and Perceptions of Kurdistan*. London: Routledge.

Østergaard-Nielsen, E. K. (2002). *Trans-State Loyalties and Politics: Turks and Kurds in Germany*. London: Routledge.

Özcan, Ali Kemal. (2006). *Turkey's Kurds: A Theoretical Analysis of the PKK and Abdullah Öcalan*. New York: Routledge.

Özoğlu, Hakan. (2004). *Kurdish Notables and the Ottoman State: Evolving Identities, Competing Loyalties, and Shifting Boundaries*. Albany, NY: State University of New York Press.

Özoğlu, Hakan. (2001). 'Nationalism' and Kurdish notables in the late Ottoman–early republican era. *International Journal of Middle East Studies*, 33, 383–409.

Philpott, Daniel. (2001). *Revolutions in Sovereignty: How Ideas Shaped Modern International Relations*. Princeton, NJ: Princeton University Press.

Pickles, J. (2004). *A History of Space: Cartographic Reason, Mapping and the Geocoded World*. London: Routledge.

Quam, Louis O. (1943). The use of maps in propaganda. *The Journal of Geography*, 42, 21–32.

Reidy, A., Hampson, F. & Boyle, K. (1997). Gross violations of human rights: Invoking the European Convention on Human Rights in the case of Turkey. *Netherlands Quarterly of Human Rights*, 15(2), 161–173.

Resnick, David. (1992). John Locke and liberal nationalism. *History of European Ideas*, 15(4–6), 511–517.

Roeder, Philip G. (1991). Soviet federalism and ethnic mobilization. *World Politics*, 43(2), 196–232. DOI:10.2307/2010471

Romano, David. (2006). *Kurdish Nationalist Movements: Opportunity, Mobilization and Identity*. Cambridge: Cambridge University Press.

Romano, David & Gurses, M. (eds.). (2014). *Conflict, Democratization and the Kurds in the Middle East: Turkey, Iran, Iraq and Syria*. New York: Palgrave Macmillan.

Rosow, S. J. (1990). The forms of internationalization: Representation of western culture on a global scale. *Alternatives*, 15, 287–301.

Sabuncu, Yavuz. (2001). *Anayasaya Giriş* [Introduction to Constitution]. Ankara: İmaj Yayıncılık.

Safran, W. (1991). Diasporas in modern societies: Myths of homeland and return. *Diaspora*, 1(1), 83–99.

Said, Edward (2003). *Orientalism*. London: Penguin Books.

Said, Edward (1994). *Culture and Imperialism*. London: Vintage.

Said, E. (1978). *Orientalism*. New York: Pantheon.

Sami, Şemseddin (1996). *Kamusu'l A'lam*. Ankara: Kaşgar Neşriyat.

Sary, G. (2016). Kurdish self-governance in Syria: Survival and ambition. *Research Paper: Chatham House MENA Programme*.

Savelsberg, Eva (2014). The Syrian-Kurdish movements. In David Romano & Mehmet Gürses, eds., *Conflict, Democratization and the Kurds in the Middle East*. New York: Palgrave Macmillan, pp. 85–107.

Schumpeter, Joseph A. (1976). *Capitalism, Socialism and Democracy*, 5th edn. London: Routledge.

Şerafeddin, H. (2006). *Şerefname: Kürt Tarihi, Etnografya ve Coğrafyası*. Translated into Turkish by Celal Kabadayı. Istanbul: Yaba Yayınları.

Şerefhan, H. (2009). *Şerefname: Kürd Tarihi*. Translation to Turkish by M. E. Bozarslan. Istanbul: Deng Yayınları.

Shain, S. (1999). *Marketing the American Creed Abroad: Diasporas in the US and their Homelands*. Cambridge: Cambridge University Press.

Shain, Y. & Barth, A. (2003). Diasporas and international relations theory. *International Organization*, 57(3), 449–479.

Shaw, M. N. (1997). Peoples, territorialism and boundaries. *European Journal of International Law*, 8, 478–508.

Sheffer, G. (2002). *Diaspora Politics: At Home Abroad*. Cambridge: Cambridge University Press.

Sheffer, G. (1986). *Modern Diasporas in International Politics*. London: Croom Helm.

Sheppard, Si. What the Syrians have wrought: The radical, unlikely, democratic experiment in northern Syria. *The Atlantic*, 25 October 2016. www.theatlantic.com/international/archive/2016/10/kurds-rojava-syria-isis-iraq-assad/505037/

Sidaway, James D. (2000). Postcolonial geographies: an exploratory essay. *Progress in Human Geography*, 24(4), 591–612.

Sirkeci, İbrahim. (2006). *The Environment of Insecurity in Turkey and the Emigration of Turkish Kurds to Germany*. Lewiston, ME: E. Mellen Press.

Smith, Anthony D. (2004). *The Antiquity of Nations*. Oxford: Polity.

Smith, A. D. (1996). Culture, community, and territory: The politics of ethnicity and nationalism. *International Affairs*, 72(3), 445–458.

Smith, A. D. (1986). *The Ethnic Origins of Nations*. Oxford: Basil Blackwell.

Smith, A. D. (1981). States and homelands: The social and geopolitical implications of national territory. *Millennium*, 10(3), 187–202.

Smith, A.D. (1979). *Nationalism in the Twentieth Century*. Oxford: Martin Robertson.

Smith, T. (2000). *Foreign Attachments*. Cambridge, MA: Harvard University Press.

Stansfeld, G. (2005). Governing Kurdistan: The strengths of division. In B. O'Leary, J. McGarry & K. Salih, eds., *The Future of Kurdistan in Iraq*. Philadelphia, PA: University of Pennsylvania Press, pp. 195–218.

Stephens, Michelle Ann. (2003). Reimagining the shape and borders of black political space. *Radical History Review*, 87, 169–182.

Stilz, A. (2011). Nations, states, and territory. *Ethics*, 121(3), 572–601.

Strohmeier, M. (2003). *Crucial Images in the Presentation of a Kurdish National Identity: Heroes and Patriots, Traitors and Foes*. Leiden: Brill.

Sykes, Mark. (1908). The Kurdish tribes of the Ottoman empire. *The Journal of the Royal Anthropological Institute of Great Britain and Ireland*, 38, 451–486.

Tahiri, H. (2007). *Structure of Kurdish Society and the Struggle for a Kurdish State*. Costa Mesa, CA: Mazda.

Tamir, Y. (2003). *Liberal Nationalism*. Princeton, NJ: Princeton University Press.

Tax, Meredith. (2016). The Rojava model: How Syria's Kurds govern. *Snapshot – Foreign Affairs*. 14 October.

Tejel, Jordi. (2008). *Syria's Kurds: History, Politics and Society*. New York: Routledge.

Tezcan, B. (2000). The development of the use of 'Kurdistan' as a geographical description and the incorporation of this region into the Ottoman Empire in the 16th century. In K. Çiçek, ed., *The Great Ottoman-Turkish Civilization*. Vol 3. Ankara: Yeni Türkiye, pp. 540–553.

Tezcür, G. (2016). Ordinary people, extraordinary risks: Participation in an ethnic rebellion. *American Political Science Review*, 110(2), 247–264.

Tezcür, G. (2014). The ebb and flow of armed conflict in Turkey: An elusive peace. In David Romano & Mehmet Gurses, eds., *Conflict, Democratization, and the Kurds in the Middle East*. New York: Palgrave, pp. 171–188.

Tilly, Charles. (1994). States and nationalism in Europe 1492–1992. *Theory and Society*, 23(1), 131–146.

Tyner, Judith A. (1982). Persuasive cartography. *Journal of Geography*, 82 (4), 140–144.

Vali, Abbas (ed.). (2003). *Essays on the Origins of Kurdish Nationalism*. Costa Mesa, CA: Mazda.

Van Bruinessen, M. (2006). Kurdish paths to nation. In F. A. Jabar & H. Dawod, eds., *The Kurds: Nationalism and Politics*. London, Saqi, pp. 21–48.

Van Bruinessen, M. (2003a). Ehmedî Xanî's Mem û Zîn and its role in the emergence of Kurdish national awareness. In A. Vali, ed., *Essays on the Origins of Kurdish Nationalism*. Costa Mesa, CA: Mazda, pp. 40–57.

Van Bruinessen, M. (2003b). Kurds, states and tribes. In F. A. Jabar & H. Dawod, eds., *Tribes and Power: Nationalism and Ethnicity in the Middle East*. London: Saqi, pp. 165–183.

Van Bruinessen, M. (2003c). The Kurds in movement: issues, organization, mobilization. Talk given to the Friends of the IISH, Amsterdam. Online.

Van Bruinessen, M. (2002). Kurds, states and tribes. In F. A. Jabar and H. Dawod, eds., *Tribes and Power: Nationalism and Ethnicity in the Middle East*. London: Saqi, pp. 165–183.

Van Bruinessen, M. (2000). Kurdistan in the 16th and 17th centuries, as reflected in Evliya Çelebi's *Seyahatname*. *The Journal of Kurdish Studies*, 3, 1–11.

Van Bruinessen, M. (1994). Genocide of Kurds. In Israel W. Charny, ed., *The Widening Circle of Genocide*. New Brunswick, NJ: Transaction Publishers, pp. 165–191.

Van Bruinessen, M. (1992). *Agha, Shaikh and the State: The Social and Political Structures of Kurdistan*. London: Zed.

Van Walt, M. & Seroo, O. (1999). The implementation of the right to self-determination as a contribution to conflict prevention. *UNESCO International Conference Report*. Barcelona: Centre UNESCO de Catalunya.

Vanly, Ismet Sheriff (1993). Kurdistan in Iraq. In Gerard Chaliand, Michael Pallis & David McDowall, eds., *People without a Country: The Kurds and Kurdistan*. London: Zed Press.

Voller, Yaniv. (2014). *Kurdish Liberation Movement in Iraq: From Insurgency to Statehood.* London: Routledge.

Vujakovic, P. (2002). Whatever happened to the 'new cartography'? The world map and development mis-education. *Journal of Geography in Higher Education,* 26(3), 369–380.

Wahlbeck, Ö. (1999). *Kurdish Diasporas: A Comparative Study of Kurdish Refugee Communities.* London: Macmillan.

Waldinger, R. & Fitzgerald, D. (2004). Transnationalism in question. *American Journal of Sociology,* 109(5), 1177–1195.

Watts, Nicole F. (2014). Democracy and self-determination in the Kurdistan Region of Iraq. In David Romano & Mehmet Gurses, eds., *Conflict, Democratization, and the Kurds in the Middle East.* New York: Palgrave, pp. 141–170.

Weber, Eugene. (1976). *Peasants into Frenchmen: The Modernization of Rural France, 1870–1914.* Stanford, CA: Stanford University Press.

Weldes, J. (1996). Constructing national interests. *European Journal of International Relations,* 2(3), 275–318.

Westermann, William Linn. (1991). Kurdish independence and Russian expansion. *Foreign Affairs,* 70(3), 50–54.

Whelan, Anthony. (1994). Wilsonian self-determination and the Versailles settlement. *International and Comparative Law Quarterly,* 43, 99–115.

White, G. W. (2000). *Nationalism and Territory: Constructing Group Identity in Southeastern Europe.* Lanham, MD: Rowman & Littlefied.

Williams, Andrew. (2002). *Nationalism and Particularity.* Cambridge: Cambridge University Press.

Wimmer, Andreas & Yuval Feinstein. (2010). The rise of the nation state across the world, 1816–2001. *American Sociological Review,* 75(5), 764–790.

Wintle, Michael. (1999). Renaissance maps and the construction of the idea of Europe. *Journal of Historical Geography,* 25(2), 137–165.

Wolff, S. & Peen Rodt, A. (2013). Self-determination after Kosovo. *Europe-Asia Studies,* 65(5), 799–822.

Wright, John K. (1942). Map makers are human: Comments on the subjective in maps. *Geographical Review,* 32(4), 527–544.

Yanarocak, Hay Eytan Cohen. (2014). A tale of political consciousness: The rise of a nonviolent Kurdish political movement in Turkey. In Ofra Bengio, ed., *Kurdish Awakening: Nation Building in a Fragmented Homeland.* Austin, TX: University of Texas Press, pp. 137–154.

Yeğen, M. (1996). The Turkish state discourse and the exclusion of Kurdish identity. *Middle East Studies,* 32(2), 216–229.

Zimmer, O. (2003). Boundary mechanisms and symbolic resources: towards a process-oriented approach to national identity. *Nations and Nationalism,* 9 (2), 173–193.

Reports

Amnesty International. (2015). Syria: US ally's razing of villages amounts to war crimes. Report. 12 October.

Conference on Security and Cooperation in Europe (1975). Declaration on Principles Guiding Relations Between Participating States, *International Legal Materials.*

Human Rights Watch (2014a). Under Kurdish Rule: Abuses in PYD-run Enclaves of Syria. Report.

Human Rights Watch. (2014b). 'Maybe we live and maybe we die': Recruitment and use of children by armed groups in Syria. Report.

International Crisis Group. (2014). Flight of Icarus? The PYD's precarious rise in Syria. Report.

KHRP. (2002). *The Kurdish Human Rights Project Legal Review.* London: Kurdish Human Rights Project. PKK website, www.pkkonline.com/en/in dex.php?sys=article&artID=210

Middle East Research Institute. (2015). Protecting Minorities' Rights in the Kurdistan Region: A Tailor-Made Model. Report.

#Tarih Dergi (2014). Kürtler: 1000 yıllık çözüm süreci. Report. Issue 6.

Primary Documents

Charter of Paris for a New Europe (1990).

Democratic Federation of Northern Syria. Social Contract. 2016 via Internationalist Commune https://internationalistcommune.com/social-contract/, last accessed 18 January 2019.

HDP General Election Manifesto. (June 2015). HDP website, https://drive.goo gle.com/file/d/0Byrzr4UgN9-0LWQxOUxpUmVFRm8/view, last accessed 2 February 2019.

Helsinki Final Act. (1975).

Kurdish Delegation to the Peace Conference. (1919). *Memorandum on the Claims of the Kurd People. Prepared by General Şerif Pasha.* Paris.

Memorandum on the Kurdish Question. (1945). Submitted to American Legation, Baghdad.

National Assembly of France. (1789). Declaration of Rights of Man and of Citizen.

Memorandum from the Kurdish Rizgari Party. (1946). Addressed to the UN through the US Legation, Baghdad.

The Text of the Fourteen Points. (1943). New York: The Woodrow Wilson Foundation.

UNESCO Division of Human Rights' Conference. (1998).

United Nations Charter. (1945).

Websites

Kurdish Institute of Paris. www.institutkurde.org/en/kurdorama/map_of_kurdistan.php

Kurdistan National Congress (KNK). Convention. www.kongrakurdistan.net/en/convention/

Kurdistan National Congress (KNC). Charter. www.knc.org.uk/?page_id=7

National Assembly of France. (1789). Declaration of Rights of Man and of Citizen. http://xroads.virginia.edu/~hyper/Paine/rightsIII.html, last accessed 18 April 2012.

The Kurdish Project. Website. https://the kurdishproject.org/kurdistan-map/kurdish-diaspora/

UK Parliament Foreign Affairs Committee. (2018). Kurdish Aspirations and the Interests of the UK.

UK Parliamentary Inquiry on Kurdish Aspirations. (2018).

UN General Assembly Resolution 1514 'The Granting of Independence to Colonial Countries and Peoples' in 1960. www.un.org/en/decolonization/declaration.shtml

UN General Assembly Resolution 1541 'Principles which should guide Members in determining whether or not an obligation exists to transmit the information called for under Article 73e of the Charter' in 1960.

UN General Assembly Resolution 2625 'Declaration on Principles of International Law Concerning Friendly Relations', 1970.

UN Twin International Conventions on 'Economic, Social and Cultural Rights & Civil and Political Rights' (1966). https://treaties.un.org/doc/publication/unts/volume%20999/volume-999-i-14668-english.pdf

US Congressman Bob Filner, Statement, 1 May 1997, Congress, available via www.c-span.org/video/?c1134998/clip-house-session&start=0, last accessed 2 February 2019.

US Congressman Frank Pallone, Statement, 6 April 2000, available via http://kurdistan.org/the-statement-of-congressman-frank-pallone/, last accessed 2 February 2019.

US Department of State Website, www.state.gov/s/inr/rls/4250.htm, last accessed 2 February 2019.

Newspaper articles and blogs

Al Jazeera. (2016). Syria civil war: Kurds declare federal region in north. 17 March, www.aljazeera.com/news/2016/03/syria-civil-war-kurds-declare-federal-system-north-160317111902534.html

Ateş, H. (2012). Barzani unites Syrian Kurds against Assad. *Al Monitor*, 16 July, www.al-monitor.com/pulse/politics/2012/07/barzani-grabs-assads-kurdish-car.html

Çakır, R. (2014). Cemil Bayık ile söyleşi' [Interview with Cemil Bayık], 3 February, www.rusencakir.com/Cemil-Bayik-ile-soylesi–Tam-metin /2439

Geneva Call, 22 June 2018, https://genevacall.org/syria-new-measures-taken -by-the-kurdish-peoples-protection-units-to-stop-using-children-under-1 8/, last accessed 7 January 2019.

Hamsici, Mahmut. (2017). *BBC Turkce*, 3 April, www.bbc.com/turkce/ha berler-turkiye–39439341

Hürriyet. (2016). Kobani'de yaşananlara karşı harekete geçilmeli [Action is needed against what's happening in Kobani], 6 October, www .hurriyet.com.tr/hdp-kobani-de-yasananlara-karsi-harekete-gecilmeli–27340041

Hürriyet Daily News. (2016). Pentagon chief praises Kurdish fighters in Syria, 18 March.

Küpeli, C. (2014). Radikal democrat hareket olarak HDP [HDP as a radical democratic movement]. *Birikim*, 17 July, www.birikimdergisi.com/guncel-yazilar/1022/radikal-demokrat-bir-hareket-olarak-hdp#.Xiqc2y2cb_Q

Rudaw. (2014). Divided Syrian Kurds reach deal in face of ISIS threat, 22 October, http://rudaw.net/english/kurdistan/221020141

Salih, M. A. (2015). With the Islamic State gone from Sinjar, Kurdish groups battle for control. *Al-Monitor*, 10 December, www.al-monitor.com/pulse/originals/2015/12/iraq-kurdistan-sinjar-liberated-isis -hegemony.html

Salih, M. A. (2014). PKK forces impress in fight against Islamic State. *Al-Monitor*, 1 September, www.al-monitor.com/pulse/originals/2014/09/pk k-kurdish-fight-islamic-state.html

Spyer, J. (2013). Say it again. Kurdish independence now, *The Tower*, 6 September, www.thetower.org/article/freedom-for-the-kurds-now/

Van Wildenberg, Vladimir. (2014). Rival Kurdish parties battle for power in Syria, *Al-Monitor*, 28 May, www.al-monitor.com/pulse/originals/2014/0 5/kurdistan-kdp-pyd-erbil-barzani-ocalan-syria.html

Van Wilgenburg, W. (2013). PYD leader sceptical of Kurdish agreement with Syrian Opposition, Rudaw, 20 September, http://rudaw.net/english/mid dleeast/syria/30092013

Wintour, P. (2016). UN condemns ISIS genocide against Yazidis in Iraq and Syria. *The Guardian*, 16 June, www.theguardian.com/world/2016/jun/16/un-condemns-isis-genocide-against-yazidis-in-iraq-and-syria

Wood, J. (2015). Why Turkey-KRG ties will likely trump Kurdish solidarity. *The National*, 27 July, www.thenational.ae/world/middle-east/why-turkey-krg-ties-will-likely-trump-kurdish-solidarity

Index